The Chaos Theory of Careers

The Chaos Theory of Careers outlines the application of chaos theory to the field of career development. This text represents a new perspective on the nature of career development. It emphasizes the dimensions of careers frequently neglected by contemporary accounts.

Key themes include:

- Factors such as complexity, change and connection
- People's aspirations in relation to work and personal fulfilment
- Contemporary realities of career choice, career development and the working world

It will be vital reading for all those working in and studying career development, either at advanced undergraduate or postgraduate level, and provides a new and refreshing approach to this fast-changing subject.

Robert Pryor has worked continuously in the career development field since 1974. For 17 years he was employed with the New South Wales government as a careers counsellor, researcher, trainer, policy analyst and team manager. He has lectured at the University of Sydney, Macquarie University and the University of New South Wales. He has been a Visiting Senior Research Fellow (University of NSW) and is currently Adjunct Professor, School of Education, Australian Catholic University. He is the longest ever serving member of the APS Ethics Committee and has published widely in the field of career development and psychological assessment. He is Elected Fellow of both the Australian Psychological Society (APS) and the Australian Association of Career Counsellors (2007), and a member of the Editorial Board, *Australian Journal of Career Development*.

Jim Bright enjoys a portfolio career that combines academic research and teaching with management consultancy and journalism. He is a partner in Bright and Associates, a career management consultancy, and Professorial Fellow in Career Education and Development, Australian Catholic University. He is a registered psychologist and has held full-time academic appointments in the School of Psychology at the University of New South Wales, Australia and the University of Hertfordshire, UK. He is a Fellow of the Australian Psychological Society and a past Chairman of the National Executive Committee of the Australian Psychological Society College of Organisational Psychologists. He is a Fellow of the Career Development Association of Australia, a member of the National Career Development Association, and an Honorary International Director of the British Columbia Career Development Association. He can be found on his blog about chaos and careers at www.brightandassociates.com.au.

Praise for *The Chaos Theory of Careers*

"In their customary style, Robert Pryor and Jim Bright engage their readers in an insightful consideration of how we live and how we make sense out of living. In this, the most recent and arguably the most comprehensive and practical explication of career chaos theory, Pryor and Bright provide a rich description of what career chaos theory is and, more importantly, how it can be used to foster positive career development in others. The writing style is interesting, thought provoking, and evocative (not comments often attributed to career development texts!). Covering topics spanning from Frank Parsons to fractal geometry and from Donald Super to symmetry patterns, this book brings important energy to a field in need of invigoration and new perspectives. I recommend it as required reading for anyone who is serious about career development theory and practice."

—Spencer G. Niles, Editor, *Journal of Counseling & Development* and Professor and Department Head, Counselor Education, Counseling Psychology and Rehabilitation Services, Penn State University

"The twenty-first century world of work is turning the career development field upside down. As a result of these radical changes, our field needs new theories to provide the knowledge base for effective, humane, and ethical counseling for the full range of working people. In adopting chaos theory, we now have a lens to understand and intervene in the work lives of people who are facing an uncertain world, at best. This book is a must-read for counselors and researchers who are trying to understand the postmodern nature of working. I strongly recommend this book; Pryor and Bright have transformed the discourse of our field, embracing the changes that we face. With this publication, Pryor and Bright are leading our field into the twenty-first century with creativity, passion, and vision."

—David L. Blustein, Ph.D., Professor of Counseling, Department of Counseling, Developmental, and Educational Psychology, Boston College

"In *The Chaos Theory of Careers*, Pryor and Bright present an innovative model that comprehends the uncertainties and complexities of the work role in contemporary organizations. Using this model, they describe creative counseling methods that enable clients to capitalize on change and chance in designing careers that enact personal meaning and social contribution."

—Mark Savickas, Professor of Behavioral Sciences at the Northeastern Ohio Universities College of Medicine and Adjunct Professor of Counselor Education at Kent State University

"This is the book we have all been waiting for. The authors present a readable and detailed account of chaos theory applied to career development. Certainly this represents one of the new faces of career development theory and practice."

—Norman E. Amundson, Professor of Counseling Psychology at the University of British Columbia

The Chaos Theory of Careers

A New Perspective on Working in the Twenty-First Century

Robert Pryor and Jim Bright

Routledge
Taylor & Francis Group

NEW YORK AND LONDON

First published 2011
by Routledge
711 Third Avenue, New York, NY 10017

Simultaneously published in the UK
by Routledge
2 Park Square, Milton Park, Abingdon, Oxon OX14 4RN

Routledge is an imprint of the Taylor & Francis Group, an informa business

© 2011 Taylor & Francis

The rights of Robert Pryor and Jim Bright to be identified as authors of this work have been asserted by them in accordance with sections 77 and 78 of the Copyright, Designs and Patents Act 1988.

Typeset in Sabon by Swales & Willis Ltd, Exeter, Devon

Library of Congress Cataloging in Publication Data
Pryor, Robert.
The chaos theory of careers: a new perspective
on working in the twenty-first century/
Robert Pryor and Jim Bright.
p. cm.
Includes bibliographical references and index.
1. Career development. I. Bright, Jim. II. Title.
HF5381.P76 2011
331.70201–dc22
2010031946

ISBN13: 978–0–415–55188–5 (hbk)
ISBN13: 978–0–415–80634–3 (pbk)
ISBN13: 978–0–203–87146–1 (ebk)

Robert Pryor
Dedicated to Jim Bright, who started me off on the voyage of chaos and who has enabled me to enjoy and value every nautical mile since.

Jim Bright
Dedicated to Robert Pryor, a strong friend who reinvigorated my passion for research and writing and whose generosity of spirit, intellect and humour continues to inspire, delight and guide.

> "Do not boast about tomorrow, for you do not know what a day may bring forth."
>
> (Proverbs 27:1)

CONTENTS

PREFACE

"Life is Uncertain"

Life is uncertain. This is one of the greatest and most perennial of "inconvenient truths" in the field of career development. Individuals approach career development practitioners seeking certainty, and many of the dominant theories that inform practice hold out promises of certainty or at least reducing uncertainty. It is an inconvenient truth because life's uncertainty tells us things about ourselves that we may not want to hear and that present challenges that we may not want to face. Ultimately it exposes our human limitations of knowledge and power.

Uncertainty reveals limitation and limitation signals vulnerability. But it also reveals something else—something about us that is less defensive and more positive, more hopeful. If uncertainty exposes our limitations of knowledge and power, it also suggests, at least, that there may be potentials within us and possibilities around us that we may currently be unaware of but that may be awaiting us if we would but have the courage to run the gauntlet of uncertainty: that is, to risk vulnerability and failure in the quest for opportunity and achievement. The failure of career development theory to provide a compelling and practical account of uncertainty is a major shortcoming because it directs focus to the probable and de-emphasizes the possible.

What new approaches are available to meet the challenges and possibilities of uncertainty? This book addresses this issue in its broadest sense. It presents a new conceptual approach to people's careers and the interconnections of those careers with the rest of their lives through the formulation of chaos theory. This forms a theoretical basis for understanding and integrating many of the realities of contemporary life and work experience. New perspectives on how to understand these realities and how counselors may be able to assist others to negotiate them effectively are also included. Strategies and specific techniques for career counseling are provided, along with research evidence about contemporary employment realities and the efficacy of counseling based on chaos theory.

In this process many of the key issues in the contemporary career development literature are addressed to demonstrate both the relevance and the contribution that chaos theory is making to this field. In particular, the contemporary need for a sense of meaning, purpose, a sense of the sacred, spiritual wholeness, community contribution and individual fulfillment are brought into focus and linked within the chaos theoretical framework of careers. This book offers a new direction that acknowledges the major contributions of the past, while also recognizing that there remain current realities that have previously been neglected and new challenges that need to be faced.

We would like to thank our families for their support during the writing of this book. We also wish to express our appreciation to those professional colleagues who encouraged us in our early endeavors to apply chaos theory to career development. In addition we also want to acknowledge all the Routledge publication staff who have contributed to the publication process.

R. P.
J. B.

CHAPTER 1

Complexity, Uncertainty and Careers

To live is to change.

INTRODUCTION

Everything in our universe is subject to change. When the rate of change is very slow we tend to ascribe "stability" to such phenomena and tend not to think of them as changeable or changing ... but they are. Human experience is often interpreted in terms of the alternation between stability and change. Some crave continual change and some seek perpetual stability. The tension between these two parameters of our being, have frequently been the focus of artistic expression. The Elizabethans, for example, having experienced the upheavals of the Reformation and the Renaissance, were almost preoccupied with coming to terms with change. They called it "mutability." The greatest writer of them all, William Shakespeare, wrote sonnets that repeatedly returned to the theme of change in human life and love, especially change in its ultimate form—the change from life to death.

The twentieth century saw the rate of change in many areas of human life and experience begin to accelerate in comparison with earlier centuries. With such acceleration came the loss of many previous certitudes (Peat, 2002). In science, for example, the beginning of the twentieth century saw the apparently immutable, generalizable and universal laws of Newtonian mechanics suddenly undermined by Einstein's theory of relativity. Then, within about 30 years, the very fundamental concepts of causality and predictability on which Einstein, not to mention Newton, had depended were themselves challenged by quantum mechanics. Suddenly it became apparent that there were parts of reality at the sub-atomic level that appeared to defy much of what science had, at least since the Enlightenment of the eighteenth century, assumed to be the way the universe worked.

As if all this were not enough, a further revolution in scientific thought was slowly, almost surreptitiously insinuating itself into various dimensions of scientific theory and practice as the twentieth century progressed (Briggs & Peat, 1989). Chaos theory, as it was subsequently to be designated, challenged traditional scientific methods of controlled laboratory experiments, of analyzing ever more specific phenomena and of attempting to control for all extraneous variables. Chaos theory pointed to the complexity of reality and its essential interconnectedness. These theorists emphasized the systemic nature of the universe and the need to consider phenomena in their totality and context rather than always reducing them to their constituents. Now it was not only sub-atomic particles that defied prediction: chaos theory pointed to the stochastic and contingent nature of all reality (Lorenz, 1993). The laws of science became understood not as immutable certainties but as statements of probability (Prigonine, 1997).

The recognition of complexity began to spawn not only change but also chance. It was not that classical physics, the theory of relativity and quantum mechanics were all incorrect or even superseded. In fact, each was and remains among the great intellectual achievements of humans' aspirations to gain an understanding of the nature of things. It was just that they were not enough. Chaos theory has come to represent the "new frontier" of human endeavor in the same quest to which such luminaries as Newton, Einstein and Bohrs had so perspicaciously previously contributed. Now chaos theory is finding applications far beyond its original fields of endeavor of mathematics, biology and meteorology. The concepts and ideas of the theory have been applied across economics, political science, aesthetics, theology and clinical psychology. In fact, aspects of chaos theory are found in various forms in popular culture, especially films such as *Chaos*, *Jurassic Park*, *Sliding Doors*, *The Butterfly Effect*, *Serendipity* and *Slumdog Millionaire*.

In this book the authors will try to document, integrate, interpret and extend previous efforts applying chaos theory to the field of career development since work remains one of the most fundamental of all human activities. Moreover, as we try to demonstrate in this chapter, work and careers have been some of the aspects of human experience that have undergone monumental change which demands new approaches in terms of career development theory, research and counseling intervention practice.

NEW REALITIES OF CAREER DEVELOPMENT

Fundamentally, our world is less predictable than was once thought. Our lives are uncertain and our work is subject to changes over which we can have limited control. Some of the "new realities" for twenty-first-century work are:

- Speed of communication
- Reshaping of organizations
- Speed and extent of change
- Need for lifelong learning
- Globalization of both consumer markets and labor markets
- Increasingly contractual nature of work
- Rapidity of technological innovation and its adoption.

Daniel Pink (2005) argued that developed economies are confronted by a trinity of challenges:

- Abundance—are the skills, products and services offered by individuals and organizations in demand when there are abundant alternatives?
- Asia—can the product be made or the service delivered more cheaply using Asian labor?
- Automation—can the product or service be made or delivered faster, better or more cheaply by a computer?

He argues that increasingly people are looking for meaning and social connection in their actions. We imbue our interactions with both people and objects with emotional value. Hence we realize that the company we keep, the jobs that we do and the products that we purchase are to some degree reflections or projections of ourselves. We are, in developed countries, confronted by choice in most areas of our lives. Literally from the choice of birthing methods, to the choice of a casket, we or our carers have an abundance of choices to make, and the way we make them is far from always being rational (e.g., Ariely, 2008).

The impact of globalization, most especially seen in the dramatic rise of Asian economic power especially in China and India, is another powerful reminder that our work practices, and hence our careers, are subject to continuous and unpredictable change. Friedman (2005) suggests that the conflagration of technology and attitude change has led to a "flattening of the world" where many more nations, companies or individuals can compete viably for business. These developments are unlikely to create the conditions for long-term stability classically associated with career development (e.g., Super 1980).

Technological advances, especially in information and communications technology, but also in medicine and robotics, have also played a major role in creating a complex, uncertain and unpredictable world, in which the notion of stable or predictable career paths becomes ever more questionable. The result of the forces of abundance, Asia and automation is uncertainty, and that is a reality that has not been addressed adequately in the career development literature to date.

CHANGE AND UNCERTAINTY

Humans struggle with the reality that uncertainty is inevitable in all of our actions to a greater or lesser degree—we want control, and it disturbs us to think that total control is fundamentally unattainable. Approaches to career development that emphasize certainty and hold out the promise of providing neat answers are attractive to people confronted by the uncertainties and complexities of their lives. It is therefore not surprising to discover that clients seek out certainty in career counseling and prefer that counselors give advice, opinions and answers (Galassi, Crace, Martin, James & Wallace, 1992). This presents a challenge because we live in a world that is not simple, certain and predictable, and a world that is populated by people who are complex, changing and inherently unpredictable.

As Taleb (2007) noted, reflection on our own experience as humans will indicate the uncertain and unpredictable nature of many events in our lives and our world. He posed the following questions:

> Look into your own existence. Count the significant events, the technological changes, and the inventions that have taken place in our environment since you were born and compare them to what was expected before their advent. How many of them came on schedule? Look into your own personal life, to your choice of profession say, or meeting your mate, your exile from your country of origin, the betrayals you faced, your sudden enrichment or impoverishment. How often did these things occur according to plan? (p. xix)

Some of the words commonly used to describe individuals' involvement with work include "vocation" and "career development," the former meaning a calling or to be called, and the latter suggesting progression. Other words that are commonly used include "transition," "change," and "outplacement." All of these terms relate to movement or shift (Bright & Pryor, 2008). Definitions in the field of human careers always come back to the acknowledgement of shift. Indeed Savickas (1997) argues that movement is the defining quality of the human condition—to live is to move. Movement is what separates humans from inanimate objects. Amundson (2003a) observed that counseling clients often present their career problems in terms of being "stuck"—in effect, being unable to move. He sees a fundamental role of career counseling as getting people moving in positive directions toward worthwhile objectives.

Evidence of shift in career trajectories is plentiful. For instance, Jepson and Choudhuri (2001) followed a cohort of 170 people over 25 years and found almost two thirds experienced changing occupational career patterns. Not only is shift the most common career experience; it might even contribute positively to satisfaction. Jepson and Choduri reported that stable occupational career patterns were associated with lower levels of career satisfaction.

Within the domain of career change, increasing attention is being given to unplanned change (e.g., Betsworth & Hanson, 1996; Bright, Pryor & Harpham, 2005; Cabral & Salomone, 1990; Chen, 2005; Mitchell, Levin & Krumboltz, 1999; Osipow, 1973). A consistent pattern emerges from studies employing a range of different methodologies including surveys and case studies that between 60% and 100% of adolescents and adults report chance events that significantly influenced their career paths.

Given the centrality of movement to career development theory and practice, it is perhaps ironic how relatively neglected movement has been in the literature in this field for most of its history. Thus two influential metaphors of career up to the present time that do not immediately imply movement are those of "career as fit" and "career as resource," yet arguably these metaphors have dominated career development theory and practice for the last 100 years. This may provide a clue as to why theory and practice in the area of shift is strangely limited.

Career as fit is typically associated with the theories of Frank Parsons (Parsons, 1909) and John Holland (Holland, 1997). The counseling focused on narrowing down options and making recommendations based on person-job fit. Much has been written about these approaches, and it is fair to say that the concept of fit between individuals and occupations as the basis for predicting occupational outcomes or as a basis for practice has been subject to an exponentially increasing critical commentary (e.g., Amundson, 2003a, 2005; Arnold, 2004; Bright, Pryor & Harpham, 2005; Patton & McMahon, 2006; Pryor & Bright, 2003a,b, 2007; Savickas 1997).

Career as resource is seen most clearly in the discipline and practice of human resources. This discipline considers the potential of the career, in combination with other resources in the process of wealth creation. Essentially, the "career" is a building block or an ingredient in the construction of wealth, and hence it is seen as a stable entity. This allied discipline has also labored under a characterization of individuals that does not encourage one to think of them as continually shifting and subject to shift. Indeed much of the change management literature appears to be predicated on the notion of coercing or cajoling individuals to accept and adapt to change regimes. Furthermore, rarely is change construed in this literature as being anything more complex than a simple movement from an "old" structure to a "new" structure. For instance, in their textbook on organizational behavior, Greenberg and Barron (2000) distinguish first order change and second order change. First order change is "continuous in nature and involves no major shifts in how an organization operates"(p. 586). Second order change is "far more complex" (p. 586) and relates to structural changes that employ *strategic planning* which "must begin with a stated goal" (p. 594). Thus through the traditional approach to strategic planning radical change is conceived of as planned behavior where the current (old structure) is changed to the future (new structure).

The dominant metaphors of fit and resource have not encouraged us to deal with the complexity of shift. Most existing career development theories fail to account adequately for one or more of four crucial contemporary elements in career development and choice (Bright & Pryor, 2005; Pryor & Bright, 2003a,b, 2007).

1. Failure to incorporate the range of potential influences on people's careers.
2. Failure to move beyond a narrow sense of matching to the dynamic, interactive and adaptive nature of human functioning in the world and in making career decisions and taking career action.
3. Failure to go beyond acknowledging to incorporating into theory the tendency of humans to construe and construct

experiences and perceptions into meaningful and often unique interpretive structures for understanding themselves, their life experience and their world.
4. Failure to adequately conceptualize unplanned and unpredictable events and experiences which are often crucial and sometimes determinative in the narrative of people's careers.

Things and people change, shift happens (Bright, 2008a), but many of our methods, our training and our clients' expectations tend to privilege certainty over uncertainty. Taleb (2007) argued that all the shifts that have really mattered in life have shared three characteristics: (a) they are outliers that fall outside the realm of regular expectations; (b) they have an extreme impact; and (c) "human nature makes us concoct explanations for [their] occurrence after the fact, making [them] explainable and predictable" (p. xviii).

The observation that we live in times of exponential change seems to be increasingly accepted. Uldrich (2008) has estimated that 95% of what we know about the human brain has been discovered in the last 20 years. If we consider the discipline of career development, we can see clear evidence of exponential shifts in knowledge. A PsycLit database search on articles relating to "careers" indicates the first listed in the database was published in the 1890s, but that just about half (49%) of the total output have been published in the last three decades. The results for papers on "career change" are even more dramatic, with 93% of them having been published in the last 30 years. While it may not seem surprising now that there is such a focus on change, would we have predicted this in the 1960s?

Dramatic change has always been a feature of human experience, but the rapid increases in communications technologies has created a more interconnected world, where the behavior of individuals separated in time and space from others can have profound, dramatic and unpredictable effects. Consider the following stories that illustrate not only the changes in communication technology, but the dramatic way in which events can influence our careers (and always have).

The first story happened to a cigar-loving army officer in the Civil War and is related in Durschmied (2000). On September 13, 1862, First Sergeant John Bloss and Corporal Barton Mitchell of the Union Army 12th corps found a campsite near Hagerstown, Maryland, that had been vacated by their enemy, the Confederate Army, earlier that day. Bloss found an envelope that contained a parcel wrapped in white paper. The parcel contained three high-quality cigars, but the paper they were wrapped in was even more important, it contained the Confederate's battle plans. This led directly to a conflict on the September 17 at Antietam, resulting in the loss of over 23,000 lives, the bloodiest day in America's history. A few days after this event, Lincoln was emboldened to announce the Emancipation Proclamation.

The second story happened on Monday, September 8, 2008, and concerns United Airlines, a regional newspaper and a lot of very fast communications technology. Share trading was halted in the stock of United Airlines following rumors that the company was filing for bankruptcy. The rumor caused a massive sell-off of stock in United and saw the stock take a dive from $12.17 to $3 (a 76% fall in less than a day). A journalist at the *Florida Sentinel* newspaper had posted a six-year-old report on its website covering the story that United were filing for bankruptcy protection. The original story appeared in the *Chicago Tribune* and was true six years before, but the rumor generated by the re-post was completely untrue. A major corporation in the US was almost obliterated by an editorial mistake in Florida.

The third story also occurred in Florida, which appears to make a habit of playing host to these dramatic shifts, as many will recall that it was there that the 2000 US Presidential election between George Bush and Al Gore was decided. Ultimately, George Bush won by 5 electoral votes, but 25 were disputed in Florida, meaning that whoever won Florida won the Presidency. The issue turned on the reliability of the voting and vote-counting process. The term "hanging chads," to denote a piece of paper not fully punched out of a (voided) voting card by a faulty voting machine, was added to our vocabulary. Thus again, unusual and unpredicted events became pivotal in the future of a nation.

PERSONAL EXPERIENCE OF CHANGE

For an individual born at the beginning of the twentieth century and living for most or all of it, the amount of change they are likely to have experienced almost anywhere on the planet is immense. Amanda Jones, an African American woman from Bastrup County, Texas, was born in 1899. In 2008 she voted for a Black President, Obama, in the Presidential elections. In between those events she would have experienced the Great Depression in the 1920s and 1930s, the two world wars, the civil rights movement and the birth of both Hollywood and Bollywood (the home of the Indian film industry), as well as the rise and fall of Communism as a global political ideology, television, mass-produced cars, computers, air travel, the iPod, jazz music, rock music, rap music, the internet, space travel, the invention of the Mars Bar, Milky Way and Kit Kat, the rise of the union movement and much more. If she had an interest in career development she would have lived through every major theoretical development in the field from Parsons to chaos theory. Sadly, she died in December 2008 just before Obama's innauguration. Her father was a slave who was emancipated, and thus Amanda's story links in part to our earlier story of the discovery of those cigars by Sergeant John Bloss in Maryland in 1862.

In Amanda Jones's lifetime we have seen a shift from the paternalistic employment practices pioneered by those chocolate barons, Milton Hershey in Philadelphia and Cadbury in Birmingham, in the United Kingdom, to more individualist and self-help approaches. Hershey and the Cadbury family both established schools, housing and whole local communities (Hershey, Pennsylvania, and Bourneville, Birmingham, UK) to enhance the well-being of their workers and their families. Amanda Jones would have experienced the social contract between worker and employer being replaced by the psychological contract (Rouseau, 1996). She would have seen education change from being a front-end process of knowledge and skill acquisition to the contemporary need for lifelong learning to help individuals confront the continually changing demands that workplaces make. She would have seen hierarchical management structures build up and up throughout the first 60 years of the twentieth century; perhaps she even saw the Billy Wilder movie *The Apartment* (Wilder, 1960), which provided such a scathing commentary on the dehumanizing effect of such structures. She lived through the remainder of the century where scores of middle managers from such hierarchies lost their jobs. Most recently, she would have lived against a backdrop of many workers losing their jobs to overseas producers.

Change from another perspective can be seen in the life of Wang Guiying, born in 1901 in southern Guizhu province in China. She was born as the Boxer Rebellion was ending. Wang Guiying avoided marriage most of her life because she was afraid of being treated poorly, since Chinese woman had few if any rights when she was young. Extreme acts, such as foot binding to make women look more attractive, were commonplace. In her lifetime Wang would have experienced the Chinese Civil war, the rise of Mao and Communism, the Cultural Revolution, the industrialization of China, the handback by the British of Hong Kong, the rapid expansion of manufacturing and electronics industries in China, and the Chinese Olympic games in Bejing. Wang was a farmer for most of her life and she may have been aware of the huge influx of workers from the country into the rapidly industrialized cities around China. The opportunities for both men and women in China have changed dramatically in her lifetime, and members of her village community may have left for the cities to do the manufacturing jobs that were once done by Amanda Jones's compatriots across America.

The lives of Amanda and Wang in so many ways are different, yet in others and from a career development perspective they contain similarities. The women lived through a time when changes in politics and human rights had a major impact for both, in negative and positive ways. They lived in a time when jobs were subject to enormous change and transformation due to war, technology and attitudinal change. Both experienced tremendous upheaval due to dramatic changes in the economy and the way their compatriots worked. These two women, at different ends of the earth, divided by geography and political systems, are united by complexity, change, chance and uncertainty. Their stories are also reminders that the current generation are not the only ones to have had to confront change. However, we may be the first to move decisively to recognize change and to face the challenge of trying to incorporate it into career development theory and practice.

CHANGE AND CAREER DEVELOPMENT THEORY AND PRACTICE

Change, technology and globalization are outpacing changes associated with the life cycle, so developmental models no longer can be seen as the primary changes we have to deal with personally or communally. In slower times, the main changes were those brought about by aging. Commonly recognized sources of change such as globalization, technology, government regulations and performance management (Greenberg & Barron, 2000) simply were not present or as prevalent or frequent in the pre-industrial world. Now we are obliged to change the way we work regularly. Many of the theories, procedures and tools designed for career development emphasize stability and characterize career development as a problem to be solved, rather than career development as an ongoing process.

If change is this ubiquitous, extensive, continuous and impactful, then it follows that there are severe limits to humans' ability to make long-range deterministic predictions. It is possible to continue to believe that we are able to do this; however, it turns out that in many fields of human endeavor the track record of such attempts reveals that we do not do it very well. Taleb (2007) makes the following point about prediction: "when I ask people to name three recently implemented technologies that most impact our world today, they usually propose the computer, the Internet and the laser. All three were unplanned, unpredicted and unappreciated" (p. 135).

Limitations in our ability to predict the future can be seen in the repeated failure of interest inventories to predict significant outcomes for clients. Arnold (2004) noted that congruence between the person and environment has been shown in several metastudies to correlate poorly (between 0.1 and 0.2) with outcome measures such as satisfaction (e.g., Assouline & Meir, 1987; Tranberg, Slane & Ekeberg, 1993; Young, Tokar & Subich, 1998). Arnold (2004) highlights the problem by observing that the concept of congruence in Holland's (1997) theory accounts for only 1%–4% of the outcome measure variance. He proposes 14 problems with the theory including inadequate conceptualization of the person and the environment, inadequate measurement of the environment, the fact that job environments are increasingly demanding variety and diversity, and that jobs are continually changing.

The continuing value of traditional person–environment fit models of career choice has been questioned since they fail to capture adequately the complexities, uncertainties and dynamic aspects of modern work (e.g., Mitchell et al., 1999; Pryor & Bright 2003a,b; Savickas & Baker, 2005) As Savickas and Baker (2005) point out, "With less stable personalities and occupations, vocational psychology's basic model of person environment fit with its goal of congruence seems less useful and less possible in today's labor market" (p. 49).

If, then, we are living in a changing world, and if, indeed, to live is to move, it is incumbent upon the career development community to embrace the concept of change or shift in their theories, practices and tools. We need to recognize that the most fundamental challenge that career counselors confront is to assist their clients to develop the skills of adaptation and resilience required to negotiate and use productively the fluctuating fortunes of their careers. It includes assisting clients to reinvent themselves continually, to identify opportunities, to recover from setbacks, to find meaningful work that matters to them and to others, and to capitalize on chance. We have defined these activities as "shiftwork" (Bright & Pryor, 2008).

Shiftwork as a concept derives from chaos theory (Lorenz, 1993). Chaos theorists have observed that change can occur in systems either gradually or very quickly. However, the effect of change is to reconfigure the system. This is usually called a "phase shift," after which the system functions in a way different from its former operational configuration. The classic physical example of this is the proverbial sand tipping into a single pile forming a pyramid shape on a flat surface. At some point only one additional grain of sand is required for the existing pile to bifurcate into two poles—a new configuration of the system. The changes and uncertainties of human experience show similar analogous reconfigurations through the slow advances of age or the dramatic impact of trauma or job loss. Such effects can be internal to the person, such as disease, or external, such as technological change. The Chaos Theory of Careers (Bright & Pryor, 2005a, 2007; Pryor & Bright, 2003a, 2007a) explicitly incorporates the concept of "phase shift" in its account of careers in terms of complex dynamical systems.

We live in a highly interconnected world that is subject to continuous, unpredictable and sometimes dramatic change. Indeed, each and every one of us is highly interconnected and continually changing because that is the life condition. As a response to these realities, the authors developed a theory of career development that has interconnection, change, chance at its heart. In the following chapters we set out the Chaos Theory of Careers, its potential for extending our understanding of the dimensions of decision making, its implications for practice in counseling and organizations, its relevance to spirituality, its challenge to research methodologies, and the possible future directions for a chaos approach to career development.

CHAPTER 2

Complexity, Uncertainty and Career Development Theory

It's not "either/or" it's "both/and."

INTRODUCTION

Typically new approaches to conceptualizing reality, nature and the world begin by rejecting and overthrowing what has gone before (Kuhn, 1962). This becomes a way to define and differentiate the new vision from the old. In this chapter, in light of the realities of contemporary career development highlighted in Chapter 1, the perspective which suggests that most of the last 100 years of career development thinking can be dismissed or at least neglected will be challenged. It will be contended that benefit has derived from earlier theory and research which needs to be not only acknowledged in passing but actively integrated into contemporary thinking about working and careers. To understand, decide and act in a complex, changing and connected career context we believe can only be successfully achieved by using the multiple perspectives of both traditional theories and recent conceptual contributions in the field of career development. A retreat into dichotomous thinking characterized as "either/or" ultimately will fail the test of real inclusiveness and cannot constitute an adequate basis on which to develop and practice effective career counseling in a complexity-laced world.

In the last 20 years there has been a steady flow of articles in the literature that draw attention to the shortcomings of what are variously described as "traditional," "quantitative," "trait-factor," "positivist" or "modernist" approaches (e.g., Brown, 2007; Savickas, 1997; Savickas et al., 2009; Super, 1992; Vondracek, Lerner & Schulenberg, 1986). Recently these criticisms have been accompanied by arguments urging the adoption of alternative approaches that sometimes focus on specific techniques such as narrative (e.g., Brott, 2001), or more conceptually on alternative theoretical frameworks such as career construction and postmodernism (e.g., Savickas et al., 2009). Savickas coined the phrase "from scores to stories" that neatly captures one of the key ideas presented by the postmodernist approach (Savickas, 1993; Savickas et al. 2009).

There is great value in much of the postmodernist agenda, but we have consistently cautioned against the risk of becoming so enamored by the novel that we reject the familiar. There is a danger of stereotyping and oversimplifying the "old." Lumping together much of the work done over the last 100 years as being inadequate for the twenty-first century risks caricaturing and underestimating the power and utility of the ideas generated in this period. For example, John Holland, a doyen of traditional matching paradigms of career development, was not oblivious to the need for creativity in career development. He wrote:

> Many people will have to create their own structure for combining incompatible work with a more satisfying social and recreational life. To deal with this need, what has been seen as career counseling may become life counseling, in which work is an important facet of creating a more satisfying life. (Holland, 1997, p. 404)

Consequently, it is useful to review some of the approaches of the past that are now being challenged so vigorously. In undertaking this task we have deliberately chosen not to attempt a comprehensive review of this material as this is not the main focus of the book. Readers can find excellent and more comprehensive summaries in Brown and Brooks (2007) and Patton and McMahon (2006).

EARLY BEGINNINGS

It is almost traditional to cite the commencement of the field of career development with Parsons (1909). Frank Parsons was a social reformer who came to realize that work was a major potential influence for the social and financial advancement of the disadvantaged and the poor (Baker, 2009). In 1905 he founded the Vocational Bureau in Boston with the aim of assisting individuals to make better career choices (Sensoy-Briddick, 2009). Parsons used a matching approach which became the paradigm for most subsequent theory and practice in the field for the rest of the century. Fundamentally, his model was that individuals had to know as accurately as possible information about themselves, especially their abilities, and also to have information about different occupations such as their duties, activities and other personal requirements. With these two types of information individuals were encouraged, with the assistance (usually the direction in Parsons' approach) of a counselor, to apply "true reasoning," which later became known as decision making. True reasoning was intended to enable individuals to link their characteristics with those of specific occupations to achieve an appropriate match of the person and the occupation. The simplicity and apparent practicality of such an approach resulted in the wide usage of matching individuals to occupations in both world wars and subsequently when career development theorists began to reflect on the nature of the career decision-making process (Briddick, 2009).

MATCHING THEORIES

The paradigm for such choice was that of matching characteristics of the person with those of particular occupations. The concept of "career" was the progressive development of a person's working life within the occupation originally chosen after leaving school, college or university. A rigorous example of the matching paradigm originated in the University of Minnesota and became known as the Theory of Work Adjustment (TWA) (Dawis & Lofquist, 1984). The fundamentals of this theory were that good occupational choices would be made when there were correspondences between characteristics of individuals and those of occupations. Thus if there was a good match between the abilities of an individual and the performance demands of an occupation, then it was likely that the person would be successful in working in this occupation. The TWA called this "satisfactoriness." If the personal preferences of an individual corresponded with the rewards offered by an occupation, then it would be likely that the person would like working in this occupation. The TWA designated this as "satisfaction." As a result, a suitable occupational choice was understood to be one in which the person was both satisfactory in performance and satisfied in preference.

However, the most well known and most influential theory based on the matching paradigm was that of John Holland (Holland, 1959, 1997). Holland's theoretical disposition to occupational choice was both minimalist and pragmatic. He sought to answer the question

"What is the simplest and yet most helpful way to assist individuals to make occupational choices?" Holland's approach was to make the match between individuals and occupations more systematic. This was achieved not by the development of normative measures of abilities, interests and values as the TWA researchers had done, but by simply asking people through a self-scored questionnaire what they thought their skills and preferences were (Holland, 1973). Holland's research generated a taxonomy both of human types and of occupational stereotypes (Pryor & Bright, 2005a). These six types were labeled Realistic, Investigative, Artistic, Social, Enterprising and Conventional. This classification has become and remains, despite its limitations (Pryor, 2002), the single most influential representation of occupational interests in contemporary career development practice. It has frequently been used also as a basis for organizing occupational information for those facing occupational choices (Spokane, Meir & Catalano, 2000).

Holland's theory continues to be researched, and a wide variety of inventories and other measures utilizing the so-called "Holland hexagon" remain in widespread use by career counselors (Shahnasarian, 2006). Other approaches that emphasize career choice as matching (e.g., Janis & Mann, 1977) propose decision-making models that typically involve collecting information, generating alternatives, weighing options, deciding between options and implementing a specific choice.

DEVELOPMENTAL THEORIES

The other dominant theme in career development after World War II was to focus less on the choice process and more on career as developmental process. The dominant figure of this approach has been undoubtedly Donald Super, who first outlined his theory in the 1950s (Super, 1953, 1957). Super is usually credited with shifting the focus of counselors and researchers alike away from "occupations" to the concept of "career." Super's theory focused on describing the process of career development, and over a 40-year period the theory evolved by incorporating ongoing thinking in other areas of psychology into his theory. Super's initial theory sought to describe individuals' careers in terms of stages: growth, exploration, establishment, maintenance and decline (later renamed "disengagement"). Originally, Super's theory considered occupational choice as a single event in this developmental paradigm. Occupational choice was seen as individuals implementing their self-concept. That is, as individuals develop through the growth and exploration stages, they develop a set of perceptions about themselves which they then seek to match with particular occupations. The closer the match, the greater the sense of personal and work satisfaction. Although broader in scope than Holland at this point, the theory does have similarities to the matching paradigm first enunciated by Parsons. However, as Super elucidated the theory incorporating life span and life space concepts, emphasizing the multiple role nature of careers, the self-concept was later conceptualized as an internalized perspective of the person's self along with the person's perception of the context in which the person lives out other chosen roles in addition to worker including parent, student, citizen, homemaker, child and leisurite (Super, 1980; Super, Savickas & Super, 1996).

This theory has been influential in the development of a range of other recent theoretical approaches including the contextual theory of career (Young, Valach & Collin, 1996; Young & Collin, 2004), which links action theory with contextual influences and the circumscription/compromise theory (Gottfredson, 1981, 1996, 2006); this incorporates aspects of both the developmentalism of Super and the interest taxonomy of Holland. Savickas (2006) has used the idea of the occupational self-concept as a basis for career construction theory (see below).

THE LIMITATIONS OF MATCHING PARADIGMS

The matching paradigms embedded in both occupational choice and career development theories outlined above are based on a set of assumptions about career development and decision making including:

- Everything is fixed—stable and unchanging.
- Choice is a matter of rationality.
- Logic is the best decision-making style.
- All the relevant information that is needed for a decision can be known.
- There is only one best decision.
- The process of career development is an orderly pattern of progression.
- Indecision is bad and decidedness is good.
- Making a decision does not affect the context in which the decision is made.

- Choice is about a long-term goal such as "the career."
- Choice implementation must be practical—grounded in reality.
- Commitment is necessary to overcome obstacles in the way of realizing one's choice.
- Other possibilities are dangerous distractions from the achievement of the original goal.

In light of the "new realities" of the world of work outlined in Chapter 1, virtually all of these assumptions of traditional theories of career choice and decision making have been seriously questioned. Increasingly, it has been noted that there is a multiplicity of potential influences on careers, that the world is continually changing and the long-term stability of occupations cannot be relied upon, that individuals are increasingly changing occupations in their careers by either choice or necessity, that individuals not only react to change but are actually active agents for change in their own lives and the contexts in which they interact, and that unplanned events play a larger role in people's lives than traditionally allowed (Krumbolt & Levin, 2004; Patton & McMahon, 2006). The traditional matching paradigm assumes that individuals have more control over their lives and circumstances and the outcomes of their actions than they actually have in day-to-day human experience (Pryor & Bright, 2003b). In fact, we rarely have complete information before we make all sorts of decisions, and even more rarely can we be assured of all the consequences of such decisions. In addition, human decision making is rarely as logical and rational as we would like to think it is. Various career decision-making styles have been identified, with being logical and rational only one of the possibilities (Harren, 1979; Osipow, Carney, Winer, Yanico & Koschier, 1987).

In fact chance (the unplanned) is one of the neglected aspects of human experience in the traditional matching paradigm (Chen, 2005). Career decision makers themselves readily acknowledge the influence of unplanned events on their lives and careers (Bright, Pryor, Earl & Wilkenfeld, 2005). Those who work in vocational rehabilitation readily acknowledge the importance and the impact of disease, misadventure, accident and medical negligence on people's ability to work. Virtually none of these types of events are expected by the hapless individuals to whom they occur, yet such influences, if they find any level of recognition within traditional theories of career development, are allocated an ad hoc place without any rationale for their occurrence other than that they cannot be denied.

NEW DIRECTIONS OF CAREER DEVELOPMENT THEORY

Amundson (2003a) summarized the change in career development theory succinctly:

> our paradigm has shifted away from stability, order, unifor-
> mity, and equilibrium towards a new order of instability, dis-
> order, disequilibrium, and non-linear relationships where small
> inputs trigger major effects. (p. 91)

Indeed, the paradigm shift has been so dramatic that it led Krumboltz (1998) to conclude that it "drives home the realization that
career counseling theory has been misleading us for decades" (p. 391).
In response to a changing world of work in which the stability of many
occupations or employment more generally is declining, labor markets
are transforming under influences such as globalization, individuals
are seeking meaning and balance of priorities in and through work,
and the complexity and interconnections of factors are impacting individuals' working lives, some new approaches to career development
theory have emerged. The two most prominent of these are career construction theory and systems theory.

CAREER CONSTRUCTION THEORY

Career construction theory (Savickas, 1997) draws on the idea of Super
that work can be understood as the implementation of a self-concept.
In career construction theory this is used to view careers as ways that
individuals impose meaning on their lives and behavior. Individuals
integrate their thoughts and experiences into a meaning pattern or patterns called "life themes" (Savickas, 2005). Such life themes can be
revealed in the personally significant stories by which people seek to
find meaning as a basis for career choice and the work roles they want
to assume. In this theory, emphasis is placed on individuals' ability to
construct their own careers by taking action to adapt themselves and
what matters to them to the transitions of career development such as
from education to work, from occupation to occupation, from work
to non-work and from one job to another job. Thus career development is a process of progressive self-definition as individuals grow,
develop, respond and change as they encounter the challenges of living and working. Career construction theory, therefore, focuses on
personal meaning and perception rather than on abilities or traits that
matching theories emphasize (Savickas, 2006). Counseling is therefore

not about discerning a good match between the person and the occupation, but rather it is about assisting individuals to identify and utilize their life themes through narrative telling and then actively constructing the future (sometimes expressed as writing the next chapter of the story). Career construction theory focuses on the importance of what matters to individuals and their capacity to influence creatively both themselves and their work contexts.

One of the challenges for career construction theory is to provide an account of the interface between individuals and the environments that they find themselves in: the point at which the person's social construction of reality interfaces with a world that exists beyond the person's perceptions of it. For some radical postmodernists this is not a challenge, because they argue that there is no reality beyond perception (e.g., Patton & McMahon, 2006, p. 175). However, others such as Savickas et al. (2009) characterize career intervention for the individual as "matching their needs to those of contexts, in particular, the context of work activities."

At some point, as Lenz (2008) points out, most people have to make a career decision about an occupation, job or course. Consequently, it is incumbent on those who argue that "counselors must discuss with clients 'how to do' not 'what to do'" (Savickas et al., p. 11) to consider how a lack of content in such interactions will benefit such a client. Furthermore, the assertion that counseling should eschew testing (scores) and focus exclusively on stories lacks any credible account of helping an individual understand how they relate to others or to external standards, barriers or realities. For example, no matter how convinced an individual may be about his or her story of becoming a neurosurgeon, it is still useful to consider that person's assessment scores because, like it or not, these will be influential or even determinative of the chances of studying medicine. That is, in career development at least, at some point phenomenology has to confront the external realities of, among other things, educational institution entry quotas, labor market imperatives and economic fluctuations more generally.

Further, career construction theory and its apparent derivative, Life Designing (Savickas et al., 2009), emphasize control as an "advantageous" strategy in responding to environmental demands and also in negotiating that environment. Counselors are called upon to identify the "control parameters of potential dynamics in their complex ecosystems" (p. 12) and then develop narratives that help clients make sense of these. While these authors use terms derived from or closely related to chaos theory, including the notion of fractal and non-linearity, they appear to believe that control parameters can be identified, isolated (or described in relation to others) and controlled to some extent through narrative. However, it is questionable whether such parameters can be identified in principle given the complexities of the human condition, and this implies very significant limitations in our ability to predict and therefore take control over future events.

There is a danger that in privileging narrative as the means to produce meaning and continuity in a person's life the degree of control and choice that people genuinely have is exaggerated. Our concern here is that postmodernist expectations about career development may be just as unrealistic as the modernist expectations they have sought to supplant.

SYSTEMS THEORY FRAMEWORK

Patton and McMahon (1999, 2006) have applied the systems theory approach of Bronfenbrenner (1979) to the career development context. Systems theory in general seeks to understand phenomena in holistic terms, emphasizing the interconnections and complexity of reality. One of the distinctive aspects of this theoretical approach in comparison to many other theoretical conceptualizations is that the Systems Theory Framework has sought to be inclusive of most of the variables that other theories and research results have identified as potential influences on career development (Patton & McMahon, 2006). The Systems Theory Framework seeks to provide the convergence of career development theories that was much discussed in the early 1990s but subsequently appeared to lose steam as the aspiration for a comprehensive vision of career development failed to emerge (Savickas & Lent, 1994).

Thus in the Patton and McMahon framework the individual is viewed as a complex system comprising various recursively interacting subsystems of influences on career development such as interests, skills, ethnicity, gender, personality, beliefs, health, values, sexual orientation and knowledge. The individual is also viewed as a system embedded in a larger social system comprising subsystems such as family, media, workplace, education, peers and community. This social system is itself embedded in a larger system designated the Environmental-Societal System, which has subsystems including globalization, historical trends, political decisions, employment markets, geographical location and socioeconomic status. This approach points to the emergent and non-linear nature of changes and the importance of context in career development and decision making. In practice, the Systems Theory Framework points to the importance of identifying patterns of development over time and contexts and to the interactive nature of these systems and subsystems as open rather than closed. The Systems Theory Framework links in with career construction theory in its emphasis on story as the major approach to understanding the patterns and relationships that individuals identify as influences on their careers.

The Systems Theory Framework has introduced a range of new concepts into career development as well as identifying influences on career development often neglected in the literature, such as geographical location and change over time. It has demonstrated the need for a complexity-based approach to careers rather than a narrow focus on a small number of factors or influences.

However, these contributions are best understood as taxonomic in nature rather than genuinely explanatory. In essence, the problem with the Systems Theory Framework (STF) is that it is more framework than theory. To illustrate, the STF rightly identifies chance as an influence on career development. However, after having been identified it is simply added to the mix of other influences without a coherent account of why or how it influences the other systems and subsystems. Butz (1995) had noted that a weakness in all systems theories other than chaos theory was the lack of a dynamic that drove the system. To put it another way, the STF is predominantly content without processes beyond mutual influence ("recursiveness") and permeability of system boundaries ("open systems"). Also, despite the authors protestations of inclusiveness of positivist concepts like assessed abilities, interests and personality (Patton & McMahon, 2006), they themselves argue that the STF (and developmental theories) "lend themselves less easily to the assessment processes of trait and factor counseling" (McMahon & Patton, 2002b, p. 54). Indeed almost all of their emphasis is on constructivist approaches to career counseling in practice (e.g., Patton & McMahon, 2006).

SOME CONCLUSIONS

Therefore having noted the limitations of earlier approaches to career choice and development, the danger is to jettison prematurely all the insights that these earlier theories provide for both practitioners and their clients. Postmodernist approaches to career development stress the agentic properties of individuals and their capacities for constructing their own careers rather than simply entering occupations or accepting jobs. Such approaches, however, are likely to overemphasize the capacities of individuals to control their lives in general and their work in particular. They typically characterize the individuals as the authors of their own story, but neglect the fact that these individuals as authors cannot completely control the plots, and indeed that in any individual's story there may be multiple independent authors. Career construction and narrative counseling approaches in general encourage clients to stress the linearity, logic and the pattern of their careers and to underemphasize the non-linear, chance and unplanned influences.

What is required is a conceptual account of career development with practical applications that accounts for both the traditional career development-matching approaches with their emphasis on identifying the enduring characteristics of both individuals and occupations and the new challenges of imaginatively navigating through the labor market and creating a meaningful life in and through work. However, such an account must also not neglect the realities of complexity and its limitations on humans' capacities for control and predictability. It is contended in the next chapter that a career development perspective based on chaos theory may be able to accomplish most if not all of these objectives.

CHAPTER 3

The Chaos Theory of Careers: Background and Development

Complexity is to blame.

This could be the epitaph for twentieth-century science. Peat (2002) chronicles the decline in certainty in scientific thinking over the last 100 years under the influence of, among other things, relativity, quantum mechanics, the uncertainty principle, irrational numbers, the three-body problem and non-linear equations. The limitations of scientific explanation (Dewdney, 2004) and of our capacity to predict (Chown, 2007) have become increasingly recognized. In the discipline of career development, the traditional paradigm of positivism, determinism and reductionism originally resulted in the pervasive dominance of the matching paradigm for most of the previous century. Occasional voices of opposition were raised, such as Warnath (1975) and Roberts (1977), but these were typically drowned out by the consensual chorus of researchers endeavoring to demonstrate either or both the predictive and discriminant validity of various career development measures such as vocational interests, work values, personality traits, decision-making style and dimensions of career maturity. It all seemed so compelling that what career counseling was all about ultimately was finding the correspondence between the characteristics of individuals and occupations (Dawis & Lofquist, 1984). For many still working in the career development field, the matching paradigm remains the basis for their thinking, research and practice (e.g., Harrington & O'Shea, 1992).

In Chapter 2 the limitations of the matching paradigm were adumbrated. New theoretical counseling approaches such as career construction theory and the Systems Theory Framework, while redressing some of these limitations, are themselves limited in their capacity to provide an adequate theoretical explanation of complexity and its consequences. This chapter proposes that the Chaos Theory of Careers is a more complete account of career development than anything that has come before it in the career development field.

BACKGROUND TO CHAOS THEORY

Chaos theory has neither a unique founder nor a specific date of formulation. Various writers such as Gleik (1987), Briggs and Peat (1989), Butz (1997) and Lorenz (1993), among others, have located its origins at diverse times and with a range of different individuals. However, there is some agreement that the use of the term "chaos" to describe the non-periodic behavior of systems is attributable to a famous article by Li and Yorke (1975) entitled "Period three implies chaos." However, the most celebrated early event in the history of chaos theory is the failure of Edward Lorenz, an experimental meteorologist, to predict the weather using computer modeling. When on one occasion Lorenz approximated the data input the next morning after interrupting its processing in order to go home overnight, he found that the results being produced by the model during processing began to diverge from previous results from the model, and the divergence became greater the longer the processing was allowed to continue. This was quite unexpected, and after seeking for an explanation it became apparent to Lorenz that it was the tiny deviation in the data occasioned by approximating the results from the night before that had been the cause. Eventually, what he came to realize was that very small changes in the functioning of complex systems have the potential to result in a total transformation of the system.

This subsequently was designated the "Butterfly Effect" on the basis that something as apparently inconsequential as the beating of a butterfly's wings has the potential to precipitate a major meteorological disaster somewhere else in the world. Lorenz (1993) went on to define the distinguishing characteristic of chaotic systems to be sensitivity to change in initial conditions, which is simply another way of stating this effect. A further way of understanding this phenomenon is in comparison with Newton's third law of motion to the effect that "for every action there is an equal and opposite reaction." This is the basis of the linear mathematics of proportionality. However, what Lorenz had identified was a non-linear effect in which the impact of a change was disproportionate to its initial cause. What happens in complex systems comprising many interconnected recursive components is the potential for amplification of the impact of a change which may concatenate in a manner somewhat akin to the ripple effect of a stone thrown into a still lake. Some scientists, such as Strogatz (2003), believe that the future of all science lies in the exploration of non-linearity in the world.

However, what Lorenz and subsequent other chaos theorists, across a variety of disciplines, actually demonstrated was not simply the temporal or practical limitations of the predictability of natural phenomena, but its impossibility (Briggs & Peat, 1989). No amount of subsequent advances in scientific equipment or methodologies, no matter how much more powerful we can make our computers, nor how much more we can theorize about and discover about ourselves, our world or the universe as a whole, will ever enable us to be able to predict precisely all natural phenomena. The fundamental reason for this is that within non-linear, iterative systems' functioning are inherent tendencies to both stability and change, which can be observed and subsequently explained but which cannot before the event be predicted with precision. To express this concisely, complexity breeds contingency. The functioning of such systems is intrinsically stochastic.

A further consequence of these considerations is the limitation of human knowledge and control. Thus Dewdney (2004) writes:

> The discovery of barriers to knowledge has been accelerating somewhat over the past two centuries, keeping pace with science itself ... There are people among us who will brook no barriers ... there are others who, like me, will find marvels in these barriers to thought and action. A barrier gives shape, after all. (p. 3)

Later in this book the idea of barriers giving shape will be taken up and explored with the chaos notion of "fractals." The fact that there are barriers to our ability to know and control our world should not be a considered a statement of defeat nor a cause for despair. Complexity reveals that while there may be things we cannot know there is still so much more that we can discover and apply. As Dewdney (2004) goes on to reflect:

> Limitations on what we can know or do, whether real or only apparent, have the salutary effect of driving the scientific and technological process forward. Based on the apparent acceleration of impossible findings, it seems safe to predict

that science will increasingly become entangled with things unknowable and undoable. (p. 6)

The nature of the changes in science that chaos theory has either reflected and/or spawned can be summarized as:

From simplicity to complexity (Gell-Mann, 1994)
From certainty to uncertainty (Peat, 2002)
From reductionism to emergence (Morowitz, 2002)
From segmentation to interconnection (Barabasi, 2003)
From linearity to non-linearity (Strogatz, 2003)
From causality to contingency (Prigogine, 1997)
From determinism to agentism (Butz, 1997)
From analysis to synchrony (Strogatz, 2003)
From order to turbulence (Kaufman, 1995)
From predictability to chance (Peat, 2002)

Briggs and Peat (1999) identify three new themes that chaos theory has introduced into science. First, chaos theory envisions a new understanding of control as limited by contingency and chance rather than as the aspiration to be able to know and manipulate everything in nature. The chaos theory approach is one of humility before mystery and of embracing uncertainties and learning to live with and through them. Second, chaos theory points to human involvement with nature as creative interaction rather than total dominance or abject submission. We are creative participants in the changing nature of the world understood as the flux of patterns. Third, chaos theory draws attention to the subtlety of the universe. Nature abounds with nuances and irregular patterns that expose the limitations of the simplistic categories that we often use to understand and negotiate our world. In this sense all knowledge and theory is an inevitable simplification of complexity and should therefore always be considered subject to revision. This subtlety also allows for the positive use of non-linearity to create major impacts from small changes, thereby opening up many possibilities and opportunities to effect change in our world.

APPLYING CHAOS THEORY TO CAREERS

Chaos theory can be understood as the study of the behavior of complex dynamical (or adaptive) systems (Kaufman, 1995). In the consideration of how such a study could be applied to the study of careers, two principles of chaos theory were identified: self-organization and change. Self-organization describes the propensity of phenomena to form increasingly complex patterns. Without such a principle at work in the universe, logically there could be no universe. To talk about the universe and anything in it presupposes some sense of discernible structure. The principle of self-organization accounts for the stability, structure, stasis, predictability and lawfulness that humans have observed, identified and utilized throughout our evolution (Morowitz, 2002). This has been the traditional province of Western science since the Renaissance as well as for the ancient Greeks. The matching tradition of theory and practice in career development outlined in Chapter 2, with its emphasis on interests, values, traits, abilities and skills, is an example of the focus on structure, stability and the congruent linking of the characteristics of individuals with those of occupations.

The second principle is that of change. Chapter 1 identified the multidimensional nature of change that is impacting on contemporary work patterns. Chaos theory characterizes change in terms of adaptation and resilience as a complex dynamical system tries to maintain its stability in the face of influences to change. However, because change can be non-linear, iterative and unpredictable (Briggs & Peat, 1989), there remains the perpetual possibility that new outcomes for the system may emerge (Laszlo, 1991; Morowitz, 2002). This is experienced in the contingent nature of human life and experience—out of any set of circumstances, various outcomes are possible but only one is ever actualized (Butz, 1997).

Human history is the interpretation and record of human contingency at the individual, social group or societal level. If the change is sufficiently impactful then the system may experience a phase shift in which the structure and way of functioning of the system may radically change (Kellert, 1993). Trauma, religious conversion, midlife crisis, redundancy or rapid promotion are examples of the kinds of phase shift changes that can occur in individuals' lives and careers. The career construction approach outlined in Chapter 2 can be seen as the current theme in career development theory and practice which emphasizes the importance, the possibility and the opportunity that self-initiated change can have in people's career development. However, it fails at the point at which change is unplanned, unforeseen and unprepared for and for which individuals may not be responsible.

Most commonly the themes of self-organizing and change have been seen as opposing perspectives for understanding and counseling in career development. Typically, the various proponents of either stability (matching) or change (constructing) pay lip service to the opposite perspective but rarely seek to integrate or incorporate the other perspective into their theoretical work. However, for the chaos theorist these perspectives do not represent opposing trends or separate perspectives (Pryor & Bright, 2006). Complex dynamical systems incorporate both stability and change, structure and surprise, as linked, recursive and perpetual potential influences at the one time in the one system. Thus stability leads to change, and change may lead back again to stability. Indeed, some parts of such systems may be undergoing change at the same time that they are establishing stability in another part.

For example, consider the situation of Max in which a potential personal change may or may not initiate work changes for him. Max might be going through a divorce in his personal life at the same time that he is informed that his company's restructuring policy will not affect his current job. Here we have both change and stability. Of course, later on the divorce may affect Max's career by contributing to his work performance decline that results in demotion or losing his job, or by freeing Max to be able to move to another part of the country where a promotional opportunity is being offered.

Complex dynamical systems incorporate both self-organizing order and the unpredictability of change as integral to their functioning. For example, through negative feedback such as thermostat the system changes to reinforce its stability and structure by temperature regulation, while through positive feedback such as in a sound system, in which amplified sound combines with the original signal in a feedback loop creating a rapidly increasing noise, the system changes lead to disorder and turbulence (Briggs & Peat, 1989). The complexity perspective results in holistic accounts of how systems work rather than trying to focus exclusively on specific components of such systems as the way to account for the whole through an amalgamation analogous to fitting together a career jigsaw. If the last 100 years of career development have taught us anything about explanation through theory, it is that the jigsaw can never be put together. The career convergence aspirations of the early 1990s amply testified to the stubborn resistance of theories to become incorporated into one another while they remain narrowly focused (Savickas & Lent, 1994).

THE CHAOS THEORY OF CAREERS

The Chaos Theory of Careers (CTC) is embedded in both a realist and a phenomenalist epistemology. Again, this illustrates the dichotomy of career development theorizing up until the present. The matching or positivist tradition is based on a realist epistemology which assumes that what is being discussed as content of such theories, including abilities, values, traits, demands of an occupation and so on, actually exists in the world as entities. The phenomenalist view, which is typically adopted by the constructivist career theorists, instead considers all content in career development to be merely social constructions and metaphors. This is in one sense simply another manifestation of a venerable dispute that has raged on and off at least since the 1930s in psychology generally and was originally designated the "idiographic-nomothetic issue."

The approach of the Chaos Theory of Careers is to break away from the dialectical oppositions that disputes like this typically generate. If complexity encompasses both the positivist and the constructivist perspectives then there appears to be no reason why it cannot also integrate the idiographic and nomothetic as well. The CTC approach is to acknowledge that there is a real world independent of human observations of it. However, this world is so complex that it can be viewed from many different perspectives. That is why we can have many different scientific disciplines all examining, for example, the human body, but using differing concepts and focusing on different dimensions of the complexity—bones, blood, nerves, brain and so on. The nomothetic perspective seeks to take observations and experiences of the world and translate them into patterns of lawfulness and predictability. The development of personality trait measures in career development would be an example. The idiographic perspective focuses on the creative, individual and unique interpretation of reality by each person. The career counseling client narrating the story of their career would be an example of this latter perspective.

How might these two perspectives be integrated? The CTC sees career development as an interlocking process of choosing (nomothetic perspective) a career and creating (idiographic perspective) a career. In career development, choosing is a creative process and creating involves making choices. For example, Mary might choose to work as a dental technician but how she negotiates her terms of employment, with whom she prefers to work, how she arranges her workplace, what meaning she ascribes to the occupation and how she links it with other important spheres of her life and experience all can involve creativity, idiosyncrasy and personal significance. Conversely, assume that Mary decides to start her own business and open a health food shop with an emphasis on gourmet health foods, since she recovered from cancer without surgery through a major alteration of her eating habits. She may even link this business with another offering alternative therapies based on health food principles. However, she will still have to comply with various health and legal codes and make financial arrangements, all of which presuppose interacting with established external systems. Thus complexity in career development frequently involves a combination of the idiographic and the nomothetic. When chaos theory career counseling is discussed later in this book it will be apparent that the CTC approach seeks to integrate both positivist (nomothetic) and constructivist (idiographic) techniques to explore the complexity of each person's career development.

The holistic conceptualization of the Chaos Theory of Careers (Pryor & Bright, 2007a) means understanding reality in terms of systems that are characterized by complexity, interconnection and susceptibility to change (Pryor & Bright, 2003a). In short, they are complex dynamical systems (Bright & Pryor, 2005a). Complex dynamical systems can self-organize into order, coherence and resilient stability but they are also at the same time "sensitive to change in initial conditions" (Lorenz, 1993). "Complexity" involves a potential multitude of components of and influences on the system. "System" implies interconnectedness, interdependence and recursiveness of influence. Being "dynamical" emphasizes that as a consequence of being both "complex" and "systemic," chaotic systems are susceptible to change that has characteristics including non-linearity (disproportion between causes and effect), unpredictability (the causal chain is too complicated to be able to identify a single cause–effect sequence), iteration (concatenated influence through a network of interconnections), vulnerability to phase shift (the configuration of the whole system's functioning can transform) and emergence (new properties and capabilities of the system develop over and above those of its components individually) (Pryor & Bright, 2003b). Thus individuals developing their careers and experiencing life transitions are complex and dynamical systems acting within a matrix of other complex dynamical systems such as particular employing organizations, community groups, the labor market, the national and global economies, and so on.

Individuals as complex dynamical systems self-organize their lives both in order to survive and to find or make meaning, as a direct result of the complexity of the human brain. Our brains enable us to successfully survive and to render our experience meaningful through our (advanced) capability for pattern making (Kurzweil, 1999). As far as we can tell, humans are the most efficient sentient beings on earth at perceiving patterns, making patterns and utilizing patterns. We see relationships, connections, regularities, causal chains, continuities of existence beyond immediate perceptions in our world (Amundson, 2003a). Contemporary thinking about metaphor (e.g., Amundson, 2009) is another example of this propensity to pattern making by understanding one phenomenon by reference to another. The same is also evident in Ormerod's (2005) depiction of economics in organismic terms.

From such patterns we draw inferences about their underlying dynamics and consistencies. This is how we develop an understanding of the way in which the world works and our expectations about ourselves and others. In addition, we inject meaning and personal significance on the otherwise jumbled sequences of experiences that make up our lives. In doing so we also impose coherence (or system) on these patterns of events through self-conscious reflection on them (Gell-Mann, 1994). This is how we derive, at a personal level, both individual integrity and human spirituality, which are fundamentally a realization of our own integration into a pattern of meaning and significance larger than ourselves. Briggs and Peat (1999) express a similar idea in relation to artistic endeavor: "Art is the expression of our faith that the universe is spiritually coherent" (p. 112).

The process of pattern identification is not just one of perception and recognition. Humans act as complex dynamical systems to create order and meaning in our experiences and our environment. We try to make the world conform to the conceptions of patterns that we learn, test and develop through our experience (Briggs & Peat, 1999). In this sense Peck (1978) is correct in viewing all human activity as forms of problem solving in which fundamental problems revolve around meaning, identity and expectations about the way the world should work. Sometimes we are extremely successful with endeavors to conceptualize and control ourselves and our environment, such as through science, and sometimes we are mistaken, as in the gambler's fallacy (that is, the belief or expectation that previous chance event outcomes such as tossing a coin can influence future chance event outcomes, such as the next toss of the coin—the fallacy being to think that such outcomes can be connected when each toss is entirely independent and the probability of any outcome always remains at chance). In this sense, chaos theory through the notion of pattern making incorporates both traditional positivist concepts such as abilities, interests, work requirements and course entry levels with constructivist aspects of current career development theory that derive from pattern perception and pattern making such as narratives (Savickas, 2005), metaphors (Inkson, 2007), maps (Pryor, 2003), journeys (Baruch, 2004) and voices (Watson, 2006). The former are nomothetic patterns and the latter are idiographic patterns.

Before exploring some of the implications of the CTC, it is appropriate to indicate why we chose to use the word "dynamical" to describe complex systems when other writers (e.g., Bloch, 2005; Waldrop, 1992) have preferred "adaptive." When complex systems respond to changes in their own internal movements or to influences outside of themselves, such changes may be adaptive but they may not necessarily be. Sometimes such changes may have no adaptive function at all and be simply incidental. For example, Gould (1991) noted that pink flamingos are pink, not because of the supposed camouflage advantage of being harder to spot in the sunset, but just because they eat nothing but shellfish. Therefore there appears no necessary reason to assume that all the changes in complex systems will be adaptive—they may be but they may not. For example, most psychological defense mechanisms, such as projection or denial, as responses to influences on individuals' lives and emotions are likely to be maladaptive (Lewis & Junyk, 1997). As a consequence, we believe that "dynamical," which emphasizes change without loading such changes pejoratively, is a more appropriately neutral appellation for complex systems in chaos theory.

SOME IMPLICATIONS OF THE CHAOS THEORY OF CAREERS

In the next chapter another concept fundamental to chaos theory in general will be explicated and applied to the field of career development, and in the chapter after that further consideration will be given to patterns in nature and human thinking. The rest of this volume will be devoted to the contribution that the Chaos Theory of Careers (CTC) can make to theory, research and counseling in the career development field. It will be claimed that the CTC has the potential to reconcile the conflict between conceptions of being and becoming; it identifies the need to consider multiple perspectives to deal with complexity; it can help us understand how chance impacts on career development and how we might deal constructively with unplanned events; it links coherently science and spirituality for understanding outcomes and individuals; it suggests how non-linearity opens up new potentials for constructive individual change; it points to the need for the recognition of patterns rather than a preoccupation with prediction; it points to human limitations as well as potentials and challenges those involved in career counseling and research to a new humility before the complexity and mystery of existence; it questions the uncritical acceptance of goal setting as the primary counseling strategy and reiterates the need for a broad vision in the practice of career development thinking.

CHAPTER 4

The Chaos Theory of Careers: Attractors

Our limits are our freedoms.

Superficially, limits such as the laws legislators make place restrictions on the way we can acceptably behave in a particular society at a specific time. In this sense they diminish our freedom. However, on reflection it should be obvious that well-conceived and wisely implemented laws actually facilitate our freedom as individuals. For example, traffic laws set up conventions for driving that allow drivers to have reasonable expectations about how other users of the road should behave. If the traffic light is red drivers should stop, we all expect them to stop and most of the time they do stop, and so on. If there were no such laws then everybody would be very free but every busy intersection of a major city would be a "free-for-all" in which accidents would be legion. Therefore having restrictions on behavior actually enables our freedom to accomplish things that unbridled license would thwart. Our limits are our freedoms.

In systems thinking, without limits there can be no system. The whole point of identifying a cluster of phenomena as a system is to distinguish those components interacting together from other systems and influences. The boundaries of some systems are relatively easy to distinguish, such as an automobile engine or a tree. However, other systems, especially as they become more complex to our purview, become increasingly difficult to delineate accurately. Indeed, the boundaries of one complex system with another may easily become arenas of dispute. For example, in most democracies there are distinctions made between the government as a system and the military as a system. However, in times of coups d'état the military dispute the boundary and often take over much the content of the system of government and then rule as a junta. Finding the boundaries or the limits of systems requires investigation into how the components of the system operate or behave.

ATTRACTION

In chaos theory in general, the ways in which complex dynamical systems behave have been identified. They are called each particular system's "attractor." Williams (1997) stated that the concept of the "attractor" is the most crucial contribution of chaos theory. The notion of "attraction" in general is not dissimilar to its popular use. Bees are attracted to pollen, moths to light, the hungry to food, enterprises to profit, governments to power, lovers to each other and so on. Chaos theory has its origins in mathematics and the physical sciences (Kaufman, 1995). In such contexts, the concept of attraction is used to give an account of how natural systems function. Any form of satellite, from subatomic particles circling a nucleus to planets orbiting our sun, can be seen as an object caught in an attractor in the form of an orbit. Gravity is identified as the force of attraction that influences our world and daily experience most obviously. How systems function may be the product of competing or resonating forces. The reason humans can walk around on the surface of the earth rather than be sucked into the earth's core through gravity is that the electromagnetic force between the earth's atoms is stronger than gravity. Thus gravity keeps us from falling off the earth and electromagnetism keeps us on its surface. The competing nature of these forces of attraction determine where and to a large extent how humans live. To use a previous example, speaker feedback is an example of resonating attraction (Briggs & Peat, 1989). A speaker sound is picked up by a microphone and heard through the speaker more loudly and picked up by the microphone, and so on, in a repeating pattern, each time amplifying the sound. Here the attractors of the speaker and microphone are not competing but reinforcing one another. The more complex systems are, the more complicated can be the forces of attraction impacting on their functioning (Briggs & Peat, 1999). If there are also subsystems within systems, each with varying attractors, it frequently becomes virtually impossible to predict outcomes of such systems' functioning with any precision.

In summary, attraction can be understood as the process by which a system self-organizes into coherence and adapts to maintain, sustain or recreate such order when subject to change from either internal functioning or external influence (Jantsch, 1980).

The characteristic pattern of this process of attraction is called an "attractor." Many delineations of the attractor concept can be found in the general literature on chaos theory (Kellert, 1993). For the purposes of applying the concept to career development, six specific and often complementary ways to understand attraction and the attractors are outlined.

CHARACTERIZING ATTRACTORS

Characteristic Trajectories

Attractors can be understood as characteristic trajectories of systems (Kaufman, 1995); that is, the typical ways in which systems operate as systems. An attractor shows a system's long-term behavior (Williams, 1997). Psychologists have been studying such characteristic patterns of human behavior for about 100 years. These have been variously designated as instincts, traits, temperament characteristics, abilities, skills, aptitudes, habits, interests and so on. Much of the practice of career counseling has been based around the identification and measurement of such characteristics (Amundson, Harris-Bowlsbey & Niles, 2005; Shahnasarian, 1994). Briggs and Peat (1999) describe an attractor's trajectory as the plot that reveals its repeating pattern. Williams (1997) has described an attractor as a system's "identity card."

Feedback Mechanisms

Briggs and Peat (1989) identify the operation of attractors in terms of the complementary forces of positive and negative feedback. Sanders (1998) views attractors as feedback mechanisms that systems utilize by which they can sustain stability, respond to perturbation and initiate change. All the time individuals are receiving feedback about what is happening both to them and to their world. Most learning, for example, is a consequence of feedback about which actions achieved the desired outcome and which did not. Action-oriented theorists such as Krumboltz (1998) suggest that just trying various occupations and processing the feedback is an effective way to improve career decision making, especially for those who become transfixed by indecision.

When confronting change in a system's functioning, negative feedback promotes stability in the system since the system is experiencing difficulties in seeking to initiate such change. In such circumstances, the system is likely to resist the impact and challenge of changing.

This might help explain the phenomenon of employees having been informed that the company is to close or relocate, and that they will be made redundant as a consequence, failing to take any action to find other employment opportunities until after the company actually makes them redundant. Initiating change is so difficult for institutionally dependent workers that they simply will not face it. The feedback on the prospect of changing is so negative that they reject the opportunity. In the process, they often exacerbate the perceived problem of change by postponing it. Then decisions about their future may have to be made under stress and financial pressure, which are typically deleterious to effective career choice. Many psychological defense mechanisms such as denial can be understood as negative feedback when a system (that is, an individual) is confronted with undesirable change (Butz, 1997).

Positive feedback in reaction to change usually means that change will be embraced since it is perceived to be rewarding to the system. Work trials for those being case managed by rehabilitation counselors is an example of the use of positive feedback as a way to develop or alter clients' attractors after a sustained period out of the open labor market. Work provides time structure, activity opportunities, social contact, a sense of identity and a focus away from a recovering individual's pain and limitations. Such changes often have positive psychological effects in assisting individuals to adjust and to find new coping strategies (Pryor & Hawkins, 2009; Rubin & Roessler, 2007; Szymanski & Parker, 2003).

End States

Gharajedaghi (1999) characterizes attractors as end states to which systems move. Kaufman (1995) describes attractors in terms of a basin of attraction and homeostasis. Human homeostasis can be physiological or psychological. Physiologically, it can be seen in the state of functioning in which the body resists changes by compensatory actions such as immune responses to germs, sweating and shivering with temperature changes and adrenalin discharge when threatened. Psychologically, it can be seen in subsequent amnesia after facing intense trauma. Butz (1997), as previously noted, identified attractors as defense mechanisms. It is not hard to see how the classical defense mechanisms identified by Freud, such as projection, reaction formation, denial and sublimation, could be understood as attractors. For example, prejudiced persons may project their own inadequacies onto a minority group in order to avoid confronting their own problems. In such a situation their existing attractor is defending their current end states from the challenges of either changing their attitudes or more generally addressing their own problems.

Attractors as end states find expression in the work of a variety of organizational experts (Covey, 2004; Peters, 1987; Senge, 1990) who have emphasized the importance of "a shared vision" within an organization in order to achieve effective responsiveness to both workplace and economic change. At the individual level, the focus on meaning, purpose and mission in contemporary career counseling (see Chapter 9 for details) represents another example of the importance of end states for career development.

Ordered Boundaries

Attractors can be understood as the boundaries of systems as they operate. Without boundaries to a system, there is no system—just absolute disorder. Attractors in this sense are the limits within which systems operate and by which systems are differentiated from one another. In career decision making this conception applies as the limits of what may be acceptable to individuals, for example in terms of their core values, interests, ethics, motivation or preferences, and the limits on their capabilities as a result of their knowledge, abilities and developed skills. Thus a person who has a strong ecological perspective may find working for a paper production company just within acceptable value limits but employment in the logging industry unacceptable.

In systems theory in general, the boundaries of systems may be more or less permeable or impermeable (Richmond, 2000). Impermeable boundaries are those that eliminate or restrict influence from outside the system. Such attractors seek to operate or function independently of the rest of the world. Some psychoses can be conceptualized in such terms since psychotic individuals frequently act in ways that demonstrate little contact with the rest of reality—hence their speech and behavior may appear bizarre, inappropriate and irrational. Less extreme examples of systems attempting to be impermeable might be the hermit, the misogynist and the extremely withdrawn or self-contained person. Some individuals adopt such a shutting-off of the outside world as a form of escape from pain, emotional vulnerability or responsibility. It is not uncommon in vocational rehabilitation for individuals who have been injured and can no longer work to withdraw from most social contact as a consequence of anger, bitterness, feelings of worthlessness or social embarrassment. The impermeability of a system's boundary has a direct relationship with "closed systems thinking" (see below).

Permeable boundaries are found in systems that are susceptible to outside influences. Individuals may actually seek out new influences, information, ideas, relationships, connections and so on outside their current contexts and patterns of operation. In personality trait terms, such permeability would be identified with "openness to experience" on the one hand and "extraversion" on the other (McCrae & Costa, 1987). Work as a social activity tends to promote permeability of boundaries since it tends to be undertaken in interpersonal, or at least relatively public, contexts, much of the activities of which are performed by interacting with others as customers, coworkers, competitors and colleagues.

Reality Visions

Spirituality has become an increasingly important issue in the career development literature (Bloch & Richmond, 1997). Attractors can be understood spiritually as visions of reality—what gives sense and purpose to living. Thus attractors can be seen to reflect individuals' values, sense of worth, identity, meaning making and sense of mission (Pryor & Bright, 2004). Attractors are the expression of what really matter to individuals. "Mattering" is becoming a foundational concept of constructivist thinking in career development and choice (Amundson, 2003a; Savickas, 2005). If individuals are to convert "preoccupations" into "occupations" (Savickas, 1997) then knowing what matters to them becomes essential to the choice process since work frequently constitutes a significant part of most people's lives and has a major impact on all other dimensions of their experience of living. Chapter 9 explores such issues in greater detail.

Equilibrium and Fluctuation

Attractors can be described in terms of their tendency toward equilibrium or fluctuation. As attractors become increasingly closed systems, they tend more toward equilibrium. As systems move closer to equilibrium, they start to exhibit repetitious behavior until a crisis occurs (Kossman & Bullrich, 1997). As systems move further from equilibrium, they experience more fluctuations owing to their increasingly open interactions with their environments. This is associated with less stability and a greater chance of system reorganization or "phase shift." Thus as attractors more closely resemble open systems, the more unstable they become but the higher the likelihood that adaptation can occur. Thus a system that has the potential to break up into chaotic disorder also has the potential to reorganize in new ways (Prigognine & Stengers, 1984). In counseling terms, this increases the possibilities for client transformation. Masterpasqua (1997), when discussing the need for disequilibrium for psychological health, observed:

> Chaos is not so much pathological as it is a state of maximum readiness for an emerging reorganized self-system ... individuals most capable of adaptation and growth are those poised at the edge of chaos. (p. 37)

This becomes a particular career-counseling issue for those who have lived in cloistered environments, such as young adults from financially comfortable families or those who have done the same kinds of work for the same employer over longer periods of time. The often coddled nature of such individuals' lives has prevented them from having to face many significant challenges. Life has been easy for them— others have shielded them from many of the contingencies of human experience. However, when suddenly faced with a major career development challenge, such as choosing a four- to six-year professional course of study or an offer of redundancy, they struggle to take responsibility for facing and meeting the challenge. Too much equilibrium in the past has not "battle-hardened" them for the inevitable uncertainties that all of us have to confront (Rescher, 1995).

TYPES OF ATTRACTORS

In their discussion of attractors, Lewis and Junyk (1997) make the following observation about attractors as accounts of systems:

> According to notions of multiple causality, human behavior is stochastic, unpredictable, and self-organizing. To describe the activities and states of a human system, then, we must map out its tendencies or possibilities, not its rules. (p. 44)

Schaffer and Kott (1985) have suggested that accounts of systems can be understood in terms of the motion within systems exemplified by different types of attractors. Chaos theorists have identified four fundamental types of attractors that describe the functioning of all systems. Pryor and Bright (2007a) have sought to apply these to career development as the point, pendulum, torus and strange attractors.

Point Attractor

This describes a system structured to move toward a fixed or single point, place or outcome. Crutchfield, Farmer, Packard and Shaw (1986) define a point attractor as representing all systems that come to rest with the passage of time. The typical physical representation of such a system is a basin or sink in which objects or fluids move or flow toward the bottom or plug hole. Psychologically, this is a description of driven thinking and behavior, "tunnel vision," exclusive preoccupation, overconfidence in decision making, fixation on a choice option, ideological or goal-dominated thinking and/or obsessional or fearful behavior. Vocational examples of such systems' functioning include professional athletes preparing for major sporting events, workaholic executives, "control-hungry" managers who cannot delegate, the belief in the "career for life," inherited careers (perhaps a farmer, or someone following in a parent's footsteps) and single-product companies. Career development theories that emphasize the idea of "fit" as a result of matching, such as Holland (1997) and Dawis and Lofquist (1984), tend in practice to be used to point people toward the best occupation based on various criteria of matching, such as personal abilities to job demands. Counselors who adopt this approach typically conceptualize careers in very individualistic terms and tend to disregard the range of broader issues that may impinge on individuals' capacity to choose and implement career decisions. They are also likely to disregard the role of chance and uncertainty and to rely too much on the predictive validity of the assessment measures, such as interest inventories, that they typically employ (Pryor, 2002).

Pendulum (sometimes called the Equilibrium, Limit-Cycle or Periodic) Attractor

This describes a system that functions by regular swings between two points, places or outcomes. The typical physical representation of such a system is a pendulum moving from one pole to the other pole of the swing, passing through a vertical point in the process. With the pendulum attractor there are competing sources of attraction that cause systems not to simply cancel each other out but rather to function in a swinging motion from one attraction source to the other.

An example of the pendulum attractor that most students of psychology come across in learning theory is the "approach-avoidance" conflict in which one option is attractive when far away and becomes less attractive as one approaches it, while in turn this results in another option previously less attractive becoming more attractive as it is moved away from. In career counseling terms we can identify such a pattern in the functioning of stressed clients who are likely to adopt dichotomous thinking strategies—everything is black or white, perfect or useless, desirable or repulsive, ecstatic or horrific. Such thinking is extreme in content and typically oversimplified in structure. Only two competing influences are contemplated and the choice of one option can only be made at the expense of the other. Work–family role conflict can be understood in these terms. The demands of each role can be competing, and sometimes people will see answers exclusively in terms of being a worker or being a parent. Of course both are legitimate choices; however, the challenge is to develop more creative and nuanced strategies to explore the possibilities of balance and adaptation and change for each individual seeking to reconcile work and family responsibilities. Other vocational applications of this attractor are role conflict, career indecision, rigid and extreme ideas, occupational stress, risk-taking sensitivity, lack of commitment, fear of failure and divided loyalties or priorities. The pendulum attractor can be seen in clients who hold rigid and extreme beliefs such as black-and-white thinking. This is generally a barrier to effective thinking and hence prevents insights and the generation of solutions.

Counselors should encourage clients to consider issues from multiple perspectives; in so doing, the clients appreciate that the problem is likely not to be reduced to a simple either/or scenario (Amundson, 2003a). Clients in the grip of pendulum thinking will rarely be able to generate win–win scenarios and, furthermore, solutions that present "balance" as the desirable outcome may be aggravating the situation by attempting to stop the pendulum at the lowest point: that is, at the point of compromise in which neither conflicting need is appropriately met, thereby aggravating both.

Torus Attractor

This describes a system that functions in a complex and yet predictable way. Such a system repeats itself either exactly or approximately over time. The typical physical representation of such a system is the maze in which there is only one way through and which leads eventually back to its beginning to start again. Once the solution is found, each new time through the maze repeats previous routes to complete the task. This is an example of the attractor exactly repeating. The self-similar variant is akin to a long piece of wire being wrapped around a donut. As the wire circles around the dough, it describes a characteristic loop, which varies only in that each successive loop is a wire's width further around the donut. For most intents and purposes, the torus attractor can be thought of as exactly repeating since the minor differences are typically of little practical consequence in this system. Psychologically, this is a description of routine, habitual and predictable thinking and behavior. In similar situations the influence of this attractor is manifested in typical, consistent, trait-like reactions and responses. Such individuals know that the world is complicated so they seek to keep control by organizing and pigeonholing both people and things. They develop systems for doing things at set times and in nominated places. Consistency, routine, classification, hierarchy and organization are their catch-cries.

In organizational terms the classic example of this is inflexible bureaucracy. Everything is systematized; there are prescriptions for all actions; work is structured around set schedules and timeframes; people and information are "processed," which usually means identified with some part of the system and treated according to standard procedures. Specifically vocational examples of torus attractor operation include the "backroom" technician who just wants to be left alone to do the assembly job he or she has always done; or the file clerk who has been with the company for many years and, though very bored, is just holding on for a few more years to retirement; or the insecure worker who finds any change in his or her work circumstances a threat and who dreads the feeling of not being in control of his or her work tasks. Such individuals may also be constrained by tradition, organizational culture, supervisors' perceived expectations and conformity to the extent that they relinquish the right and responsibility of individual decision making of any real consequence. For some counseling clients the power of the predictable repeating pattern of the torus attractor results in them making the same mistakes, such as reverting to addictions or abusive relationships, over and over again (Briggs & Peat, 1999).

Obsessional and paranoid behavior patterns also are likely to be described by the torus attractor. Fear, insecurity, self-consciousness, uncertainty, worry about failure, desire to "play it safe" are sources of motivation that frequently constrain those in the torus attractor. When the illusion of their control is shattered by a major negative unplanned event, they typically try to regress to an earlier mode of coping, refuse to consider the consequences of change, deny or hope that it does not affect them, or simply lose all confidence in their ability to respond to the new set of circumstances confronting them.

Strange Attractor

This describes the functioning of a system that is complex in the sense of being potentially susceptible to a wide range of influences and having the capacity for complicated internal relationships among its components to develop. In this sense it resembles the torus attractor. However, there are some fundamental differences. The principal difference is that strange attractors exhibit a defining characteristic of chaos: sensitivity to change in initial conditions (Lorenz, 1993). This sensitivity to change is a consequence of two inherent characteristics of strange attractor systems. First, such systems repeat themselves as do torus attractors; but unlike torus attractors, strange attractors never exactly repeat. This is one of the reasons why such systems may appear literally "chaotic," that is random and unpredictable. The pattern or order in the system emerges from the self-similar but never identical movements of the system over time.

The second reason for the sensitivity to change of strange attractor systems is that, unlike torus attractors, they are open to influences beyond themselves. This is why in physics and other sciences they are identified as "dissipative" in nature (Prigonine, 1997), following the second law of thermodynamics (Gell-Mann, 1994). Such systems can interact with other systems in mutually influential ways—often in systems theory designated "recursion." The result of this is that the number of potential change influences becomes, at least in theory, virtually infinite. In practice many factors will limit this number, but the crucial point is that such systems are susceptible to a wide range of both endogenous and exogenous influences. The typical (and historical) physical exemplar of such a system is the weather. Owing to the multitude of interacting factors combining complexly, the precise prediction of the weather beyond about a week, in most parts of the globe, is unreliable. However, over time emergent patterns of order in terms of seasons and climate are clearly discernible. Psychologically, the strange attractor is the "edge of chaos" where the human potential to adapt, develop and grow is manifested along with human limitations of knowledge and influence. The edge of chaos is where change and chance are not seen as opposing forces to order and stability but rather as integrated realities of the fabric of existence. It is the meeting point at which the processes of self-organization and stability in systems coalesce with the contingency of human experience and the creativity of human potential. In vocational terms, the edge of chaos (EOC) is the conjunction of rational/logical planning and action with originality and imagination in decision making, to confront the threats and opportunities inherent in the uncertainty of our work, our lives and our world.

SYSTEMS THINKING

The potential of the attractors conceptualization for an understanding of individuals' problems has been evident to psychologists working in clinical and rehabilitation contexts. Butz (1997) observed that much maladaptive thinking and behavior such as neurosis can be understood in terms of clashes of attractors within individuals. Moran (1998) argues that clients can be usefully considered to be strange attractors (and hence open systems). In the clinical realm, Moran argues that when behavior becomes closed and periodic it is often a clinical marker for mental illness. Torre (1995) noted that under stress individuals tend to regress to more rigid attractors. Marks-Tarlow (1995) identified limit-cycle attractors (such as the pendulum attractor) as regressive defense mechanisms characteristic of compulsive behavior. Livneh and Parker (2005) have applied attractors to an understanding of adaptation to chronic illness and disability.

The four attractor types outlined above can be classified into either open or closed systems categories. The Chaos Theory of Careers contends that virtually all significant career development counseling problems can be understood in terms of individuals trying to impose closed systems thinking on an open systems reality (Pryor & Bright, 2007a). Point, pendulum and torus attractors are all examples of closed systems thinking. In essence, closed systems thinking is an attempt to simplify reality in an endeavor to achieve order and control.

Closed Systems Thinking

Humans goal-set, dichotomize and make routine their worlds in order to control, master and manage unwanted change. Such strategies can be successful in the short term or with a limited range of activities or when the system is free from disorder (Strogatz, 2003). In such circumstances, closed systems thinking works and there seems no reason to believe it would not go on working. However, complexity will have its way with us all eventually (Taleb, 2007). At some point unplanned change will intrude into the apparently closed system world, often with profound and sometimes disastrous effects. Such moments of crisis or opportunity will cause the closed systems thinkers to reassess their view of the world, themselves, their destinies, their aspirations and their values. Thus for example, the 35-year-old up-and-coming sales executive who seeks career counseling after receiving a diagnosis of cancer is likely to be confronting a challenge not only in health but also in meaning, purpose, values and beliefs. The illusions of stability, control and predictability have been exposed, and the challenges of disorder, contingency and uncertainty need to be addressed, not only in treatment but also in career and life. The reality of life as an open system has finally exploded into his or her world of hard work, talent, promotion and success in the company.

While there are important differences between those who are dominated by the point, pendulum and torus attractors, there are some fundamental similarities as well. Such closed systems thinking is characterized by expectations that the unexpected either will not or should not happen. These individuals may believe that they are virtually invincible and in control, and have the belief that life should be fair and that they should, as a consequence, be treated fairly in their own terms. They are likely to have a strong sense of personal control and not to give very much consideration to the contingent nature of human experience. Such individuals are likely to derive great confidence from perceived order, pattern and stability in the past, and as a consequence to believe that while change can occur it is likely to be linear in nature and therefore still able to be controlled through appropriate future planning. Where change does occur or something unexpected happens, this is regarded as in some sense extraordinary. As a consequence, it has comparatively little impact on their general beliefs about the person having sufficient knowledge and control of their life circumstances. In particular, this closed systems thinking tends to limit the number of inputs into the system to which responses are made. In this sense, this thinking is an attempt to simplify reality in order to gain a sense of control over one's experience. Moreover, insofar as this has worked in the past it will tend to be repeated. Thus people are likely to keep doing what they have always done on the basis that it has worked before, whereas the strange attractor demands open systems thinking.

Open Systems Thinking

Strange attractor or open systems thinking is premised on the idea of the limitations of human knowledge and control of reality including the system represented by the strange attractor itself. Masterpasqua (1997) noted when considering complex systems that there are no closed systems with the possible exception of the universe itself. Open systems thinking is characterized by a recognition that the unexpected can and sometimes will happen. As a result, individuals are vulnerable at least some of the time to change over which they have no control. While they would like life to be fair, they recognize that life itself has no guarantees. While seeking to control some parts of the functioning of the system, this approach acknowledges human limitations in terms of control and the realities of contingency. While order, pattern and stability are recognized from the past and passing into the present, the reality of major change in the configuration of the system and the experience of one's life are also acknowledged as continually potential. This thinking appreciates that the past does not guarantee the present, nor the present the future. Also acknowledged is the possibility of change being non-linear in the sense that a small difference may result in very major reconfiguration of the system. Therefore the unplanned and the unexpected are not simply exceptions to the stability and order of reality but are part of its very nature (Rescher, 1995). Once this is accepted, instead of being perceived as a perpetual threat to be warded off or a specter to be fled from, change can be construed as a reality to be created and influenced at best and accepted and submitted to at worst (Pryor & Bright, 2007a).

FROM CLOSED TO OPEN SYSTEMS THINKING

In its ultimate inability to deal with unexpected change, closed systems thinking is frequently characterized by a failure to recognize, utilize and create opportunities. There is a fundamental inability to acknowledge what can and cannot be done or known in response to the complexities of reality. Closed systems thinking attempts to deny the non-linear nature of change by believing that change should be and can be controllable. Further such thinking believes that if change is not able to be controlled then reality should not be like this. In essence, closed systems thinking fails to recognize the potential of emergence (Morowitz, 2002) as a consequence of change when new states of the system and the environment in which the system functions develop and need to be responded to in a proactive way.

Bright and Pryor (2008) identified the change from closed to open systems thinking in terms of "shiftwork" in which 11 paradigms shifts are necessary to deal with working in an open systems world. These shifts are:

Shift 1: From Prediction to Prediction and Pattern Making
Shift 2: From Plans to Plans and Planning
Shift 3: From Narrowing Down to Being Focused on Openness
Shift 4: From Control to Controlled Flexibility
Shift 5: From Risk as Failure to Risk as Endeavor
Shift 6: From Probabilities to Probable Possibilities
Shift 7: From Goals, Roles and Routines to Meaning, Mattering and Black Swans
Shift 8: From Informing to Informing and Transforming
Shift 9: From Normative Thinking to Normative and Scalable Thinking
Shift 10: From Knowing in Advance to Living with Emergence
Shift 11: From Trust as Control to Trust as Faith

In subsequent chapters the counseling implications of closed and open systems thinking will be further explored. However, a simple model of the use of the chaos theory in counseling can be adumbrated as a four-step process:

1. To identify, where operative, clients' closed system thinking strategies.
2. To help clients to realize that such efforts at control, certainty, knowledge and predictability are crucially limited.
3. To assist clients to recognize and utilize the stabilities and surprises of living in the strange attractor.
4. To enable people to be able to both perceive the dimensions of complexity and to acknowledge and effectively negotiate uncertainty, change and chance in constructive ways to fulfill their deepest aspirations.

In the next chapter the ways in which attractors can be identified and have been used will be explored through the concept of fractal patterns.

CHAPTER 5

The Chaos Theory of Careers: Patterns and Fractals

We live between dimensions.

Career counselors sometimes use a technique called a timeline. Basically counseling clients are asked to draw a line that represents their lives either as a whole or up to the present. Many people draw the line as in a graph, gradually rising or falling depending upon the highs and lows of their experience. Some clients will draw their line as a shape such as a circle, seeking to convey the idea that life is a series of recurrent patterns. Of course, there is no one right answer to such an exercise. The counseling goal is to assist clients to reflect on their experience and draw potential implications for further action. However, some thought about the task would lead to a consideration that the task itself is unrealistic since if we tried to draw a line through time to depict our experience it would be continuously moving. If it were not moving, it actually would mean we are dead! Thus the moving timeline we should draw would have greater dimensionality than a single line but it would have less dimensionality than a figure such as a circle or a square. In fact, it would have a fractional dimensionality somewhere between one and two. This is one way to understand the notion of a "fractal" first coined in the context of classical Euclidean geometry by Benoit Mandelbrot (1975), who pointed out that once you allow shapes to move the traditional notions of pattern as dimensional space become inadequate as descriptions of reality. Applying this to lives and careers, the outstanding implication is that we live our lives and develop our careers between the dimensions with which we typically construct our understanding.

Chaos theory replaces the line with an endlessly complex figure of fractal dimension. At every scale of magnification, the fractal reveals new patterns and intricacies ... What may look from a distance to be linear reveals on closer examination the twists and turns and arabesques of infinite fractal detail. (Briggs & Peat, 1999, p. 126)

HUMANS ARE PATTERN PROCESSORS

Humans are pattern identifiers. We recognize similarities between the people we encounter and the events we experience. We link such similarities in ways consistent with our developing schemas about how we think reality works. In so doing, we infer causes and effects. Experience becomes the testing ground for our schemas and for the validity of the patterns we identify. As the patterns humans identify and create include more elements and become more complicated and interconnected, we often describe such patterns as "systems." Chaos theory conceptualizes all of reality in terms of systems. Although the term "chaos theory" tends to imply that its focus is on disorder, system turbulence and unpredictability, the focus is equally on order and stability. The Chaos Theory of Careers conceptualizes reality in terms of existents as systems in relation to other systems. Thus individuals developing their careers and experiencing life transitions are complex dynamical systems acting within a matrix of other complex dynamical systems such as particular employing organizations, community groups, the labor market, the national and global economies, and so on.

Understanding the fundamental importance of patterns in human functioning provides a framework for considering how pattern processing lies at the heart of career counseling techniques such as pattern identification (Amundson, 2003a) and narrative (Bujold, 2004) and how these relate to the Chaos Theory of Careers. The ability to identify and create patterns is an essential and inescapable feature of human thought and adaptation. New information is acquired by our senses, which automatically convert sights, sounds, textures and smells to patterns of neuronal activity. We synthesize these rudimentary patterns into more sophisticated patterns by creating links between existing stored patterns and the newly perceived ones. Through a process of aggregation we categorize patterns into reusable categories such as plants, animals, and buildings (Holland, 1995). Patterns also form the basis of creative thought, which can be thought of as combining elements of, or even whole, existing patterns into novel new concepts (Duggan, 2007).

In career counseling the ability of counselors to see patterns is essential to their ultimate effectiveness:

> Counselors need the ability to recognize patterns because most clients cannot say who they are or articulate their life theme. The essence of people, their unique spirit and activating force, can be seen only in the whole pattern, not in the individual traits, but clients find it easier knowing and reporting their traits that are so embedded in their own pattern that they do not realize they have one. (Savickas, 1997, p. 10)

The ability to see patterns is complemented by the ability to compare, contrast and synthesize patterns.

Identifying similarities between patterns involves some form of tagging process (Holland, 1998) that highlights specific local characteristics in each pattern. For instance, a pattern of a car may contain four round patterns that we might tag as "wheels," or the pattern in a career might be the striving for peer acceptance across different roles. This tagging process is essential because when next we encounter a similar pattern we can classify the pattern as belonging with the car pattern or the pattern of needing recognition. We can also divide our category into patterns with two wheels and those with four and tag them as motorcycle and car respectively. Such processes apply across all human experience and for instance underpin the marshalling of armies on a battlefield or rallying supporters at a political rally, or the adhesion of antibodies to antigens (Holland, 1995). In addition to tagging, there are other fundamental processes that underlie pattern processing.

At the heart of pattern processing are the notions of regularity, similarity and symmetry. Human beings are particularly sensitive to regularities in their environments and encode these regularities in the absence of conscious efforts to do so. For instance, Bright and Burton (1994, 1998) demonstrated that people show a sensitivity to regularities apparent in stimuli in the absence of any intention to learn about the regularities and the absence of any conscious awareness they had acquired this information. In one study people were asked to rate the aesthetics of clock designs without being told that every design presented bore a time that fell between 6 and 12 o'clock. Subsequently when shown some new clock designs, participants indicated they had seen before those clocks whose time fell between 6 and 12 o'clock, despite both the design and the specific time depicted being novel.

Regularity can derive from the presence of the same tags across a stimulus, such as the presence of wheels on a car. They can also derive from the presence of the same tags across different stimuli such as the presence of wheels on different models of cars. Regularity is most often thought of in terms of physical properties such as visual, auditory, tactile or olfactory repetition. However, regularity can also be generated psychologically, for instance in noting the frequency of occurrence of certain behaviors such as that the television news is always broadcast at 6pm, or that the postman always rings twice.

Similarity involves the psychological linking between two or more experiences. The similarity may be relatively superficial and based upon the physical properties of the stimuli. Alternatively, regularity can derive from the creative act of analogous thinking whereby a new stimulus is classified as "sort of like old" (Brooks, 1978). Many theories of human memory (e.g., Hintzman, 1990) are based upon the idea that we store experiences as memory traces, and when we encounter a new stimulus we attempt to match it against previously stored traces. This matching process permits us to make judgments about similarity. It also allows us to combine the new and the old into novel combinations. Creative thinking often results from such novel combinations of the new and the old (Duggan, 2007).

Symmetry is an essential element in many patterns, and one for which humans have a particular affinity. Symmetrical patterns have a precise correspondence of form and constituent configuration. Symmetry implies design and purpose, and it is perhaps not surprising therefore that symmetrical patterns are commonly found in religious iconography including: Christian (Cross), Jewish (Star of David), Hindu (Om), Islamic (Crescent), Buddhist (Wheel of Dharma), Shinto (Torii Gate), Sikh (Chakkar), Baha'i (nine-pointed star), and Jain (raised hand). In nature, symmetries abound, and can be seen in the delicate pattern of a snowflake, in the robust structure of a tree, in a honeycomb and in the structure of DNA. Humans are attracted to symmetrical patterns, and more broadly the concepts of evenness and balance. We have an aesthetic preference for symmetrical faces (Mealey, Bridgstock & Townsend, 1999).

Self-similarity is a special form of similarity that is actually a form of symmetry. It has been defined as "symmetry across scale" (Gleick, 1987, p. 103) or magnification symmetry. This means that the pattern of an object is repeated across all scales of the object. A simple example of this idea is Russian Dolls where within each doll is another smaller but identically featured doll (see Figure 5.1).

Figure 5.1 Fractal patterns of Russian dolls.

The centrality of pattern processing in human thinking is reflected in the large number of patterns that hold special meaning for us. Commonly employed patterns in career counseling include narrative, metaphor, maps, journeys and voices. Before considering the connections between these patterns and the Chaos Theory of Careers, we need to return to a special form of pattern that is the signature of chaos.

FRACTALS: THE SIGNATURE OF CHAOS

When we attempt to reproduce or represent nature we simplify reality and create a pattern that is an approximation of what we perceive. The most influential example of this is Euclidian geometry, which has given us circles and triangles. Most of us learned this geometry at school and were encouraged to use the Platonic shapes of triangles and circles as resemblances to reality. However, as Benoit Mandelbrot famously pointed out, "Clouds are not spheres, mountains are not cones, coastlines are not circles and bark is not smooth, nor does lightning travel in a straight line" (Mandelbrot, 1982, p. 1). In fact most things in the world, apart from those that have been man-made using Euclidian geometry, such as windows, wheels and cogs, turn out to be wrinkly, rough, jagged and irregular. They present in a "fractured" form. This is the other dimension of the term "fractal"—the first being "fractional," which was referred to earlier in this chapter.

Mandelbrot found that there were certain odd shapes that mathematicians had discovered years before that provided a way of modeling the roughness and wrinkles observed in the world. The shapes were "pathological" because they were created by the repeated application of the same process in a recursive fashion (Dewdney, 2004).

Recursion means simply that the output of a process is fed back into the process as the input. When this repetition happens sufficiently often, the results are intricate and elaborate patterns that can often resemble patterns that naturally occur in nature. Briggs (1992) identifies the link between recursion and fractals in terms of the activity of systems: "Fractal geometry describes the tracks and marks left by the passage of dynamical activity" (p. 22).

A classic example of a "pathological" function can be observed in Koch's snowflake. Starting with a triangle (Figure 5.2), the function is a simple rule of adding another triangle at the midpoint of each line (Figure 5.3). After seven iterations of this simple rule, the resulting pattern looks remarkably like a snowflake (Figure 5.4), and the precise straight lines of the triangle have been transformed into ever more wrinkly and bumpy surfaces. Such patterns have another important feature. They are self-similar at every level of scale.

Benoit Mandelbrot (1975) coined the term "fractal" to describe patterns that are self-similar across scale. We are surrounded, immersed and comprised of fractal patterns. As Briggs (1992) observed:

> Most natural objects, including ourselves, are composed of many different types of fractals, woven into each other with "parts" that have different fractal dimensions. (p. 71)

The branching of trees and plants, the coastline of Britain, clouds, our circulatory system and our brains are all structures that demonstrate fractal patterns (see Figure 5.5).

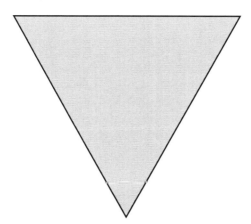

Figure 5.2 Koch snowflake.

Figure 5.3 Next iteration of the Koch snowflake.

Fractals come in various different forms. There are so-called linear fractals that demonstrate exact self-similarity at every scale. More complicated fractals are said to be non-linear in that they are generated by non-linear equations. The resulting fractal patterns do not consist of straight lines as in the Koch snowflake (Figure 5.4); rather, they include curves and swirls. This makes the self-similarity at

Figure 5.4 Koch's snowflake, further iteration.

Figure 5.5 Fractal patterns in nature.

different scales deformed and unpredictable, but nonetheless there is some degree of similarity that can be observed. Finally, the most complicated fractals have a random component which introduces even more "roughness" into the patterns, which even better resemble some naturally occurring patterns such as mountain ranges and tree branches (Figure 5.6).

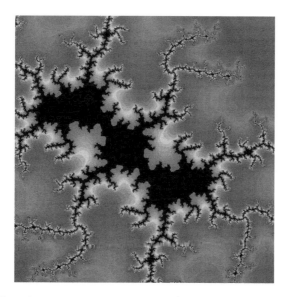

Figure 5.6 Fractal pattern in the Mandelbrot set.

Fractals are visual traces of the action of a chaotic system. In the previous chapter, the defining feature of chaos—the strange attractor—was described. The pattern of a strange attractor is a fractal. Chaotic equations in mathematics are "pathological" in that they generate patterns when many iterations of the equation take place. Therefore over time the pathology or pattern can be ascertained as the emergent pattern of the fractal. Given the nature of the strange attractor, the fractals produced are self-similar yet at the same time inherently unpredictable. Furthermore, the trajectories evident in the fractal never exactly repeat and over time the fractal may radically change its pattern. In a literal sense, a fractal combines pattern and surprise. "Fractals record what happens in the transition between order and chaos" (Briggs, 1992, p. 13).

FRACTALS AND CAREER DEVELOPMENT

Within the Chaos Theory of Careers, individuals are understood as complex dynamical (e.g., chaotic) systems, and thus their behavior is recorded in fractals. Even if individuals start life with identical genetic blueprints, as in the case of identical twins, because of the sensitivity to initial conditions of chaotic systems every individual develops both a unique general fractal and subsets of fractals. The complexity of human beings suggests that non-linear or even random fractals are likely to provide the most compelling descriptions of human behavior (Strogatz, 2003).

Considering behavior in fractal terms provides a framework to consider the relationship between patterns of behavior and apparently random or unexpected behaviors. Fractals illustrate the complexity and inherent unpredictability of human behavior and hence careers. The concept of a fractal pattern of behavior provides a mechanism to link existing concepts in vocational psychology such as traits (Dawis, 1996), Holland codes (Holland, 1997), stories (Bujold, 2004), metaphors (Amundson, 2009; Inkson, 2007), maps (Pryor, 2003; Savickas, 1995), journeys (Baruch, 2004), trajectories (Mercer, Nichols & Doyle, 1988) and voices (Watson, 2006).

It is through these processes of repetition, similarity and symmetry that we are able to create meaning and to understand our world. From this perspective we can see that a narrative thread describing a person's career path serves to highlight regularities, similarities and symmetries in the person's experience (Briggs & Peat, 1999). Our ability to appreciate similarities is so ingrained that we do so automatically and unthinkingly. For Mandelbrot (1977), "the most important instrument of thought is the eye. It sees similarities before a formula has been created to identify them"(p. 26).

Constructivist career counseling techniques such as those adumbrated by Savickas (1995) can be seen as attempts to encourage clients to get an appreciation of their fractal patterns, and hence to get some indication of possible future trajectories:

> Clients review their lives and focus awareness in an effort to grasp the theme; that is, to construct the whole that will clarify the parts. They will eventually resume forward movement and use the newly clarified and refined life theme as a map with which to plot a new location for themselves. (p. 366)

And in 1997, Savickas wrote:

> The essence of a person, her or his unique spirit and activating force, can only be comprehended as a whole pattern, not trait pieces. (Savickas 1997, p. 9)

The *theme* Savickas conceptualizes can be clearly interpreted in Chaos Theory of Career terms, as the emergent fractal pattern that results from the individual's complex behavior over time. The idea of the life theme as a map closely resembles the concept of a fractal in that a fractal illustrates both the potential and the limitations of a complex system. Savickas' map plays a similar role. In the second quote, it is clear that Savickas has something very akin to a fractal in mind when considering the uniqueness of an individual. This is exactly the conclusion of Briggs (1992): "Chaos affirms that individual details matter" (p. 30).

FRACTALS AND STORY

Savickas uses "story" as the method of capturing the fractal. Stories are the method through which counselors "gain access to a person's spirit and life theme" and "stories are modes of knowing that capture the richness, uniqueness and complexity of what life means to a client. From these stories about their torments and elements, their preoccupations and projects, I look to find the theme" (Savickas, 1997, pp. 9, 11).

A clear description of the role of narrative in career counseling is provided by Christensen and Johnson (2003):

> A career narrative is basically a story about a career. It is a story that connects the … client's past to the present in the sense that it conveys how the protagonist came to be what he or she is presently. This retrospective aspect of narrative is supplemented with the career story's progressive aspect, in which the narrative puts into words the future that the protagonist is approaching. A story is therefore both an account of how the protagonist came to be what he or she presently is, and furthermore, what future is expected for the protagonist to enact based on his or her particular past and present being." (p. 151)

This description of narrative illustrates the tendency to characterize narrative as providing an almost complete description of the client. Rarely in the literature on narrative is there any recognition of the limitations of the narrative approach, the recognition that narrative does not capture all of the complexities of the client or their circumstances (Pryor & Bright, 2008; Taleb, 2007). It would be a mistake to equate a narrative with a person's strange attractor, as any one narrative is inevitably a simplification of reality whereas a strange attractor is a far more complex structure. In many regards the use of narrative techniques in career counseling was a response to the perceived over-simplification of matching-based assessment paradigms. Using the metaphor of the Koch snowflake, labeling a client using a three-letter Holland code might be akin to reducing the snowflake to a simple triangle. The subsequent more complex iterations of the Koch snowflake are analogous with the client's story. As more iterations are performed, the pattern becomes more complex and more closely resembles a snowflake in the same way that a client's narrative more closely resembles the client than an abstract three-letter code.

However, the Koch snowflake is a linear fractal and repeats in a simple manner. Likewise, narrative has a linear structure that links one life event after another into an explanatory structure (Savickas, 1995). The simple repeating patterns of the Koch snowflake, or the repeating structure of the client preoccupation captured in a narrative, represent a simplification of, and therefore incomplete account of, reality.

Consider the more complex fractal depicted in Figure 5.4. This fractal clearly has an emergent pattern, but it is not one that can be neatly captured in a linear form within a story, or for that matter within the confines of a psychometrically derived category or value. Elements of the pattern do exhibit relatively simple structure, but over time the patterns change in an unpredictable fashion that adds significantly to their complexity. This fractal graphically illustrates the limits of predictability in career development. Short-range predictions are reasonably accurate, but over time such simplifications are usually inadequate. From a career counseling perspective, it reminds us that over-reliance on any one method is likely to be inadequate, and will fail to capture much of the inherent complexity of clients viewed as systems embedded in other complex dynamical systems. Using a range of different techniques is more likely to provide greater insights into the nature of the client's fractal.

FRACTALS AND METAPHOR, PATTERN IDENTIFICATION, MAPS, JOURNEYS AND VOICES

Metaphor has gained a lot of attention as a powerful career counseling technique in the practice of career development (e.g., Amundson, 2003a; Inkson & Amundson 2002; Inkson 2007; Sagaria, 1989; Spain & Hamel, 1993). For Inkson (2007), considering a range of metaphors leads to true understanding. So presumably, in Inkson's terms, a fractal can be fully understood by adopting a range of metaphors. This suggests that different metaphors will provide insights into different aspects of the fractal, and hence metaphors may provide a way of navigating around and understanding fractals.

Metaphor involves the implicit description of one concept in terms of another. Metaphors therefore involve the pattern-processing component of similarity. A single metaphor therefore cannot capture the reality of a situation, but rather it illuminates an aspect of reality. It draws links between particular aspects of a person's career and other aspects of reality independent of the career. Metaphors provide insight by translating portions of some unknown pattern (the career) and highlighting the similarities to some well-known pre-existing pattern, for instance comparing career development to a game or pastime (Pryor & Bright, 2007b), or comparing career development to established ideas in physics (Amundson, 2003b).

In fractal terms metaphors are useful ways of navigating around the fractal. Adopting different metaphors is akin to adopting different perspectives to view the fractal. The sheer complexity of fractals means that radically different patterns can be observed depending upon the perspective taken by the observer. Simple patterns like circles do not change at different levels of magnification; simply less and less of the pattern is seen as one zooms in. A fractal pattern, on the other hand, reveals a continually changing pattern from different perspectives.

Journey is one of the most over-used metaphors in the career development world, to the point that its deployment by an individual often belies a tragic lack of imagination and a somewhat fixed view of their own career. A journey can be thought of as a series of moves that, when joined together by plotting them, identify a trip that has followed a particular route. So in some senses a journey is not unlike the idea of a trajectory—the path of a moving object or projectile. Trajectory is a term that is commonly applied to describe the motion of a strange attractor as it reveals its complex pattern in computer simulations based on chaotic equations. For instance, Edward Lorenz's "butterfly" fractal, when plotted out over time, looks like a spiral shape, before suddenly the plot deviates to map out a second joined spiral shape, hence creating the two wings of the butterfly (Lorenz, 1993).

Thus when one goes on a "journey" along the trajectory of a strange attractor, that journey is going to be complex, ever changing, and subject to unpredictable and sudden deviations. Consequently, one way of considering the metaphor of journey is to see it collectively as the trajectories that make up a fractal. The benefit of fractal analysis is evident in that the trajectories of strange attractors are not linear, nor are they predictable. Thus the fractal perspective actively promotes a more complex understanding of behavior and avoids seeing journey narrowly in linear and predictable terms.

Interestingly, clients often use "journey" retrospectively as a way of describing the journey so far, rather than in prospective terms, the journey ahead. This retrospective usage is akin the concept of the emergent pattern within the strange attractor—a pattern that cannot be predicted in advance but can be appreciated and described over time and after the fact.

Amundson's (2003a) Pattern Identification Exercise (PIE) is another explicit example of pattern-based counseling. In PIE, clients reflect on activities they enjoy. They then consider times when the activity was and was not enjoyable. In so doing, clients are encouraged to explore their feelings on each occasion, and the context (i.e., others present, thoughts, challenges, successes and motivations). From this, they are invited to consider what patterns are suggested by the elicited information.

The underlying premise in PIE is that the dynamics that drive career exploration can come from any aspect of a person's life experiences. Amundson argues that any aspect of a person's life can be scrutinized to reveal "common life patterns." This is a fractal notion—that if you look at any aspect of the pattern, the common life patterns (i.e., fractal patterns) will be evident. Amundson is essentially talking about symmetry of scale when describing the PIE technique. In fractal terms, what the PIE method is doing is plotting out in some complexity a portion of the fractal, and then asking the client to step back and identify the emerging patterns. Similar processes operate in asking clients to set out career maps, or asking them to consider and analyze the different voices that are relevant to their situation.

FRACTALS AND ASSESSMENT

Typically books written on the general topic of fractals contain many photographs of fractal structures either occurring in the natural environment, such as the profile of a mountain range, or generated by human activity, such as dazzling displays of computer graphics. The photographs are time-limited records of the dynamical actions of systems. Pryor (1979) identified inventory test scores in similar terms as a photograph. It was asserted that a test score or profile of scores is a record of the behavior of individuals at a specific moment in time. These scores are standardized ways of identifying the relation between the person and the environment, in this specific instance the test task (Pryor, 1987, 1991). The reason for recording this relation rather than any number of a virtually numberless set of others is that research over most of the last century has shown us the practical utility for career decision making of having some idea about individuals' characteristics such as, among other things, reasoning abilities, specific skills, vocational interests, work values and personality traits.

Just as there are limitations to any photograph, such as the quality of the camera, the skills of the photographer, the physical characteristics of the environment and the demand characteristics of the situation, to name but a few, so any test score may be influenced by a wide range of factors, most of which may have no relevance to the actual relation that the assessor is attempting to measure (Goldman, 1972). Indeed, many of the technical developments of psychometrics were generated as ways to reduce such deleterious effects, with varying levels of success across different assessment tools, including reliability, validity, standardization and meta-analysis.

In a directly analogous way, test and profile scores, can be understood as fractals—the record of the interaction of the person as a system with the environment as a system. However, since we are dealing with complex systems it must be noted that many fractals can be observed recording such interactions—not all of which can be assessed psychometrically. Moreover, as we know from quantum mechanics, sometimes the very act of assessment may change what it is that we are endeavoring to assess. For example, it is not especially uncommon for a career counseling client who reports having no idea what sort of occupation he or she likes to be given by the counselor an interest inventory to complete. When the counselor subsequently asks about the individual's reaction to the inventory, the person may assert that the results are not valid because "I changed my mind while I was filling it in." The person is in fact reporting that the assessment process itself distorted the assessment results. When systems are dynamical (e.g., individuals on the verge of a phase shift such as choosing a career) such occurrences should not be particularly unexpected. Some fractals are much more temporary than others; thus, the fractal pattern of a city may be changed within a day by a cyclone crossing the coast at that point.

The more recent trend toward qualitative assessment in career development (e.g., Gysbers, 2006; McMahon & Patton, 2002b) seeks to capitalize on the process of change by encouraging questioning, exploration, subjectivity, speculation, creativity and feedback.

In the minds of some writers (e.g., Goldman, 1972; Savickas 1997), career counselors should prefer qualitative assessment techniques to quantitative (i.e., psychometric) approaches. From a chaos theory perspective (Bright & Pryor, 2007a), complexity demands multiple perspectives in order to be able to assess both the convergent and the emergent characteristics of individuals' strange attractors. Fractals are the records of the stability and change exhibited by the functioning of strange attractors. Taking sides in the quantitative–qualitative debate is simply a form of pendulum attractor thinking and leads to needlessly limiting the range of assessment techniques that may be employed by counselors to assist individuals in their career development. As we have elsewhere concluded:

> The Chaos Theory of Careers provides an integrated account of the interdependent relationship between stability and change. Hence, the CTC links the apparently different aspects of process and product, qualitative and quantitative and stability and instability. (Bright & Pryor, 2007a, p. 45)

FRACTALS AND HUMAN BEHAVIOR

Fractals have been usefully employed as tools to analyze a diverse array of human behavior. Fractal patterns in family therapy have provided useful insights into the interdependent behaviors of family members that sustain and/or conceal dysfunctional behavior (e.g., Miermont, 1995). The sheer complexity of fractal patterns containing, as they do, repeating elements as well as uncertainty and radical transformation has been linked to Adler's individual psychology. It is perhaps not surprising that such links have been made given the close affinity with Savickas' career construction theory which incorporates many of Adler's principles and fractals (Savickas, 2009).

Jung's Archetypes can be seen as fractal patterns, and have also been linked to narrative in career development (Pryor & Bright, 2007b). In economics, fractal patterns have been used to analyze the behavior of financial markets (e.g., Peters, 1994).

SOME CONCLUSIONS

That humans understand reality in terms of patterns is not particularly controversial. However, in our anxiety to meet the twin objectives of developing understanding and banishing uncertainty, we can all be lead easily into the trap of over-simplification. Much of the debate that has existed in the career development literature between positivist, modernist or matching paradigms, and the recently revisited humanistic, constructivist or post-modern paradigms, between the quantitative and the qualitative, between reductionist and holistic approaches, has amounted to efforts to supplant one form of simplified pattern processing with another.

The explicit, or more recently implicit, goal of these endeavors has been to predict some form of outcome: be it the best fitting occupation (Holland, 1997) or the next chapter of the client's life (Savickas, 1997). The methods of all of these schools of thought and of their proponents follow a similar pattern. First, discern patterns in the client's past; and second, assume that these patterns will project into the future through resemblance to an interest category, or through the process of discovering the individual's preoccupation through thematic questioning.

Essentially the debate between these broad churches revolves around the degree of complexity of the patterns that form the basis of analysis, ranging from the unapologetically simple in the case of Holland interest categories, to the more complex but ultimately still linear and simple narratives of Cochran, Bujold and others. The common claim is that a life can be encapsulated, summed up, captured in a three-letter code, or in a narrative, and that past behavior predicts future behavior.

Fractal geometry and especially the fractals created by strange attractors provide a more complex way of considering individuals and their careers. Only linear fractals conform to the maxim that past behavior predicts future behavior. Non-linear and random fractals do not conform to this maxim, yet at the same time they do exhibit structure, form and some stability. This structure is far too complex and non-linear for any technique, qualitative or quantitative, to capture adequately in isolation.

The philosopher of science Kuhn argued that scientific advances do not come gradually and linearly, but rather they represent sudden bends in a road. Like Kuhn's (1962) bend in the road, what comes next in a career may not be easily understood by what went before. Unless you happen to be standing at the bend in the road, you are unable to see clearly what went before, and what comes next. Imagine standing not at a bend in the road, but on one of the many bends on the trajectory of a strange attractor. From this perspective, we would be right to be humble about our capabilities to understand the trajectory and cautious in making any long-term deterministic predictions about the future. The Chaos Theory of Careers draws attention to the limitations of our simplifications and the challenges of living uncertainly in our unpredictably complex world.

CHAPTER 6

The Chaos Theory of Careers: Research Support

Life is empirical.

Life is more than theory and conceptualization. It is about acting, trying things, seeing what works and what does not. Every culture throughout history has collected observations about the behavior of its people and its environment. The methods used to capture and communicate these observations are as varied as mankind itself, but some methods have stood the test of time better than others. Eye-witness accounts, narratives, drawings, maps, recipes and receipts are common to many cultures as empirical methods, and since the eighteenth-century period known as the Enlightenment, the scientific method has established a dominant place in understanding the mysteries of the universe. Therefore since the field of career development claims to have its foundations in empirical science it is legitimate to ask: What empirical evidence is there to support the Chaos Theory of Careers?

As presented in earlier chapters, the Chaos Theory of Careers seeks to account for, among other things, three key elements in career development. These are:

- Complexity of influences
- Change
- Chance events.

There is empirical support for each of these elements. This chapter reviews both the specific empirical evidence in support of the CTC and, more broadly, the available evidence in the career development literature that is consistent with, and therefore supportive of, the major propositions of the theory.

SOME GENERAL OBSERVATIONS ABOUT RESEARCH AND THE CTC

In terms of complexity of influences, there is a plethora of studies that have focused on particular influences on career development. Virtually any annual review of the career development literature (e.g., Patton & McIlveen, 2009) adumbrates numerous studies that demonstrate the influence on career development of parents; the media; gender-role stereotyping; the economy; education; injury; illness; globalization; unemployment; geography; family structure, and many others. Indeed, Patton & McMahon (2006) provide an extensive taxonomy of such influences.

Taken together, these studies suggest that there are a complex range of influences that come to bear upon the individual when making career choices. However, although the sheer number of these studies and the diverse range of factors they cover are suggestive, it is still possible to argue that they are merely reflecting differences between different people making career decisions. In other words, for any one individual it is, typically, possible that relatively few of these influences are actually in operation. Under such a model, there is relatively little complexity of influence, and career decision making would be straightforward.

Stronger evidence for the complexity of influence must therefore be found in studies that have attempted to measure this complexity within each subject. Studies that present a wide range of potential influences for participants to endorse as influential are one way of measuring the complexity of influence. Of course, such studies suffer in that they are limited to only those influences that participants are consciously or readily aware of; however, they represent stronger evidence than the plethora of studies more narrowly focused on fewer influences.

Yet another approach that avoids the distortions of subjective perceptions is to observe patterns of career behavior in the presence or absence of a range of factors. Such studies make no attempt to measure how participants experience the various influences; they are more concerned with establishing reliable correlations between factors and behavior. A less direct way of establishing the importance of complexity, change and chance is to look at the effectiveness of counseling interventions that focus on these factors compared to more traditional interventions that focus on stability and fit. If it can be established that interventions addressing the key elements of the Chaos Theory of Careers are more effective than traditional counseling, this provides indirect evidence in support of the Chaos Theory of Careers.

One may reasonably ask why not look for chaotic patterns in career paths by applying mathematical modeling. If it were possible, such an approach would hold out the potential for the strongest evidence for the operation of chaotic principles in careers. However, there are significant challenges in attempting such an analysis. Essentially, such an approach entails modeling a chaotic algorithm to career patterns. Immediately, such an approach comes up against an intractable problem in the shape of non-linearity and sensitivity to initial conditions. Chaotic equations depend critically upon the initial parameters (Lorenz, 1993; Abraham & Gilgen, 1995). Parameter tweaking has bedeviled computational modeling approaches in other areas of psychology such as memory and face recognition, even though the models used in these areas typically do not exhibit sensitivity to initial conditions to anything like the extent seen in chaotic models (e.g., Stewart & West, 2007).

In practical terms, this means that even if chaotic models could be made to fit, one could not escape the charge of parameter tweaking. Furthermore, given the asserted complexity of influences that come to bear on career behavior, deciding what could plausibly be initial conditions becomes a non-trivial task. This problem rapidly falls into an infinite regress when one considers that genetics is likely to play a significant role in career development. Genetic endowment certainly influences career-related behavior in physical domains such as professional sport and athletics, music, and possibly jobs involving significant physical labor, and may plausibly be influential in cognitive-related work too. Not wanting to enter into the sterile nature–nurture debate, it is sufficient to observe that such debates exist, and any conclusion that includes a role for genetics in career behavior necessarily spells trouble for chaotic modelers.

Savickas (2009) has called for researchers to adopt an additive approach akin to that of medicine. To build upon the work of others, it is necessary to have a rich base of empirical work in the first place. Consequently the evidence reviewed in the rest of this chapter in support of the CTC is derived from existing research findings that support the key assumptions of the theory, in particular the notions of complexity of influence, change and chance. In addition, given that the CTC claims to have practical career counseling applications, research into the effectiveness of CTC-based interventions is also reviewed in support of the theory.

In this chapter we review the current state of empirical evidence related to the Chaos Theory of Careers. The evidence is arranged around the organizing principles of complexity of influence, change, chance and outcome studies. Before presenting our own work we review other research into the applications of chaos theory to career development.

COMPLEXITY OF INFLUENCES

One of the major contributions to more recent efforts at career development has been identification of the need for research with perspectives broader than the individual and provision of insightful and comprehensive taxonomies of contextual variables (Lent et al., 1994; Patton & McMahon, 1999, 2006; Szymanski & Hershenson, 1998). In relation to career decision making, however, it still appears that research into the kinds of contextual factors identified by these theorists is rudimentary and underdeveloped compared to research into person variables (such as cognitive abilities or vocational interests). Lent et al. (2002) examined perceived influences on 31 college students comprising undergraduates and graduates. They identified six categories that influence career choice. These were interests; direct exposure to work-relevant activities; vicarious exposure to work-relevant activities; work conditions or reinforcers; thinking one is good at an activity; and leisure experiences. Other categories that were influential in positive or negative choices included family, friends and teachers. They concluded that choice barriers and supports include generic factors and others that differ as a function of an individual's circumstances and experiences. Poole and her colleagues have collected longitudinal data on the career intentions and paths of students dating back to 1975 (e.g., Poole, Langan-Fox, Ciavarella & Omodei, 1991; Poole & Langan-Fox, 1992; Poole, Langan-Fox & Omodei, 1993). They found that contextual variables such as socio-economic status (SES), parental education, educational resources, support structures and parents significantly influenced career choices. The significance of such research from our perspective is that it provides some insights into the way contextual variables impact the career decision-making process.

Looking across the relevant literature of the past 50 years, there is plenty of evidence that specific environmental factors are important considerations in career development (Bronfenbrenner, 1979, 1989; Collin, 1990; Ford, 1987; Krause, Bochner & Duchesne, 2006; Leong, 1996; Patton & McMahon, 1999; Sears, 1982; Vondracek, Lerner & Schulenberg, 1986). However, much of this research has focused upon a very narrow range of variables in isolation rather than attempting to assess a broad range of factors influencing individuals simultaneously.

One example of an attempt to measure a wide range of influences simultaneously can be found in Bright, Pryor, Wilkenfeld and Earl (2005). In contrast to the qualitative approach adopted by Lent et al. (2002), this research focused on quantitatively measuring the impact of environmental influences on career decision making simultaneously. An attempt was made to measure subjective influences on career behavior in line with much of the previous work in this area, but there was also an attempt to measure objective influences on career behavior. Perceiving that something influenced one's career behavior does not necessarily mean that it actually has influenced that behavior. If, in addition, consistencies between the objective presence of that influence and the expressed behavior of the person can be indicated, however, this would provide further converging evidence to support the conclusion that a particular influence has had some material impact upon the career behavior. Influences can be divided into structural and personal environmental influences. In the personal category are included parental and family influences, friends, teachers, trainers and bosses, colleagues, and chance encounters with key individuals. The structural context would include opportunities to engage in different activities or vocations, socio-economic factors (personal finances, state of the economy, job stereotypes), geographic factors and educational opportunities.

The results from a sample of 651 high school and university students confirmed that there were a wide range of influences upon career decision making. These can be seen in Figure 6.1.

A factor analysis revealed four major factors of influence, which were labeled Media; Teachers and Lecturers; Family and Friends; and Unplanned Events. These data provide support for the CTC's claim that career decision making is subject to a complex array of influences.

This research also found evidence of the dynamic and changing nature of these influences. For instance, the influence of family was seen to diminish across the sample as a function of their age and educational stage, with high school students reporting greater levels of influence than postgraduate students (see Figure 6.2). Further studies that explore an even broader range of influences may find that the vacuum left by the receding parental influence is filled by either new or other influences.

Unusually in this study, we were able to examine "objective" relationships between parental occupations and student course choices; that is, between jobs parents were actually doing, and courses actually selected by students, a measure of the expressed behavior of both parties. We found that there was a reliable association between the occupations of the fathers and the students' choices of courses when

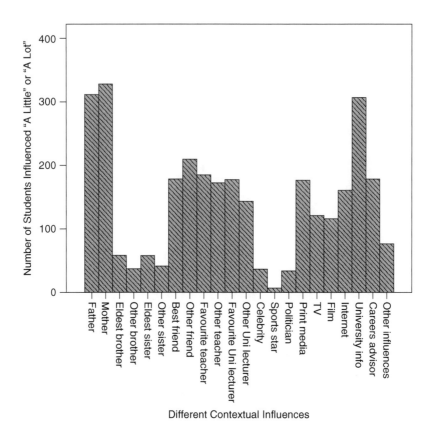

Figure 6.1 The range of influences on career decision making. (From Bright, Pryor, Wilkenfeld & Earl, 2005)

both were classified into the Holland taxonomy of occupational stereotypes. Owing to the large number of mothers who were not engaged in professional-level employment, such a relationship did not obtain overall for mothers. However, when the subset of professional working mothers was considered, a similar pattern of results was revealed.

These results confirm that a wide range of different influences come to bear in career decision making, that these changed over time, and that contextual influences such as parental occupation were reliably associated with student career decisions. The study provides some evidence for the basic assumptions of the Chaos Theory of Careers in that, for this sample at least, career decision making appeared to emerge from a complex array of different influences that also changed over time.

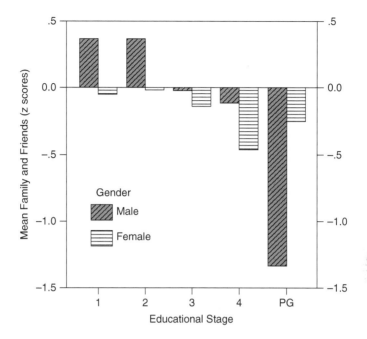

Figure 6.2   Graph showing the influence of family and friends on career choice as a function of stage of education.

More studies of this type will help to determine the extent of the influences and begin to address the dynamic nature of those influences. Furthermore, by considering subjective and objective measures of influence, there is in principle an opportunity to tease out some of the relative contributions of social constructions about the world and contextual influences.

CHANGE

A search of the PsyLit database in May 2009 retrieved 736 matches to a search on the terms "Career Change." Figure 6.3 shows, decade by decade over the last century, the distribution of these publications. It demonstrates dramatically that the notion of career change was rarely explicitly addressed in the research until a dramatic explosion of interest in the 1980s that appears to be continuing unabated. (The figures for the latest decade end in 2008, and thus may be an underestimate of the number of publications on career change in this decade.)

This suggests that although it is now well established, expected even, for individuals to change careers, the expectation appears to be

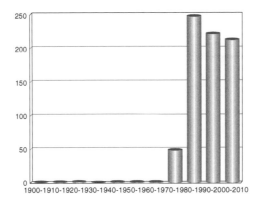

250

200

150

100

50

0
1900-1910-1920-1930-1940-1950-1960-1970-1980-1990-2000-2010

Figure 6.3 Graph showing PSYLIT search results for search on term "Career Change" over time.

a recent phenomenon, perhaps reflecting the enormous political, social and economic upheaval the world has experienced in the past 30 years from a combination of globalization, technological advances and the exponential increase in the number of liberal and democratic systems of government and society over the past 100 years.

It is not surprising, therefore, that the notion of change within career theories has been a relatively neglected topic until recently, and that most established theories of career development, especially those that trace their roots to the 1950s or earlier, either neglect or downplay change, or characterize it in a purely personal developmental manner. Again, empirical evidence that change is a constant in career development as the CTC contends is an important cornerstone in establishing the credentials of the theory. Because of the paucity of earlier research, there is relatively little empirical evidence but a lot of anecdotal evidence attesting to rapid career change in our current age. In particular, the more powerful longitudinal data are even more lacking in this area than in the career development field generally. One of few exceptions to this conclusion was the research conducted by Jepsen and Choudhuri (2001). They followed 170 rural high school students from a single grade cohort over 25 years. They found that one third of the cohort experienced stable occupational career patterns (that is, they stayed in the same occupation) over their entire working career sampled. The other way of interpreting these data is to point out that two thirds (i.e., the majority) changed occupations in the period under study. A similar proportion of women in a 10-year study also changed occupations (Betz, 1984). Furthermore, the career changers in Jepsen and Choudhuri's study were almost twice as likely to report that their careers had been "better than I expected" (64% to 34%). It seems that changing careers is not only the norm, but is beneficial for career satisfaction.

CHANCE EVENTS IN CAREER DEVELOPMENT

Despite chance events being included in the career development literature since the 1950s, there has been comparatively limited empirical research in this area. The literature has used various terms, including *chance* (Roe & Baruch, 1967), *serendipity* (Betsworth & Hanson, 1996), *happenstance* (Miller, 1983) and *synchronicity* (Guindon & Hanna, 2002).

Despite the different terminology and subtle definitional differences found in the literature, chance events generally relate to "unplanned, accidental, or otherwise situational, unpredictable, or unintentional events or encounters that have an impact on career development and behavior" (Rojewski, 1999, p. 269). Most of the research that has been conducted suggests that individuals' career decision making is influenced by chance events to a considerable degree (Betsworth & Hanson, 1996; Hart, Rayner & Christensen, 1971; Roe & Baruch, 1967; Williams et al., 1998).

Roe and Baruch (1967) found that the participants focused on the contingencies and external influences that had influenced the course of their careers rather than on logical progressions. Hart et al. (1971) examined the career histories of 60 men and the degree of planning, preparation and chance involved in occupational entry at professional, skilled and semiskilled levels. They found that the vocational histories of skilled and semiskilled workers were quite often influenced by chance encounters. For the professional workers, on the other hand, chance had much less influence because they relied on planning and preparation. Betsworth and Hanson (1996) found that of their sample of older adults, 63% of men and 58% of women indicated that their careers were influenced by serendipitous events. Williams et al. (1998) studied the contextual factors surrounding chance events and the perceived impact of chance events on the career choices of academic women in counseling psychology. They found that at least one serendipitous event had a significant effect on each of the 13 women.

Some research suggests that contingency factors (e.g., awareness of skills and abilities and perception of interests) are more likely to be perceived as having an influence on career patterns than chance factors (Salomone & Slaney, 1981; Scott & Hatalla, 1990). Salomone and Slaney (1981) studied chance and contingency factors influencing career choice in nonprofessional workers. They found that they were more likely to view their career decisions as rational, based on contingency factors such as personal qualities, than as the result of chance. However, the participants did indicate, in addition, that some unexpected events influenced their vocational decisions.

Scott and Hatalla (1990) conducted a similar study with college-educated women and found that of the top nine factors, only one, unexpected personal events, was a chance factor. However, this chance factor was perceived as influential by more than 60% of the participants.

A possible deleterious and confounding influence on research asking people to review their career development experience may be due to the way people perceive their past. In retrospect, individuals may attribute planfulness and rationality to their career decisions that to an outside observer may appear accidental (Salomone & Slaney, 1981; Williams et al., 1998). As Caplow (1954) noted, "error and accident often play a larger part than the subject is willing to concede" (p. 214). According to the Fundamental Attribution Error, people have a tendency to attribute behavior to dispositions rather than to situations (Ross & Nisbett, 1991).

Framing chance events in the context of other factors, as in Salomone and Slaney's (1981) and Scott and Hatalla (1990) studies, may reduce the amount of influence attributed to chance events as individuals strive to find a rational reason for their decisions and negate the influence of chance. Thus chance may be underrepresented, as participants may have been influenced by chance events, but not have reported it as such. In comparison, Betsworth and Hanson (1996) and Williams et al. (1998), who found chance events had a significant impact on career decision making, did not ask participants about planful behavior and events. The exclusive focus on chance events may serve to minimize the tendency to provide post hoc rationalizations of career decisions.

Career decision making encompasses both educational and occupational decisions. Consequently, research on the influence of chance events has studied both students and individuals who have already entered the workforce. However, no research has been conducted to determine whether the influence of chance events differs depending on an individual's career stage. The Chaos Theory of Careers (Pryor & Bright, 2003a, 2003b, 2007a) emphasizes career decision making as the result of short-term decisions made as situations and opportunities arise in the environment, and not primarily as the result of long-term rational planning. Therefore, it could be reasonably expected that the influence of chance events will be greater for individuals who have been in the workforce longer as they have experienced a greater number of such experiences. The research conducted by the authors reported below investigated this proposition.

Several theorists have suggested that the relationship between personality and chance events needs more exploration (Cabral & Salomone, 1990; Mitchell, Levin & Krumboltz, 1999; Osipow, 1973). Therefore in order to determine the influence of chance events on career decision making, knowledge about an individual's personal attributes is required, In particular, individuals' perceptions of the degree of chance and control in their career decision would appear to be worth investigating. The personality construct locus of control, as conceptualized by Rotter (1966) and thoroughly discussed by Lefcourt (1966), describes the extent to which individuals attribute the occurrence of environmental events to internal factors under their control (e.g., ability, skill and effort) or to external factors outside their personal control (e.g., chance factors and difficulty of the task). Individuals with an internal orientation tend to view themselves as having control over and personal responsibility for the direction of their lives. Externals, on the other hand, are more likely to feel themselves powerless to control events.

It could reasonably be expected that chance events are likely to be perceived to play a more influential role in career decision making for individuals with an external locus of control. They may believe they have little control over their vocational decisions and that they are more likely to be influenced by chance events. Locus of control has been shown to be associated with career planning (Marecek & Frasch, 1977), career indecision (Taylor, 1982), career maturity (Gable, Thompson & Glanstein, 1976), and self-efficacy for career decision-making tasks (Brown, Glastetter-Fender & Shelton, 2000). Locus of control has also been shown to be associated with career decision making specifically (Denga, 1984). Denga found that male Nigerian school students with an internal locus of control were likely to choose their occupations based on intrinsic influences (e.g., interest and ability) whereas students with an external orientation were more likely to indicate that chance and good fortune influenced their career preferences.

Bright, Pryor and Harpham (2005) provide more evidence for the role of chance events, and this research tested the hypothesis that there is a relationship between locus of control and the influence of chance events on career decision making. They reported two investigations into the incidence of chance events in career decision making. In the first exploratory study, the extent to which chance factors were perceived as influencing career decision making was investigated. It was also specifically hypothesized that more chance events would be reported as a function of educational stage—specifically, university students would report more chance events than high school students. This prediction was based on "the differential exposure hypothesis" that, on the whole, university students will be older and therefore more likely to have been exposed to more chance events than their younger counterparts. Also, it was hypothesized that high school is a more cloistered and controlled environment than university, leading to fewer unplanned experiences.

In the second study, the prevalence of chance events in career decision making was further examined and the issue of whether locus of control could account exclusively for the reporting of chance influences on career development was addressed. More specifically, it was hypothesized that:

1. A significant proportion of participants from both samples will indicate that they have been influenced by chance events.
2. The influence of chance events will be greater in the sample of older participants than in an undergraduate sample.
3. There will be a relationship between locus of control orientation and the amount of influence of chance events on career decision making. Participants scoring higher on the locus of control scale (i.e., external direction) will be more likely to indicate that they have been influenced by chance events than participants scoring lower on the scale (i.e., internal direction).
4. There will be no relationship between locus of control orientation and the amount of influence of chance events when rating another person's career history.

It was found in a sample of 772 high school and college students that the majority reported chance events that had significantly influenced their career decision making. Almost two thirds (60%) said an unplanned previous work or social experience had significantly influenced their career decisions: 44% said a personal or work relationship had significantly influenced their career plans; 43% of respondents said an unplanned positive work experience had influenced their planning (Bright, Pryor, Wilkenfield & Earl, 2005). This serves as a timely reminder that not all unplanned events are negative, something we will explore in greater depth a little later.

The sample in this study was young, with an average age of about 23 years. Furthermore, across the age range captured in the sample there was no observed increase in reporting of chance events, further suggesting the ubiquity of chance events at all ages and stages of career development (cf. studies of older populations found in Betsworth and Hanson (1996), Williams et al. (1998) etc.).

In the second study reported in Bright, Pryor and Harpham (2005), college students and adults were presented with a scenario derived from real life of a local celebrity who had experienced a significant career-enhancing chance encounter. Again, we found high levels of personal reporting of chance events, with 74% of the sample reporting chance events in their own careers. Only 10% of participants reported that chance played no role in their careers. Furthermore, there were no differences between the younger and older samples in the reporting rates of chance events, further supporting our contention that such events are ubiquitous and inherent in careers. On this evidence, it is quite insufficient to characterize the human experience of chance events in careers as occasional flashes of lightning.

Attributional style measured as locus of control correlated 0.29 with reporting of chance events, so that more externally orientated participants reported more chance events. The tendency of the externally oriented type to attribute causes of events to things external to themselves is consistent with explanations of chance events, which tend to be almost exclusively external. It is interesting that if we change our plans because of an idea "popping" into our heads we think of this as intuition, but if another person influences our plans because of them acting upon an idea that popped into their heads, we are more likely to think of this as chance. Part of our understanding of what is chance is biased toward externally caused events, whereas the CTC predicts that chance events can also emerge from the internal workings of the system.

These results are consistent with the few earlier studies on chance. Roe and Baruch (1967) conducted a study on 30 participants from different work professions and found that most participants attribute their career influences to a myriad of chance events. Likewise, Hart, Rayner and Christensen (1971) examined the career histories of 60 men at different occupational entry levels and found that the vocational histories of skilled and semiskilled workers were often influenced by chance events. In a study of 917 nonprofessional workers, Salomone and Slaney (1981) found that chance events were perceived to have an impact on the workers' vocational decisions. Scott and Hatalla (1990) also found similar results in a study on the career patterns of college-educated women.

Chance events do not always occur in isolation, although there is a tendency to treat them in this fashion in theories of career development.

Through the use of case studies, Guindon and Hanna (2002) found that participants revealed accounts of the presence and influence of a series of connected chance events on their career paths. Williams et al. (1998) observed the presence of multiple chance events reported by some participants in their study on career development. Wiseman (2004) also observed the influence of multiple linked chance events on some of his participants' career choices. Thus while the incidence of multiple chance events on careers appears evident from these studies, there has been no research to investigate the impact of single chance events in comparison with multiple chance events on individuals' careers. Also the issue of whether there is a difference of impact if multiple chance events are perceived as connected or discrete has not received empirical attention.

Bright, Pryor, Chan and Rijanto (2009) explored the role of multiple chance events and also the way chance events are recalled. It can be useful to consider chance events in terms of the dimensions of severity and personal control because not all chance events have severe consequences and not all chance events are, as is popularly thought, uncontrollable. Indeed, we were interested to ascertain whether the popular characterization of chance events as uncontrollable might be explained in terms of people's memory bias for them.

On one occasion the authors recall a fellow researcher questioning why we were interested in researching chance events—after all, chance events were "chance" so how could you research them? This sentiment nicely captures the fatalistic attitude toward chance events, and may go some way to explaining why they have received such little emphasis in the mainstream career development literature, let alone in policy initiatives. It seems that chance events are the inconvenient truth of career development. If people systematically tend to recall only the most dramatic and uncontrollable chance events, then it is understandable that researchers, practitioners and clients might see little point in exploring them more deeply. However, if it can be shown that this characterization of chance events is the result of a bias, then awareness of this biased perception may provide an opening to research and, with clients in practice, work with the other types of chance events.

To investigate this, Bright et al. (2009) presented participants with scenarios that conformed to one quadrant of a 2 × 2 categorization of chance events as high or low control, and high or low level of influence. Control in this context does not mean control over the onset of the event (it would not be a chance event if there was control over this); rather, it refers to control over the aftermath of the event. A low level of control might obtain when a person has been badly injured in a motor vehicle accident and is obliged to undergo a long period of rehabilitation—there really is little other option. A high level of control might be present after a person has had a chance encounter with a potential employer at a social function and has been asked to call the employer the following day to discuss a possible job. Here the person has almost total discretion over whether or not to make the call (barring acts of God or telephone technical failure!).

When the participants were given an unexpected test of their recall of the different scenarios, they displayed very strong memory bias. They recalled more accurately scenarios that were high in influence but low in personal control, such as the motor vehicle accident rather than the chance encounter at a party. This result may go some way to explaining why chance events are so often treated in such a fatalistic manner. Clearly, one of the challenges for practitioners is to normalize chance events and to emphasize the large number that can be influenced (Chen, 2005).

In a second study also reported in Bright et al. (2009), the nature of multiple chance events was investigated. Chance events can be positive or negative in their impacts and outcomes. They can occur singularly or in multiples. Multiple chance events can either be a series of events that are not linked to one another, or they can be related (concatenated). When participants were asked to recall chance events in their own lives, 82.3% recalled single positive events, 66.1% recalled single negative events, 64.5% recalled concatenated positive events and 58.1% recalled concatenated negative events. The least recalled were multiple independent events, with 54.8% recalling positive examples and 46.8% recalling negative examples. Without exception, the positive chance events of all types were considered to be more influential on the participants' careers than the negative ones. Furthermore, the expectations of the participants were for more positive future chance events than negative ones.

In a third study also reported in Bright et al. (2009), participants were asked to judge scenarios that depicted the various forms of independent and multiple chance events. We included familiar scenarios such as accidents, redundancy and promotion. The results indicated that negative events were perceived as having a disproportionate impact on individuals' ratings and recall, suggesting that avoiding negative chance events takes precedence over embracing positive events.

Bright et al. (2009) provides further support for the CTC contention that chance events are central and ubiquitous in career development.

Furthermore, these results shed some light on how chance events are perceived and on the reality that chance events are frequently multiple in nature and often related. The results add to a small but growing body of evidence that is demonstrating the relevance and importance of chance events in career development.

CAREER DEVELOPMENT INTERVENTIONS BASED ON THE CHAOS THEORY OF CAREERS

In this section, a different type of empirical support for the CTC is presented, focusing not on the individual components or premises of the theory but rather on the validity and utility of this approach when used with clients. A career development theory should be able to provide new perspectives on counseling (see Chapter 7) and to generate new techniques for practice (see Chapter 8), and be shown to be effective in assisting those with career development problems. These latter data constitute an important additional level of empirical support for any career development. Therefore some evidence of the effectiveness of the CTC in practice is outlined here.

Outcome studies in the career development literature are few and far between, and outcome studies that incorporate control treatment groups and longitudinal follow-ups are exceedingly rare. In a study reported by McKay, Bright and Pryor (2005), career counseling based on the Chaos Theory of Careers was compared with trait-matching career counseling and a wait-list control group. Sixty university students who attended the Careers Research and Assessment Service at the University of New South Wales seeking career advice were randomly assigned to the chaos intervention, the trait-matching intervention, or a wait-list control group.

In chaos counseling, issues of complexity, change, adaptability, uncertainty and chance are likely to figure prominently (Bright, Pryor & Harpham, 2005; Pryor & Bright, 2003a, 2003b). Consistent with writers such as Gelatt (1989), the Chaos Theory of Careers does not claim that decidedness is always the best outcome from career counseling—sometimes undecidedness can be the most appropriate and the most adaptive response in a complex, changing, and unpredictable world (Pryor & Bright, 2003a, 2003b).

In traditional trait-factor counseling, the focus is more upon measurement of interests and transferable skills, and the matching of these to suitable occupations in series of recommendations. The aim is to seek clarity and increase career decidedness while at the same time reducing career uncertainty. In any form of counseling, background information such as demographic information about the client is collected for use in interpretation and personalization of the results of the counseling or in any report that is produced. Usually, most counseling also includes a general interview to ascertain the client's expectations and thinking to date about career-related matters.

In the study, trait-matching counseling consisted of the initial interview, administration of a personality inventory, and administration of a vocational interests inventory based upon Roe's (1956) taxonomy of interests. After completion of both inventories, participants received feedback about their personality profile and their vocational interest code, which was then used to match participants to specific occupations. The feedback across both measures took approximately 30 minutes. Chaos counseling consisted of the initial interview, an interactive card sort that was the analogue of the personality inventory used in the trait-matching group, and a vocational interests card sort that was also the analogue of the inventory used in the trait-matching group. The feedback for the members of the chaos counseling group was ongoing because of the collaborative nature of the card-sort activities.

Both groups were given an initial interview. The trait-matching interview covered traditional topics such as expectations of the counseling, current situation (both study and work), strengths and weaknesses, likes and dislikes, vocational interests, and career options considered. The chaos interview consisted of the following: expectations of career counseling, influences that led to current situation (both study and work), themes and patterns of influence on career decision making, unplanned events, and what constitutes their "ideal" vocation. The Circle of Influence Task worksheet (Bright & Pryor, 2003) was presented during the chaos interview to enhance participants' thinking regarding influences on their career development. The initial interviews lasted approximately 30 minutes.

A series of measures of the effectiveness of the counseling as well as reactions to the counseling were taken immediately before counseling, immediately after counseling and one month later. Participants received questionnaires that measured the impact and outcomes of the counseling experience. The pre-counseling questionnaire contained two scales: the Irrational Career-Related Thoughts scale (lCRT) and the Career Decision Making Self-Efficacy scale (CDMSE; Taylor & Betz, 1983). The post-counseling questionnaires contained three scales: a Satisfaction scale, the ICRT and the CDMSE.

Participants' satisfaction with the career counseling approach was measured using items such as "I would recommend this career counseling experience to a friend: strongly disagree (1) to strongly agree (5)." Participants' irrational career-related thoughts (ICRT) were measured using an 11-item scale developed for the study. These items built on previous work on irrational career-related thoughts encountered in vocational counseling (Nevo, 1987). A sample item from the scale is: "There is only one vocation in the world that is right for me."

Both chaos and trait-matching counseling had a positive impact compared to the wait-list control; however, chaos counseling had a more lasting effect. Figures 6.4–6.6 illustrate the nature of the results. In Figure 6.4, it can be seen that the CTC approach resulted in a more positive change in self-efficacy than either the traditional approach or the control group, comparing one month after counseling to immediately after counseling. Confidence in personally collecting occupational information is also greater in the CTC group than in either of the other groups one month after counseling. Finally, satisfaction with CTC counseling remained high after one month, but was beginning to drop off for the traditional group and started from a slightly (non-significant) lower point initially.

The results are encouraging for the CTC because they demonstrate that an approach that emphasizes uncertainty, complexity, chance and change can be equally or more effective than more traditional approaches. Clearly more research is required, but it should be noted that there is a paucity of intervention effectiveness studies based on established theory in the career development literature, in contrast to, for instance, that in the clinical psychology literature.

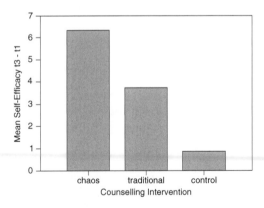

Figure 6.4 Difference in mean levels of self-efficacy pre-counseling compared to one month post-counseling.

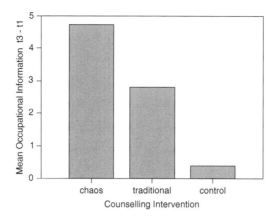

Figure 6.5 Difference in mean levels of confidence in locating relevant occupational information pre-counseling compared to one month post-counseling.

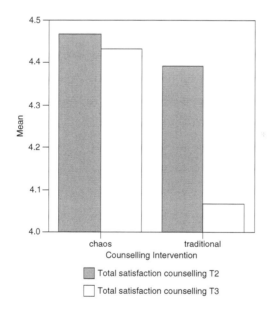

Figure 6.6 Levels of satisfaction with chaos and traditional counseling immediately post-counseling and one month later.

Other evidence for the efficacy of the CTC is provided in Borg, Bright and Pryor (2006), which reports on the implementation of a simplified CTC model for use in counseling high school students. The authors produced a "butterfly" model of careers that closely resembles Lorenz's butterfly attractor. The model is shown in Figure 6.7.

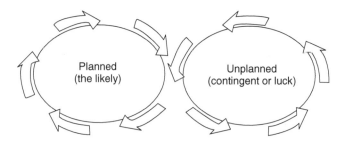

Figure 6.7   The Butterfly model of careers.

Essentially, the model serves as a simple way of explaining the interplay between planned and unplanned events in careers and reminds students of the need to be contingent in their career development planning. The model is also dynamic in that careers emerge from a continual cycling through periods of planful and periods of unplanned behavior.

The model has been successfully implemented in high schools, and the evaluations by students, their parents and senior teaching staff has been very positive. The model was incorporated into training provided to all careers teachers in one state in Australia as part of a School to Work training initiative, and similarly was well received.

Davey, Bright, Pryor and Levin (2005) reported on the application of the CTC in video-based career counseling of university students. In this study students attending the Careers Service at an Australian university watched a video containing two graduates discussing their career in CTC terms such as the non-linearity of change, the necessity of taking risks, the unknown, the influence of unplanned events, the inevitable limitations of our current information and the value of intuition versus rational thinking in decision making. Their career decision-making self-efficacy was measured pre and post the video presentation, along with a measure of their career exploration behavior —measured using the Career Exploration Survey (Stumpf, Colarelli & Hartman, 1983)—and their career intentions and plans.

The results indicated increases in self-efficacy for the students, and this increase was observed to last at least until the one-week follow-up. The study is important because it suggests that exposing people to discussions about the uncertainties and irrationalities in career development does not necessarily undermine their confidence but can serve to improve self-efficacy. Enhanced self-efficacy is an important predictor of a range of positive career behaviors (e.g., Betz & Klein, 1997; Blustein, 1989; Blustein et al., 1994).

In one unpublished study, the authors demonstrated the effectiveness of ideas based on the CTC in a change management program in a large organization, and in another the usefulness of the CTC approach allied to attribution training to enhance career behavior of university students was demonstrated.

Overall, there is a growing body of empirical data from a converging range of sources that provide support for the foundational assumptions of the CTC and evidence of the practical effectiveness of interventions informed by this theory. Obviously, further research work is required to continue to evaluate specific dimensions of the Chaos Theory of Careers. However, the body of data already available does indicate that the major conceptual components of the theory have significant research evidence to support them.

CHAPTER 7

Strategies for Chaos Theory Career Counseling and Assessment

Life is limited.

All human beings are limited in time and space. We are limited in our capacities: as the old saying goes, "The greatest fool may ask more than the wisest man can answer." Chaos theory, in particular, draws attention to our limitations of knowledge and control even over our own lives and circumstances. Moreover, when discussing "attractors" in Chapter 4, the notion of "boundedness" was introduced. Attractors are descriptive accounts of how complex dynamical systems function. Attractors are limited by their boundaries. Further, it was noted that without boundaries there can be no systems: there would only be oneness, or whatever there was in the universe (if that is not a contradiction) before the Big Bang. Thus chaos theory enables us to see that limitations are necessary and essential for coherence and stability in the universe. It also points us to the startling reality that it is our limitations that define us.

For example, in the strict sense of the word, no one can think the thoughts of anyone else. We can agree, empathize even, but we cannot actually do someone else's thinking. This is what makes them "them" and me "me." The metaphor of a song illustrates this idea. A song is defined by its limitations. A song has certain lyrics, the music has chord progression and melody, all of which combine to produce the song's unique identity. If there were no limits to the chord progressions or melodies, the song would not be recognizable as such. Indeed, with no limits whatsoever the music would descend into white noise. The strength and identity of the song derive from its limitations.

Existential thinkers such as Sartre (1966) recognized this with dictums such as "we are our choices." To choose is necessarily to limit ourselves to the option chosen, and to relinquish others. To a greater or lesser extent, our career choices contribute to our identity and our sense of career through the possibilities that we did not elect to pursue. Because work usually determines and reflects so much about us, "What do you do?" is one of the questions most commonly asked of a new acquaintance.

As a consequence, the limitations of life are not contingencies to be denied or lamented. However, most people would like to be something more than they are—smarter, wealthier, more beautiful, healthier, more athletic, more popular, more creative, and so on. This can cause great frustration, resentment and unhappiness. This is often seen when a phase shift has occurred in individuals lives that has ongoing restrictions as consequences. For example, the professional cyclist who has devoted all her energy, thinking and waking hours to achieving elite performance has made many personal sacrifices to pursue such a career and may have overcome many previous obstacles such as lack of finance, performance disappointment, injuries and the demands of rehabilitation, and conflicts with coaches and sport officials. One day, while doing some on-road training, her bike is hit by a car being thoughtlessly driven by a driver distractedly searching for his sunglasses or talking on a phone. As a result of the injuries sustained in this accident, the professional cyclist never quite achieves her pre-injury levels of performance. She no longer is good enough to win races or maintain her position on the cycling team. She becomes "not quite elite" as a performer. Her frustration, distress, grief and even anger and aggression are both natural and understandable responses to the limitations she now experiences. All her efforts and sacrifices appear to have come to nought. She is likely to need support to work through these thoughts and feelings, but work through them she must since there is "no future in frustration," as Bishop Stanway, a famous African missionary, is reported to have said. Our professional cyclist is eventually going to have to consider what, from her past, she still has now that she can utilize for her career future: her competitive experience, her network of individuals involved in sport, her knowledge of health, exercise and nutrition, her technical cycling skills, her capacities for strategizing, and so on.

Ultimately, most of us would not like to have at least some of our limitations. However, continuing to deny or lament them may not get us very far, other than to make ourselves and others miserable and depressed. If it is our limits define us, as chaos theory suggests, then herein lies a basis for career counseling. That is to say, within our limits lie our potentials. The very fact that individuals are limited in their levels of knowledge and control leads to the conclusion that we therefore cannot be certain what we are capable of achieving. Uncertainties, while sometimes perceived as threats and problems, can also be opportunities and options. This is the fundamental basis for chaos theory career counseling. Within this framework, career success relies upon the felicity with which we manage our limitations.

The most general aims of such counseling for clients are:

1. To explore and learn to accept clients' limitations, i.e., to respect stability.
2. To push the boundaries of clients' limitations to explore how rigid or flexible they might be, i.e., to develop capacities for change.
3. To develop ongoing skills to understand and to utilize the interactions between stability and change.

If, in general terms, CTC-based career counseling addresses client issues such as what we are, what we could be, and what we cannot be, then in what ways does this translate into how career counselors understand their work and how they might go about doing it? Career development theory can provide counselors with a map of the career counseling issues and processes that derive from it. A good theory provides a general survey of the landscape, identifies important landmarks and signposts, suggests alternative routes, outlines likely useful resources for traveling, and provides a vision of the destination. Chapters 2 and 3 outlined a landscape of complexity change and connection. Chapters 4 and 5 enunciated landmarks and signposts in terms of attractors and their fractals. Chapter 8 provides examples of resources likely to be useful in applying concepts from chaos theory. The rest of this chapter will adumbrate likely counseling routes based on chaos theory and a set of outcomes or destinations derived from a chaos conceptualization. Immediately following is a general framework for conceptualizing and strategizing using a CTC viewpoint; then how such a conceptualization links both positivist and constructivist currents in contemporary career development practice is outlined. After this, some assessment and counseling implications are surveyed. Finally, the paradigm dimensions of the Chaos Theory of Careers are canvassed.

CHAOS THEORY CAREER COUNSELING FRAMEWORK

This framework is structured around the career counseling process in terms of the initial stage of counseling (client expectation); the central stage of counseling (career development issues); and the final stage of counseling (outcomes).

Clients' Expectations

What clients actually bring to the career counseling context will often determine the whole of the rest of the process. Thus, if individuals seek career counseling with expectations such as "I want to know what the tests say I am best suited to" then such expectations will influence their participation in the intervention process, their perceptions of their counselor, their decision-making processes and the outcome they will seek and be satisfied with. Without addressing clients expectations, both counselors and their clients may be communicating at cross purposes, and what one may view as success the other may perceive as failure.

As a consequence, the first thing that a CTC-based career counselor will need to do is to review and (if necessary) reframe client expectations in line with the realities of a chaos-filled world of complexity, change, chance and interconnection. This involves:

Recognition of the Influence of Chance

Chen (2005) indicated that "one of the major goals of career counseling is to normalize chance." That is, to help individuals recognize and accept that unplanned and unforeseen events may have a significant impact on their lives and careers.

Acceptance of Human Limitations

This is, of course, a direct consequence of the recognition of the influence of chance (see above). Chaos theory calls upon individuals to confront their limitations in terms of knowledge and control. This, however, applies not only to individual clients, but also applies to their counselors. While professionally trained and experienced counselors can claim to bring considerable expertise to the career counseling context, they must also acknowledge to both their clients and themselves that they too are limited in what they know and can control. We are all in the same boat when it comes to uncertainty, non-linearity, emergence and phase shifts. Career counseling, therefore, is not, from a CTC theoretical perspective, viewed as telling clients what to do, but is about collaborating with clients to negotiate as well as they can, for the benefit of those clients, a chaotic reality in which no one has all the answers.

Valuing the Uniqueness of Clients

Almost inevitably humans compare themselves to others, identify more or less with others and often seek to be like others. Now, while there is nothing wrong with having role models or even heroes, the chaos theory's emphasis on the contingent nature of all experience indicates the danger of so far identifying with others that individuals relinquish their own uniqueness. While others may guide, inspire and instruct, individuals themselves must make their own unique way in the world rather than slavishly imitating or helplessly depending on others. The valuing of uniqueness may ultimately result in consideration of career choices which are atypical, unusual and idiosyncratic. Thus although there are far more sales assistants and clerks than there are buggy-whip makers, this does not preclude individual clients pursuing a career in buggy-whip making.

The Cost of Change

The CTC's focus on ongoing change draws attention to the inevitability of the experience of change and the necessity of responsiveness to such change. Many clients seek career development with as little personal change as possible. Typically, they want others or the world around them to change in order to accommodate them. Of course, most would rarely express such sentiments so boldly and so baldly—but their expectations typically reveal a responsiveness to change characterized by denial, defiance or defeatism. Those who deny change fail to see the necessity for themselves to change. They are "OK the way they are" and are quite prepared to watch the world change, until one day they wake up to find that not only has the world passed them by, but it has gone so far that it is now out of sight. We have termed this phenomenon "slow shift" (Bright & Pryor, 2008). Then the victims of change suddenly find themselves with obsolete skills and task approach strategies and inflexible beliefs and habits, all adversely impacting their ongoing career development prospects.

Similarly, those who defy change while recognizing its reality refuse to consider that change is essential for them. They are discomforted by change and so they resist it. They will not use new technologies saying things like "email is so impersonal" and "I don't want a machine to tell me what to do." They abhor the "mania for speed" of the world of work and "just want to keep things simple." They pounce on any event at work or elsewhere, in which technology breaks down, causes a problem or is used for illicit purposes, as justifications for doing a job that does not require the use of any technologies that are not at least 25 years old.

Such a response to change also characterizes the defeatists, only they reach this point much sooner than those who deny or defy change. These individuals give up almost immediately in the face of change. They are the proverbial old dogs who cannot learn new tricks—or so they tell themselves. When change is demanded of them through new work systems—recruitment, performance evaluation, promotion, accountability, communication means or service responsiveness—they collapse under the strain. Everything becomes difficult. They catastrophize their mistakes in trying to adapt to the new systems.

In a sense all three reactions to change outlined are attempts to avoid paying the price of change. Many people find change disturbing, disruptive, threatening and anxiety-provoking. It usually demands effort to challenge established patterns of thought and behavior and to learn new ways of thinking and acting. Many experience this as a form of suffering—it is often painful to make changes. Peck (1978) observed that most neurotic behavior arises from a desire to avoid legitimate suffering. Some career development counseling clients will struggle to come to terms with the suffering involved in confronting change in their own lives and in the world in which they seek to live and work. Such individuals need to be able to face and articulate these fears and pain as soon as possible in the career counseling process. Otherwise such clients are likely to become uneasy about the chaos career counseling process and decline to continue with it, usually by finding some excuse such as "I did not feel I was getting anywhere" or "we did not talk about occupations much at all."

Understanding the Relevance of Purpose and Values

The CTC's concept of the boundedness of individuals' attractors is attributable to those individuals' purpose and values. That is, why we will think and act in some ways but not others is usually a consequence of how we see the world and what matters to us in that world (Gell-Mann, 1994). Super (1980) and his followers drew attention to career development and decision making as "the implementation of an occupational self concept." Theorists such as Savickas (1997) have conceptualized career development counseling as a process of "making meaning" (p. 81). The CTC's emphasis on the systemic interconnectedness of all components of the strange attractor indicates that aspects of working and career are unlikely to be able to be kept separate from individuals' fundamental sense of purpose and values. Since work typically constitutes a major contribution to and influence on individuals' sense of identity and lifestyle, it is almost inevitable that issues of what really matters to people in their lives as a whole will be canvassed, or at least at some point intrude, in counseling.

Discussing such issues may be difficult for career counseling clients because they can be seen as "too personal or private," and some people feel threatened by having to explore and articulate such issues. For this latter group, issues of meaning and purpose in counseling are merely activities of "morbid introspection." Of course, career counselors cannot demand or compel their clients to address issues of purpose and values. However, they can seek to outline the relevance of such issues through the basic tenets of the Chaos Theory of Careers. If clients persist in their unwillingness to discuss such issues, career counseling will proceed and in our experience these issues will eventually emerge from the process at some time. This will then become a "crisis point" for clients at which either personal insight will be achieved or they will simply persist in their attempts to cordon off work from the rest of their life.

Career Development Issues

The central component of the CTC career counseling process is dealing with the major challenges that the theory identifies as likely to be relevant to individuals facing career decisions. These issues are not totally independent of one another. Frequently they interact in a complex way for individuals. However, seeking to "disentangle" them to some extent through counseling and assessment has the advantage of clarifying issues for clients and thereby making the challenges of career development appear more manageable for them. In addition, this process of disentanglement can assist the counselor to identify particular techniques that may be most appropriate for helping clients address such issues at appropriate points in the counseling process. Chapter 8 outlines some of the techniques that have been developed and can be used for such purposes.

While some of the issues outlined in the earlier discussion of expectations may emerge subsequently in career counseling, the following issues are challenges that individuals encounter in CTC career counseling. Individuals are likely to have to deal with one or a combination of these issues.

Complexity

In appreciation of the multitude of potential influences on careers and the countless ways in which these may interact as well as the sheer impossibility of being able to anticipate or understand such influences and processes, some career counseling clients will simply feel overwhelmed. There seems too much to take into account, and even if that appears possible there are always other influences of which no one is aware, which may undermine all the decisions and actions taken on the basis of what the clients thought they knew. In the face of complexity, some feelings of personal inadequacy are not only understandable but can actually be reasonable and helpful. Of course, this appears to contradict some of the contemporary "positive psychology" movement tenets about assuming control and building self-esteem and confidence. From the CTC perspective, inadequacy in the face of complexity is helpful if it leads not to helplessness but to humility on the part of both clients and their counselors. Peck (1993) observed: "It is scary to think that we really don't know what we're doing and that we are intellectual infants stumbling around in the dark. It's so much more comfortable, therefore to live in an illusion that we know much more than we actually do" (p. 75). Peck (1993) attributes individuals' failure to accept the limitations of their knowledge to fear and laziness. If clients in career counseling react in either of these ways then their counselors need to help them "face their fears" or to expose their laziness and its potential consequences such as overconfidence, ill-considered decision making and disengagement (Amundson, 2003a).

More generally, CTC career counseling clients need to have their feelings of being overwhelmed and being "in over their heads" acknowledged as a realistic reaction to complexity. However, this feeling should not lead to a sense of powerlessness which is destructive and useless. Rather, it can lead to an appreciation of human limitations and of the need to develop ongoing strategies to take into account new influences as they emerge and the non-linear effects of change.

Chance

This is the challenge to accept and embrace unpredictability and uncertainty as ongoing career development realities. Most people want and expect to be treated fairly: effort should be rewarded; success should be commensurate with talent and dedication; we should (in biblical terms) "reap what we sow." While this may often be the case, it is not in every case. Not every good or bad consequence for individuals is a result of their own behavior. Some passengers may survive an airplane crash that others do not, purely on the basis of events unforeseen and uncontrolled by either group of passengers. As a consequence, life's vicissitudes, especially those that generate very negative outcomes for some individuals, can be frustrating and seem so unfair (Athanasou, 1999). In the vocational rehabilitation context in particular, clients with acquired disabilities through accident or misadventure frequently express such thoughts and feelings. As with clients' negative responses to complexity, it must be acknowledged by the counselor that such reactions are natural and understandable. They need to be expressed and worked through in counseling. However, ultimately such reactions are not constructive for career development. If allowed to persist, those feelings can harden into attitudes of cynicism, bitterness, catastrophizing and pessimism, which give rise to a sense of victimization and malaise.

Ultimately, clients struggling with coming to terms with chance and uncertainty need to appreciate and interject two new ideas. The first is that the reality of chance and unpredictability does not entail the uselessness of making and endeavoring to implement career development plans and choices. It is at least as likely for some individuals to exaggerate the effects of chance on their lives and careers as it is for others to deny it. The CTC indicates that order and disorder exist as composites in complex dynamical systems. Neither should be exaggerated or overlooked. They interact as general dimensions of the system but it is virtually impossible for one to somehow cancel out the other. Therefore insofar as individuals can expect stability within themselves and their world, they should take positive action on that basis. Of course, that does not guarantee the efficacy of the outcomes of such actions. Clients need to develop the perspective that some strategies will fail and that new ones will need to be developed. This may be disappointing, but it is rarely a cause for despair. It also suggests the danger of putting all one's career development "eggs into one basket": that is, prematurely focusing on one career option or course of action or making decisions which effectively close off too many other possibilities. An example would be clients who commit themselves financially to a course by paying for the whole program before having a clear understanding of its relevance to their purpose; if some other need or possibility arises, they may be unable to recoup their expenditure for another purpose. They would have been better advised to have invested in the course on a "pay as you go" basis.

The second response to the reality of chance and unpredictability in careers and life is that such uncertainty may also present opportunities for action to enhance individuals' career development and life prospects. Fear often means clients will only focus on the negative possibilities of chance rather than seek to develop a mindset that focuses on its positive possibilities. Regrettably, many individuals use their imagination to worry about negative consequences that may never eventuate instead of using their imagination to create opportunities.

Constructive Change

Some career counseling clients present with the perception of having no options. They doubt the transferability of their skills, they believe their work experience is very narrow and specialized, and they cannot see any way of breaking out of their existing situation such as an uninspiring job or being unemployed. In CTC terms, they feel imprisoned in a torus attractor—repeating the same unsatisfactory patterns of life and work. Chaos theory career counselors seek to ignite the flame of such clients' own creativity and imagination as a way to commence constructive change. Constructive change is client-initiated action aimed at achieving a more fulfilling life and career. Many clients underestimate their creative capacities to envision and implement a better work life for themselves. They need encouragement to dream and hope; to see their situation from a different perspective; to utilize the power of intuition and imagination to consider creative possibilities (Amundson, 2003b, 2006). It may mean experimenting with some possibilities and taking some risks. It may mean making mistakes without believing that in the process they will become failures (Edelman, 2002). People will often censor and limit their hopes and dreams by a perceived need "to be practical and realistic." They focus on the obstacles and difficulties first and dismiss opportunities prematurely. They will underestimate their capabilities in order to avoid putting in the effort to develop such capacities in new ways. They will fail to consider other ways of structuring their careers and working lives, such as starting their own company, volunteering to develop skills, developing portfolio and protean careers (Hall, 2002), working from home, tele-commuting work, mail-order businesses, family partnerships, internet service provision or marketing, and so on. Many of the techniques outlined in Chapter 8 are aimed at helping career counseling clients to begin thinking in new ways about their careers.

Contribution/Meaning

Harvey and Harrild (2005) have observed that the only way clients can shift to "comfortable chaos" is by coming to understand what it is that they really want and what are their fundamental priorities. Meaning, purpose, commitment, spiritual aspiration and the desire to contribute are self-organizing principles by which individuals intentionally define the parameters of their identity, motivations, thoughts and actions. Some clients have difficulty identifying such profoundly personal concerns. Others find it difficult to bridge the gap between their stated aspirations and their actual words and behavior (Zander & Zander, 2000). The career counseling that derives from the Chaos Theory of Careers can assist clients to come to an understanding of the essential nature of these four major career development issues and how they may impede individuals from successfully negotiating a chaotic reality. Butz (1997) observed that most adjustment problems could be understood in terms of clashes of attractors. In CTC terms, the clash of attractors occurs when individuals try to use closed systems thinking strategies and assumptions in an open systems reality (Pryor & Bright, 2007a). In Chapter 4 the differences between closed and open systems thinking were adumbrated. Fundamentally, CTC career counseling is an endeavor to move individuals away from oversimplified thinking and the exaggerated belief in personal control (closed systems thinking) toward thinking that recognizes complexity, change and uncertainty with a realization of the limits of our levels of control and the freedom to risk making a better life and career (open systems thinking).

Counseling Outcomes

From a positivist theoretical framework such as Holland's (1997) matching model, a career counseling outcome would be expected to be (or at least implicitly be expected to be) a choice of a course or occupation. Savickas (1997) drew the distinction between the positivist and the constructivist approach as a change from fitting individuals and careers to enabling individuals to find and make meaning through work. Most of the time clients seek career counseling help when they perceive themselves as needing to make a decision. The CTC career counseling framework acknowledges the validity of such a request and the significance of such a need. However, if clients' needs extend beyond the need for information and confirmation support for already chosen options, then the CTC outlines counseling outcomes intended to assist clients to develop their career through enabling them to negotiate effectively and construct meaningful lives and careers in a world that is intrinsically chaotic. The CTC suggests that encouraging and empowering career counseling clients in this way will lead to outcomes of ongoing ownership of action, pattern identification, living with uncertainty, open systems thinking and the ongoing quest for meaning.

Ongoing Ownership of Action

The desire to have the security of a sense of being in control frequently results in individuals—even while accepting the reality of uncertainty arising from chaos—actually continuing to deny chaos in their own lives. Such career counseling clients will either consciously or unconsciously continue to cherish the belief that the unexpected always happens to someone else. Of course, most of the time they are correct but there is no guarantee that such events could not and would not happen to them. Chaos theory career counseling encourages clients to recognize this possibility and to own personally the realities of human potential (responsibility) and limitations (contingency). Such ownership is the strategic basis for acting as effectively as possible in a chaotic world. If it is avoided or denied then these clients will inevitably revert to closed systems thinking and the oversimplification of reality and human experience that it entails. Some of the career counseling implications of this ownership are outlined later in this chapter.

Pattern Identification

In traditional matching approaches to career counseling this is sometimes referred to as "self awareness" and/or "occupational awareness." However, since the Chaos Theory of Careers emphasizes the complex interconnections between career influences, clients are encouraged to begin to develop capacities for identifying not just single influences but also patterns of influence on themselves and on their work context. Often when individuals refer for career counseling they feel anxious and stressed. They cannot make enough sense of their situation to be able to take constructive action or make effective decisions. After acknowledging clients' emotional state and allowing them to ventilate their disruptive feelings, CTC career counselors will begin to encourage their clients to identify the order emerging from this perceived disorder of their lives and current experiences. Such recurring patterns initially at least tend to be maladaptive ways of thinking or acting. Cognitive behavior therapists such as Ellis (1969) have identified maladaptive thought patterns such as needing to be liked by everyone; thinking we can be happy all of the time; and believing we can be competent at everything we might consider doing. However, some patterns identified can also be positive and helpful, such as the "life themes" of career construction theory (Savickas, 2005), which may constitute the basis of meaningful decision making. The chaos concept of self-organizing systems (Bloch, 2005) may also have strategic value for clients in assisting them to initiate the emergent order that will lead on to constructive career development (Amundson, 2003a).

In the external world of work, a consciousness of pattern identification may also be useful in discussing entrepreneurial opportunities for business and employment (Gladwell, 2000). The globalization of markets, the continuing rapidity of technological development, the continuing demands for security in response to terrorism, the volatility of global financial markets, demographic changes, and new methods of money handling and purchasing as well as the developing consumer markets Asia and South America are among the kinds of emerging patterns likely to influence individuals' work opportunities both now and in the future.

Living with Uncertainty

For some people there is a compelling need for certainty. They feel they must be able to predict outcomes from actions. These individuals believe in the primacy of cause and effect. The patterns they identify usually relate to what has happened in the past as the only basis for what should happen in the future. They do not want or look for new emergent patterns. The contingent nature of reality discomforts them, makes them nervous and confuses them about how to respond. Typically, they respond by reverting to closed systems attractor behavior: goal-drivenness, role balancing or planning/controlling. These clients constantly overestimate their levels of control and repeatedly underestimate the incidence and impact of chance in daily life (Rescher, 1995). Therefore one of the desirable outcomes of CTC career counseling is that clients become more able to acknowledge, live with and actually utilize the uncertainty of a chaotic reality. This is often achieved by being able to contingency plan on the one hand and to think magically on the other (Gellat, 1991).

Drawing on the work of Neault (2002) and Mitchell, Levin and Krumboltz (1999), Pryor and Bright (2005b) identified eight dimensions of "luck readiness" that form the psychological basis of being able to respond constructively to the uncertainty of unplanned events in people's lives or careers. The eight dimensions are flexibility, optimism, risk taking, curiosity and open-mindedness, persistence especially in overcoming barriers, self-efficacy, strategic thinking and a belief in one's own luckiness. More details about these dimensions and how they can be assessed are provided in Chapter 8. Pryor and Bright (2005b) provide a list of activities and techniques to assist both career counselors and their clients to improve their luck readiness.

Open Systems Thinking

This has been a consistent theme in this account of chaos-based career counseling and therefore it should not come as a surprise that it would also be considered as a desirable outcome of the counseling process. Clients need to be encouraged and empowered to become more original and lateral in their thinking about themselves and their careers, to consider the non-linearity of change through resonance and synergy and the possibilities of phase shift (Bright & Pryor, 2008). For example, it is regrettable that those facing redundancy either in process work or middle management as organizations' hierarchical patterns flatten often wait till they no longer have jobs before they being the process of considering new options. They may be hopeful of a last-minute employment reprieve, that the firm might secure another lucrative contract that will save their jobs or that the market will suddenly pick up with a consequent increase in demand. In our experience, these things rarely occur or, if they do, they constitute only a temporary reprieve before the final axe of job loss actually fails.

Open systems thinking suggests that individuals need to be aware of the perpetual possibility that even the most secure of jobs may not be immune from disappearing and that in some industries such as, among others, manufacturing, construction, information technology, the media and politics, the chances of job loss can be quite high. There-fore, an open-mindedness toward change, an increased vigilance for new opportunities, and a willingness to take risks and experiment along with a proactive desire to avoid perceiving oneself as a helpless and hap-less victim of circumstances are all part of an open systems mindset. Such a mindset does not just react to change when forced to do so. Open-minded individuals will seek to explore the unlikely, the seem-ingly impossible, the idiosyncratic, the unique and the "crazy" as poten-tial options. Clients are encouraged to develop and use their creative resources as an outcome of CTC career counseling: not starting with the barriers and the problems but with the possibilities and the benefits of new options and ways of thinking. Chapter 8 outlines some techniques developed to facilitate such an outcome.

The Quest for Meaning

Increasingly there have been calls for the incorporation of spirituality into counseling (Weiler & Schoonover, 2001). To confront complex-ity and its implications individuals need to seek an overarching per-spective—what matters to them, what sort of person they want to be become, what kind of life they want for themselves and those they care about and are responsible for. Further, as Rescher (1995) observed, the crucial influence of luck on people's lives is recognized and felt only when something unexpected and unpredicted impacts on what really matters to them. Smith (1999) has highlighted the importance of courage as a spiritual resource tied to a sense of purpose and calling that is necessary to cope with the exigencies and vicissitudes of human experience and career development. The quest for meaning may need to be ongoing and may not be formulaically achieved through career counseling (Weiler & Schoonover, 2001). Bissonette (1994) points to the motivational power of a sense of purpose in career development and employment acquisition. Savickas (1997) views what is important for individuals as the basis for constructive action and decision mak-ing in career development. The strange attractor perspective of the Chaos Theory of Careers is consistent with these views. CTC career counseling seeks to foster clients' exploration and appreciation of their own unique sense of meaning, purpose and core values as a fundamen-tal basis for living and working in a world of both predictability and unpredictability, order and disorder, stability and turbulence (Pryor & Bright, 2004).

CHAOS THEORY CAREER COUNSELING PERSPECTIVES

The counseling framework outlined above points to the convergence of two different perspectives of career development counseling. Over the past 20 years or so what Savickas (2005) described as an "epistemic war" has been going on either explicitly or implicitly between what could variously be designated the modernist, objectivist, positivist perspective and the postmodernist subjectivist constructivist perspective. The former approach focuses attention on assaying individuals' characteristics (abilities, preferences and traits) and relating those to the requirements of various occupations. The better the fit, the more suitable the occupation. The latter perspective focuses attention on discovering themes and purpose through narratives with the goal of creating a meaningful life incorporating work.

The Chaos Theory of Careers provides a theoretical method for resolving this conflict and ending the war (Pryor, Amundson & Bright 2008). Bright and Pryor (2007) proposed that the positivist and the constructive perspectives actually correspond to the two dominant categories of characteristics of complex dynamical systems. Using the term "convergent" perspective to correspond to the positivist approach, it was suggested that the focus was on the stable, identifiable, ongoing characteristics of individuals. This perspective seeks to identify "probable outcomes" based on past behavior and knowledge. Such a decision-making counseling perspective has characteristics that include:

- Background information gathering
- Quantitative assessment
- Researching objective occupational information
- Identifying general stable patterns
- Using rationality and logic and linearity
- Weighting various options
- Studying economic and social trends
- Seeking to maximize certainty.

On the other hand, the constructive perspective that Bright and Pryor (2007) designated the "emergent perspective" is more concerned about disorder, change and the unlikely. This perspective seeks to foster the construction of "possible outcomes" based on the pursuit of purpose and passion. The decision-making counseling perspective has characteristics that include:

- Gathering subjective information
- Qualitative and open-ended assessment
- Exploring specificity and the exceptional
- Creating opportunities
- Using originality and intuition
- Being curious and willing to take risks
- Living with uncertainty.

The convergent perspective draws attention to the ordered patterns that are identifiable within complex dynamical systems as a basis for narrowing down (converging) options in order to make a satisfying and effective choice. The emergent perspective points to the susceptibility of change within complex dynamical systems. From instability, inter-action and forming new connections of influences within the system, new characteristics develop (emerge). For example, from a convergent perspective someone making a decision is an individual evaluating skills and personality to match with an occupation. However, from an emergent perspective such an individual could be perceived as part of a complex network of influences mutually influencing one another out of which a sense of purpose emerges through which a congruent work context is constructed.

It still may appear that these two perspectives—the convergent and the emergent—remain as contradictory as the positivist and construc-tivist approaches. However, this is exactly the kind of dichotomous thinking that views order and disorder as opposites when in fact in the Chaos Theory of Careers they are viewed as composites of complex dynamical systems. Through the CTC it can be seen that the insights of both the convergent and the emergent perspectives make a contribu-tion to a further understanding of the individual's personal story and self-concept on the one hand, and how such insights may correspond to a broader understanding of how society arranges work, reputation and the demonstration of abilities for work entry and performance on the other. There seems little point in knowing how your abilities and interests compare with those of other people (convergent perspective) if the utilization of such personal characteristics lacks meaning for you (emergent perspective). Conversely, simply focusing all one's attention on visualizing a fulfilling lifestyle incorporating work (emergent per-spective) if that vision has no chance of actually being realized through the world of work suggests the need for objective occupational infor-mation (convergent perspective).

It is at this point that the relevance of an earlier claim about the Chaos Theory of Careers becomes particularly germane. A point was made in Chapter 2 that the CTC incorporated both realist and constructivist epistemologies. The CTC refuses to see these two approaches to understanding the world as distinct and unrelated. They can be separately delineated but they cannot, in a chaotic world, be separated. The CTC acknowledges that human knowledge and experience comprise an inextricable blend of the objective and real with the subjective and perceived. Each is linked with the other and each influences the other. Thus, to return to an earlier example, if an individual has a passion for making buggy-whips for a living then in order to do that this the person is likely to have to seek out niche markets for such a specialized product and may even have to change the place of residence to be closer to such markets. If this is too high a cost then the person might seek to develop a new passion more congruent with his or her fundamental priorities and a realistic context in which to pursue them. Clive James (2006) makes the point that if one cannot excel in a preferred field, one can still make a meaningful and satisfying contribution by providing service to that field.

Thus it can be seen that the convergent and emergent perspectives constitute a dialectic of influence reflective of the continuous interactive impact of order and disorder within all complex dynamical systems. Therefore, CTC career counseling utilizes both perspectives and the relevant techniques that reflect either perspective. Moreover, it is possible to develop and use techniques that incorporate both perspectives and in the process also blur the distinction between assessment and counseling. Traditionally, the positivist perspective emphasized the assessment of content as a basis for differentiation of the characteristics of both individuals and occupations. The CTC's convergent perspective reflects this emphasis in its focus on the ordered and stable characteristics of complex dynamical systems (both individuals and occupations). The constructivist perspective emphasizes the process dimensions of career development as a basis for personal discovery and meaning making. Analogously, the emergent perspective of the CTC highlights the change capacities of complex dynamical systems as a means to develop, adapt and reconfigure priorities.

Pryor (2007) has demonstrated how both convergent and emergent perspectives can be utilized in career development assessment. He used the Congruence Interest Sort, a vocational interest card sort that is a work-related activity. The 64 cards are grouped psychometrically to measure the eight interest dimensions identified originally by

Roe (1956). The assessment approach is to administer the cards like a standard inventory, asking clients to sort the cards into five preference categories according to how attractive or unattractive each activity is for them. When this is completed, the sorted cards can be scored by allocating a number from one to five corresponding to the strength of preference categories. This is the essence of a convergent perspective of assessment—identifying stable and generalizable patterns characteristic of individuals. The assessment could end at this point with the highest scored scales being then used as a basis for occupational exploration and matching.

However, it is possible to develop the assessment in further constructive (or emergent) directions. Pryor (2007) outlined three examples. First, ask clients to sort through the stack of cards they placed under the "Extremely Attractive" category. Then invite them to see if they can identify any particular patterns across two or more cards. Can they name these patterns? Repeat for the "Extremely Unattractive" cards. A second example technique is to randomly select two cards from one preference category extreme and one from the other extreme. Then invite clients to see if they can perceive any way in which the two cards from one extreme differ from the other card activity. Ask them to name the difference if they can. Third, ask clients to pick up the cards at one extreme preference category and invite them to sort through the cards once again. This time they are requested to add any activities not included on the cards that they love or hate doing. These responses provide insights into the passion and mattering of the clients. This is an illustration of an emergent perspective for career development assessment. Individuals are being encouraged to interpret their own personal constructs and to explore their own deepest preferences and sources of joy. As a consequence all the data generated—convergent and emergent—can then be discussed and compared in a collaborative and supportive relationship between clients and their CTC counselors.

Super's (1980) conception of work as the implementation of the person's self-concept in an occupation implies that work as paid employment has a very central role in individuals' lives. In endorsing this notion, career construction also sees work as a primary means by which people create meaning and fulfillment. However, this is not universally true. For some people work has a comparatively peripheral role in their lives. They may have no paid employment at all or they may engage in such work but view it as a means to another more meaningful end. Douglas Jardine, the infamous English cricket team captain in the 1930s, was once reputed to have said, "The law is my livelihood but cricket is my life." In doing so, Jardine was expressing this utilitarian approach to work. Those who work in the career development field and for whom this work is interesting and important may overestimate others' level of commitment to their jobs. Some workplaces and some occupations offer little in the way of personal fulfillment or sense of overriding meaning and purpose. People often do such work out of perceived economic necessity rather than passion. Some may support themselves and/or their families and others may support avocational activities such as a specialized hobby, opportunities to travel, a humanitarian, social justice or community welfare cause, or a desire to pursue artistic endeavors such as novel writing or landscape painting.

The CTC does not presuppose the configuration of individuals' strange attractors other than the basic dynamics of complex interconnection, self-similar patterns and non-linear change. Career counseling based on the CTC is therefore accepting of the levels of centrality of work in individuals' lives as part of their quest for meaning and spirituality. Spirituality and meaning are themes that will be examined further in Chapter 9.

COUNSELING PARADIGM DIMENSIONS OF THE CHAOS THEORY OF CAREERS

This chapter has outlined a framework in which CTC career counseling can be conceptualized and planned out. The two often competing counseling and assessment perspectives of the current career development literature were then integrated into the chaos theory conceptualization of the interplay of order and change within complex dynamical systems. In this section the distinctive aspects of the Chaos Theory of Careers approach to career development counseling are outlined.

Prediction and Pattern Making

In reality we all make predictions every day. We expect the world in which we interact to be generally the same as it was yesterday and we anticipate (predict) that it will probably be the same tomorrow. Virtually everyone thinks, plans and acts on such general assumptions. Most of the time it works and that is why we persist in thinking and behaving in the ways we do. It is also the reason that closed systems thinking is so compelling and convincing. However, often in career development this leads individuals to focus on just a small number of influences and personal characteristics as they move toward important career decisions.

CTC career counseling suggests that prediction has to be tempered by pattern making. Pattern making involves considering the complexity, changeability and interconnected nature of potential and actual career development influences. Our predictions are rarely if ever totally accurate because the possibility of the influence of factors we did not take into account is always very real. Pattern making is the retrospective process of identifying previous thinking and behavior patterns that have emerged and perhaps repeated themselves in our past. As Bright and Pryor (2008) observe, "learning to see our patterns in all their complexity will present strategies to confront, cope with and capitalize on future changes in our lives" (p. 66).

Plans and Planning

Career counseling clients continue to perceive career development in terms of making plans for a particular choice. The problem is that career development is a continuous process and change can be non-linear. The consequence of these two realities is doggedly adhering too closely and for too long to plans that may result in achieving what is no longer relevant or meaningful to us. This is to revert to closed systems thinking, such as the point attractor where all vision and effort is devoted to a single goal or set of goals. The weakness of such thinking is that it overestimates human control and underestimates contingency and change.

The CTC counseling approach supports the action of making plans in career development; however, it also advocates regular and ongoing monitoring and evaluation of plans in light of current and anticipated changes. Sometimes plans need to be expanded, modified, refocused or even abandoned as new developments emerge either within or external to individuals seeking to develop and pursue their working lives. An analogy of CTC-based career counseling would be that of a financial planner (Watts, 1996). CTC career counselors seek to foster and develop ongoing relationships with their clients. Usually clients initiate going to see a financial planner because they face some form of monetary problem. Good financial planners will not only help their clients with a particular decision but will also outline strategies for ongoing financial management with implications for further decisions. They may also provide contingency strategies in the event of unplanned changes in individuals' circumstances, such as income protection and professional indemnity insurance. Since financial management should be an ongoing process, akin to career development, clients will periodically seek and receive evaluations of their assets and liabilities as well as knowledge about new financial instruments (such as changes in taxation laws) to which their clients may need to respond. Plans and planning go together on a continuous and interactive basis. Insofar as is practicable, the CTC counselor also seeks to encourage such an ongoing perspective in the clients' thinking and decision making. Just as individuals' financial priorities may alter, so too may their career and life priorities. Like career development itself, CTC counseling is an ongoing process of helping clients to anticipate, monitor, identify, create, resist and adapt to both the planned and unplanned influences on their lives and careers.

Openness

Since the CTC notes the incompleteness of the knowledge with which individuals make career decisions, all such decisions need to be construed as provisional. Clients cannot be sure that decisions will have the outcomes they expect and hope for. The expected sets of consequences of individuals' actions are those decisions' provisos. If everything does not go as planned, then further corrective action may need to be taken. It may even require a phase shift in thinking and acting, for example if someone failed to obtain entry into the only course offering the training for the occupation on which that person had set his or her heart. Openness is a mindset that seeks to consider and utilize the advantages of being undecided and still vigilant for new opportunities. Openness takes into account diverse influences and seeks to promote linkages in clients' thinking about these as a constructive way to develop career options and gain new insights about themselves and what is happening in the world of work.

Openness is a component of what the CTC calls open systems thinking, in contrast to closed systems thinking in which individuals limit perspectives, focus only on linear change, assume predictability, and exaggerate their capacity to control decision outcomes.

Risk as Endeavor

Life's uncertainty exposes everyone to risks. Risk suggests the possibility of failure, and fear of failure can be a major deterrent to individuals' career development actions. It typically results in loss of creativity and self-limiting thinking and behavior (Tseng & Carter, 1970). The Chaos Theory of Careers accepts life's uncertainties and therefore is open to the likelihood of failure on occasions. In fact, given the limitations of human knowledge and control in a complex, changing and connected world, failure is almost a logical consequence (Ormerod, 2005). The only real way to avoid failure would be to do nothing—and in fact some career counseling clients actually end up in this state by the time they seek assistance. They become so anxious about not making "the right choice" that they become totally incapable of making any choices and taking any constructive action toward a choice.

The CTC views mistakes as experiments, attempts to find possible solutions from which important information can be derived. Mistakes can be legitimate efforts to constructively negotiate the challenges of career development that did not work, or at least did not achieve the hoped for outcomes. Humans frequently seek to explore, discover, learn and achieve simply by trying things. Science, for example, at the experimental level is largely based on hypothesis testing, which is simply a form of seeking knowledge and insight through failure as much as through success. CTC counselors should not condone thoughtless, reckless and dangerous risk taking. The downside consequences of risks need to be considered if they can be estimated. However, simply because a career development action or choice may result in failure is not by itself sufficient reason for not acting. Failures as learning experiences often constitute the knowledge and courage to refine possibilities and options on which fulfilling career development is based.

Scalable Thinking

Classic psychometric thinking is based around the Normal or Bell-Shaped Curve. Fundamentally, this assumes that populations' characteristics and the probability of occurrences follow a pattern where the most likely possibilities are close to the average and become systematically less likely moving toward distribution extremes. Population norms for many inventories and tests used in career development assume this pattern of the occurrence of scores. This is designated "normative thinking." Given the widespread mathematical utility of the normal curve, this thinking is equivalent to what would be expected on the basis of past experience, "all other things being equal."

However, as Taleb (2007) observes, all other things are quite often not equal and the Normal Curve is limited in its application to complex systems. Normative thinking does not work well when systems begin to experience unpredictable and non-linear change. Merely always assuming the average or most typical outcome fails to take account of individuals' uniqueness. Merely placing people on the basis of scores in various quartile ranges, while it can be informative, fails to capture important aspects of their career development relating to scalability. Scalability thinking focuses on the unlikely, the disproportionate, the outlier, the idiosyncratic and the unpredicted. Taleb (2007) notes how pervasive and often crucial such influences are in determining the nature of our world and the consequences for humans. Scalable thinking respects the possibility that things in life and career may not progress as they have in the past. It considers the potential value of one idea event or speech in changing people's lives and careers. It always keeps open the role that chance, luck, the unplanned, the unforeseen may play in human life and work.

For example, consider a person seeking career development counseling who tells his counselor that he wants to be "a rock star." If the counselor only thinks in normative terms that counselor will probably think this is so far from what the average 16-year-old actually ends up doing for work that this client might be more realistic seeking a trade and playing music in his spare time. However, scalable thinking would focus on the reality that some 16-year-olds end up becoming rock stars—after all, all rock stars over the age of 16 must have been 16 once! Therefore rather than focus on the average or most likely outcome, such a counselor would encourage the young man to explore the implications of such a choice, to consider downside failure, to think open-mindedly and to take action in light of such considerations.

In conclusion, this chapter has outlined an overall strategy for applying the Chaos Theory of Careers to career counseling. A significant amount of this material can be found variously scattered through the existing career counseling literature. However, the CTC's application to career counseling demonstrates how these apparently disparate insights can be integrated into a coherent strategy framework based on the recognition of the interplay of stability and change, control and limitation, planning and contingency. In this process it has also been demonstrated that the CTC provides distinctive contributions to the understanding and practice of career counseling including open systems thinking, the integration of convergent and emergent perspectives, risk and failure as endeavor, pattern identification, scalable thinking and the place for courage and suffering in career development. In colloquial terms, this chapter has been, with respect to career development counseling, a "what to" adumbration. The "how to" of career development counseling with respect to the CTC's contribution to career development practice will be found in the next chapter.

CHAPTER 8

Practical Applications: Counseling and Assessment

Life is helping and being helped.

In the preceding chapter the conceptual and strategic issues relating to the Chaos Theory of Careers counseling approach to dealing with complexity, uncertainty, change and limitation were detailed. This chapter describes a range of techniques that can be used to help achieve the counseling outcomes that the CTC approach deems as crucial for twenty-first-century career development. Uncertainty poses challenges and provides possibilities. From a counseling perspective there is the challenge for the counselor of encouraging individuals to recognize uncertainty in their lives. From a theoretical perspective, there is the challenge of developing useful and practical tools and processes to apply the Chaos Theory of Careers to career development counseling. This chapter reviews some tools and processes that can be applied when working with clients using a chaos perspective. Some of these tools and processes were developed specifically by the authors as a response to the need for practical ways of applying the CTC, whereas other techniques are included that have clear application within a chaos perspective and were developed by others working in the careers field.

The tools and techniques adumbrated in this chapter are presented using a framework we developed for one particular technique—Creative Thinking Strategies—since we believe it provides a useful way of conceptualizing the counseling process. This framework also highlights how particular tools and techniques may be applied for specific purposes in the counseling process.

The Creative Thinking Strategies process has four foci: Challenges, Probabilities, Possibilities and Plans.

- "Challenges" in this context refers primarily to how individuals think about their circumstances, and particularly whether they are harboring "faulty cognitions" (Zunker, 2006).
- "Probabilities" refers to acknowledging likely or immediately plausible outcomes. In this context it also refers to the likely way in which individuals are likely to respond to, think about or make sense of their own experience. In particular, the CTC perspective focuses on individuals' attitudes, responses and strategies when confronting opportunities, risk, uncertainty, complexity of influence, non-linearity, and open and closed systems.
- "Possibilities" refers in this context to employing "strategies which are more future focused and which emphasize probabilities rather than problems" (Amundson, 2009, p. 112).
- "Plans" refers to techniques that can assist the individual in developing strategies for active engagement to address the challenge they are facing. In particular, they encourage the adoption of practical steps to address identified challenges.

CHALLENGES: FAULTY COGNITIONS AND THE VITAL ROLE OF THE REALITY CHECK

Individuals' perceptions of themselves, situations, events and experiences can be mistaken in much the same way that doctors may not wish to rely on patients' self-appraisals of their health for it is well established that people systematically underestimate their weight and overestimate their height (Australian Bureau of Statistics, 2008), gaining an insight into how clients perceive a situation can influence the strategy of the counselor. Zunker (2006) argues that these mistakes in self-appraisals results from faulty cognitions that "inhibit systematic, logical thinking and can be self-defeating" (p. 163).

A challenge for the counselor adopting the CTC framework can often be to help their client appreciate the fundamental realities of change, chance and uncertainty. Very often it will be these very factors that resulted in the individual seeking or being referred to a career counselor. Furthermore, it is likely that those who experience change, chance or uncertainty in terms of personal or career destabilization have already framed their experience in terms of control, certainty and stability and are very likely to seek or expect the promise of such conditions as the product of their counseling.

There is a general expectation that career counseling will provide a sense of personal control and certainty (and therefore the ability to predict the future) as well as offering a future vision of stability. Indeed, many of the dominant paradigms (e.g., Trait-Factor theories of person-job fit such as Dawis & Lofquist, 1984; Holland, 1997; Williamson, 1950) in the career development field are predicated on the notion that we can as counselors assist our clients to find their "ideal" occupation. Presumably, if this perfect occupational choice is ever arrived at the dividend will be certainty, control and stability.

Clearly, the CTC formulation seeks to challenge such notions about a career, and therefore it is often necessary to assist clients to an appreciation of the limits of control, certainty and prediction. To that end we have found three contrasting techniques to be particularly useful.

The Reality Checklist

The Reality Checking Exercise (Pryor & Bright, 2006) is a technique that invites individuals, either before or in the counseling context, to examine some of the myths, misconceptions and mistakes in their thinking about the realities of contemporary career development. The exercise itself is based on an idea contained in Gelatt (1991) which was developed into a 20-item checklist that can be used in either individual or group counseling (for complete details, refer to Appendix 1). Individuals indicate whether they agree with statements about work and life experience. They can then be invited to discuss which responses they disagreed with since the actual statements all accord with chaos theory principles.

The ideas, principles and issues from the responses made that the counselor is likely to draw out include:

- Our limited knowledge and control of the future
- The non-linear nature of some changes
- The influence of unplanned events
- The inevitable limitations of our current information
- The strengths and weaknesses of goal setting
- The value of intuition in decision making
- Our capacity to distort reality
- The necessity of risk taking.

Such discussions can then become the basis for testing individuals' expectations about how the world of work actually functions and their own beliefs about what can and cannot be achieved.

Signature Exercise

This is a straightforward technique that can be used at any stage of the career counseling process to illustrate the nature of reality as a combination of both self-organizing and chance principles. It addresses the issue of whether stability and change are mutually exclusive opposites or whether they can co-exist and mutually impact on one another—the latter, of course, being the chaos perspective. It is sometime thought that chaos theory suggests that there is no pattern, order or meaning to human experience or career development. Others may have difficulty acknowledging that these are aspects of their experience over which they can have very limited and sometimes absolutely no control (other than their reaction). Some who have been trained in applied science fields such as engineering may have fairly rigid positivist perceptions of reality such as "Science works by cause and effect—once you know the cause you can predict the effect."

In the Signature Exercise individuals are simply asked to write their signature as many times as they can within a limited timeframe. Either with the aid of a partner or just individually, they are asked to consider whether the signatures are recognizably the same or similar. Everyone agrees that signatures are recognizably similar or virtually the same. They are then asked to look for variations between the various signatures. Virtually all agree that the signatures are never identical. The implications of these conclusions are discussed in terms of recognizable patterns existing with chance variations (Pryor & Bright, 2006).

Limitations of Knowledge in Decision-Making Exercise

The CTC draws attention to the complexity and changeability of dynamical systems. One implication of this is that it is virtually impossible to have anything like complete or even sufficient knowledge for totally rational career decision making of significance. It is rare for anyone in daily life to have sufficient knowledge of most situations to be certain of the consequences of most of our decisions. It is right and proper that we gather information, seek opinions and research the subject before making decisions, but even experts often disagree about which choices are best and what the consequences of different decisions are likely to be. In fact, rather than rational, much of our decision is "predictably irrational" (Ariely, 2008).

In particular, the more important the decision is and the more long term its implications may potentially be, such as choosing a university course or entering an occupation, the more difficult it is to have anything like adequate knowledge of what the implications of such decisions might be. More generally, it is simply mythical to believe that totally accurate and comprehensive information is ever going to be available (Isaacson & Brown, 2000).

Coming to terms with this uncertainty is the goal of the "Limitations of Knowledge in Decision Making Exercise" (see Appendix 3 for details). Basically, individuals are asked to examine and reflect their past decision making in terms of sources of information, information discovered after decision making and the implications of what was not known prior to choosing. The exercise is expressed in terms of a group exercise for decision makers. However, replacing the other group members with the counselor to the point of pairing up, and obviously not having a plenary session, will allow this technique to be used in an individual career counseling context as well. This technique also works best with people who have some experience of having made significant decisions for themselves. Thus it may not work as well with junior high school students.

PROBABILITIES

One way to conceptualize order and stability and chance and change is as different perspectives for decision making. Using CTC, two perspectives have been adumbrated (McKay, Bright, & Pryor, 2005; Pryor & Bright, 2006). Order and stability can be characterized as a convergent perspective, whereas chance and change can be understood as an emergent perspective. Pryor, Amundson and Bright (2008) linked these perspectives to probable outcomes (convergent) and possible outcomes (emergent).

The convergent perspective on career decision making focuses on seeking to identify probable outcomes. The aim is to converge, through processes of analysis, elimination and logic, to one or a few choice options that could most likely be implemented. The convergent decision-making perspective has the following characteristics:

- Performing a detailed analysis
- Assessing the likelihood of outcomes
- Using standardized instruments
- Gathering reliable information
- Proceeding with caution
- Studying economic and social trends
- Searching for good opportunities
- Making educated guesses
- Weighing carefully the evidence

- Incorporating rational decision making
- Focusing on relatively few variables
- Assuming that "irrelevant" variables will have no systematic effect
- Seeking a single description of a situation
- Seeking a complete description of a situation
- Maximizing certainty.

(from Pryor, Amundson & Bright, 2008)

Complexity Perception Index

The Complexity Perception Index (CPI) (Bright & Pryor, 2005b) is a psychometrically constructed inventory designed to measure an individual's typical reactions to continuous change as a consequence of complexity. It measures an individual's perception (and hence reaction) to the key elements of change and complexity as adumbrated by the CTC.

Specifically, it measures the following dimensions: acceptance of continual change; need for control/certainty; non-linearity; phase shift; emergence; goal or point attractor; role or pendulum attractor; torus or routine attractor; strange or complexity attractor; and purpose/spirituality. More complete descriptions of these dimensions can be found in Bright and Pryor (2005c) and brief summary descriptions are included in Figure 8.1.

Development of the Complexity Perception Index (CPI)

Originally the CPI was developed as an in-class test as a way of illustrating to students the key elements of the CTC, but also to highlight the practical application of the CTC. Then the CPI was developed from a 47-item scale to a 137-item scale. The longer version was then subjected to reliability analyses, which resulted in a refined index of 97 items. The final 10 scales have alpha reliabilities ranging from 0.74 to 0.82 indicating the potential of the CPI as a quantitative measure of chaos theory constructs.

The CPI has proven useful in counseling a wide range of clients. In vocational guidance settings, the CPI helps focus both the counselor and client on some of the key aspects of change. The CPI client profile provides normative data that can help both parties understand both the focus and intensity of any barriers to change. Consequently, it plays an important role in influencing possible counseling directions and interventions as well as providing rich insights that enhance interpretation of other measures such as temperament, work rewards, values and interests.

DESCRIPTION LOW SCORERS	COMPLEXITY PERCEPTION FACTORS	DESCRIPTION HIGH SCORERS
Do not see the need to consider the challenge or impact of change. Believe that change can be resisted or avoided.	Continual Change	Recognises and expects change to be part of human experience. Acknowledges the limits of human control and challenge to adapt.
The future is pictured as unpredictable. Human plans are limited in their capacity to manipulate reality and need to be responsive to the unexpected.	Control/Certainty	See the future as predictable and ordered. Believe control and certainty can be achieved through personal effort and vision.
Overlook details and exceptions. Impressed by static order and stability. May not see the possibility or need for change. Disregard minor events and see no significance in them.	Non-linearity	Understand the potential of apparently minor events and behaviours to have profound impacts. Sees the possibilties for change in details and in "small steps."
Tend to see their lives in terms of stability and control. They do not expect substantial changes in their lives and may react badly to them.	Phase Shifts	May have experienced and expect radical changes in their lives. They recognise the potential for this change to be unexpected.
Do not see patterns emerging in their behaviour or work, they are more likely to want to plan and predict their work.	Emergence	Recognise that patterns of meaning emerge over time and that thinking after acting can be more beneficial than before.
Complexity is not sought to be controlled by goals and achievement. Things are allowed to evolve. Can be fatalistic and undisciplined.	Point/Goal Attractor	Complexity is reduced to goal driven behaviour. Determination, focus, vision, clarity and commitment are the means to control and achievement. Chance and change are barriers to be overcome.
Complexity is a source of competing demand resulting in role conflict and inability to fulfil expectation. Vacillation, and frustration in decision making are likely results. Chance and change only complicate.	Pendulum/Role Attractor	Complexity is not viewed in terms of conflicting demands, guilt and frustration. Does not have difficulty working out priorities resulting in integration, balance or indifference.
Complexity is dealt with by using rules, procedures and precedents. There is no vision, only process and routine. Chance and change are irritations requiring unwanted effort.	Torus/Routine Attractor	Complexity is handled without rigidity. Chance and change are seen as variety providing interest and opportunities amidst repetition.
Chance and change viewed as threats to identity and stability. Uncomfortable with the creative challenge of the unexpected.	Strange/Complexity Attractor	Chance and change viewed as sources for new opportunities. Enjoys the creative challenge of the unexpected. Pattern and surprise are embraced as complex realities of living.
See their work predominantly in utilitarian terms. Work is a means to an end and is not seen in broader terms such as contribution or purpose.	Purpose/Spirituality	See how their work relates to other people and how they fit into a larger order. They recognise limits to their knowledge and control.

Figure 8.1 Summary of the Complexity Perception Factors.

The Complexity Perception Index (CPI) focuses on assessing the content of the chaos dimensions incorporating complexity and change in particular. However, given the integral place that unplanned events have in the functioning of complex dynamical (that is, chaotic) systems and the recent attention that chance has been receiving in the literature (see below), we also considered that being able to measure what Neault (2002) has designated "luck readiness" (the psychological dimensions of recognizing and utilizing unplanned events) was another crucial assessment challenge.

Luck Readiness Index

The influence of unplanned events is widely acknowledged (e.g., Betsworth & Hanson, 1996; Bright, Pryor, Chan & Rijanto, 2009; Bright, Pryor & Harpham, 2005; Bright, Pryor, Wilkenfeld & Earl, 2005; Krumboltz & Levin, 2004; Neault, 2002; Patton & McMahon, 1999; Pryor & Bright, 2004). Luck readiness is defined as recognizing, creating, utilizing, and adapting to opportunities and outcomes occasioned by chance. The Luck Readiness Index (Pryor & Bright, 2005b) assesses eight dimensions: flexibility, optimism, risk, curiosity, persistence, strategy, efficacy and luckiness. Brief descriptions of these dimensions are included in Figure 8.2. Fuller descriptions can be found in Pryor and Bright (2005c).

It can be useful in helping to diagnose potential strengths and limitations in individuals' ability to use luck, to stimulate creative responses to career development of those who feel "stuck" in a particular job, to encourage a positive response to change among those who feel threatened or "victimized" by unplanned events often beyond their control, and to guide those who want to improve their "luck readiness" as part of the development of an entrepreneurial strategy for their future. The potential for the LRI to be used for career development research, team building, staff development and organizational change adaptation also appears promising.

Development of the LRI

Two earlier versions of the LRI dimensions with varying item content were piloted extensively in counseling and were subject to psychometric analysis. The subsequent third version of the Luck Readiness Index was administered to 65 university students. Using the same item analysis strategy as for the CPI focusing on item homogeneity and reliability, the 95 theoretical items were reduced to 52. To assist in validation and interpretation, a 30-item adjective checklist was also administered

DESCRIPTION LOW SCORES	LUCK READINESS FACTORS	DESCRIPTION HIGH SCORES
Try to avoid change or respond minimally to it. Like to keep the same thoughts and habits. New ideas and situations are disturbing. Describe themselves as easily disheartened and as a negative thinker.	Flexibility	Prepared for and responsive to the need to change. Do not find it hard to alter thinking or behaviour. Do not feel threatened by the new or unfamiliar. Describe themselves as adaptable, brave and adventurouc.
Believe that situations are likely to deteriorate rather than improve. Focus on problems and barriers to action and achievement. Do not consider themselves free to think and act. Describe themselves as pessimistic and a negative thinker.	Optimism	Expect situations, even bad ones, to improve and therefore keep trying. Believe they have enough control to be able to make decisions freely. See opportunities rather than problems. Describe themselves as hopeful, adaptable and open to new experiences.
Disconcerted by the challenge to make decisions in changing or uncertain conditions. Lacking confidence in their choices in new situations. Fear failure. Describe themselves as pessimistic and a negative thinker.	Risk	Feel confident to be able to make decisions in response to change. Recognise the possibility of failure but not deterred by it. Not dominated by fear. Describe themselves as adaptable, hopeful, open to new experiences and adventurous.
Do not seek out new information or experience unless it is obviously of use. Dislike learning or study for its own sake. Are content with what they already know. Describe themselves as pessimistic.	Curiosity	Explore and seek new knowledge and experiences. Like to learn from study and from others. Can be disciplined in their efforts to discover new things. Describe themselves as adaptable, adventurous, open to new experiences, persevering and inquisitive.
Distracted, discouraged and unpersevering if something becomes difficult to do or achieve. Tend to give up in the face of problems and barriers. Describe themselves as pessimistic and a negative thinker; fatigue quickly and are disorganised.	Persistence	Able to endure boredom, frustration and disappointment to achieve a goal. Obstacles do not discourage and are seen as oppurtunities to find new solutions. Describe themselves as confident, persevering, hopeful and tenacious.
Reluctant to try to create new opportunities. Fatalistic in the face of problems and uncertainty. Have difficulties planning ways to improve situations. Describe themselves as lacking in resolution.	Strategy	Actively seek out opportuinties and possibilities to improve chances of achieving goals. Believe that luck can be both influenced and expected. Plans ways to win in uncertain situations. Describe themselves as daring, adventurous and adaptable.
See self and situation as the result of external influences. Believe that they can do little to alter their situations. View their well-being as dependent on circumstances and others. Focus on problems and limitations. Describe themselves as pessimistic, a negative thinker, unprepared, cautious and easily distracted.	Efficacy	Believe that luck, circumstances, problems and others do not have to determine their choices or destiny. Seek to take control of their lives and what can be influenced or changed. Focus on opportunities and capacities. Describe themselves as confident, likes variety, hopeful, likes learning and tries new things.
Fail to believe or expect to have good luck.	Luckiness	Believe or expect to have good luck.

Figure 8.2 Summary of the Luck Readiness Factors.

to the sample at the same time and then correlated with the resultant seven dimensions of the LRI. The scale alphas obtained ranged from 0.68 to 0.76.

The CPI and the LRI provide new taxonomies for both understanding and classifying major career development problems and for suggesting counseling response strategies to address such career decision-making difficulties.

The CPI and the LRI are attempts to address what Harkness (1997) sees as a chaotic world requiring new skills and traits to thrive. In this venture, we are concerned about the welfare of career decision makers in times that are replete with both disorientating complexity and unparalleled opportunity. Closed-systems thinking and lack of luck readiness may make some individuals bewildered victims of the unpredictability and continual demands of change in the future.

Archetypal Narratives

Narrative has become increasingly popular as a counseling technique in career development, reflecting the importation of ideas from the clinical counseling realm (e.g., White, 2007). Narrative (or story) is a useful, indeed compelling medium with which to understand the world. We seek to understand and interpret our experience by looking for patterns in that experience. Narratives reveal fundamental structures of interpretation of human experience (Amundson, 2003a). They uncover individual frameworks for understanding personal experience.

The extent of meaning to be found in narrative provides counselors with a rich seam to mine. Most treatments of narrative practice (e.g., White, 2007) focus almost entirely upon the meanings of narratives and are almost completely silent about the structure of narrative. While the meanings of stories can be compelling and are most certainly personal, themes emerge across narratives, people and cultures, for if they did not we would find it exceptionally difficult to understand stories. Perhaps part of the explanation of narrative's popularity rests on the familiarity of the structure of stories. The mere exposure effect reported by Zajonc (1980) indicates that people prefer things that they have previously been exposed to. In the case of narratives, in some sense we have all heard the story before. If we had never been exposed to the structure of stories, how could we experience anticipation, suspense, surprise and a panoply of other emotions? For the enjoyment of narrative involves the twin chaotic imposters of pattern and surprise.

While each individual's experience (and therefore narrative) is unique, we all have to negotiate a common range of developmental challenges as part of living (Bujold, 2004). If this were not the case then it is difficult to see how narrative endeavors such as art, history, philosophy, spirituality and literature would be meaningful to any one other than the individuals responsible for creating them. Indeed, this is explicitly recognized in that the literature in the career development field has drawn upon such materials as bases for counseling, including fables (Fergle, 2007), myths (Green & Sharman-Burke, 2000), movies (Pryor & Bright, 2003a) and parables (Pryor & Bright, 2006).

The underlying patterning of these stories of common experience as revealed in world literature has been surveyed to reveal seven archetypal plots (Booker, 2004). These seven plots, identified by examining 4,000 stories across cultures and time are:

1. Overcoming the Monster
2. Rags to Riches
3. Voyage and Return
4. The Quest
5. Comedy
6. Tragedy
7. Rebirth.

Pryor and Bright (2009) have identified how the notion of archetypal plots can be used within the CTC. While the seven archetypal plots cannot be directly equated with any one of the CTC attractors, identifying the plots underlying individuals' stories and the attractors they represent provides new insights into the nature of such counseling clients' difficulties. In addition, these insights can provide alternative strategies for choosing new stories that will orient the person toward open systems thinking and away from unrealistic expectations about human knowledge and control. The counseling application of this is to help individuals to question the plot that they have been telling themselves as the story of their career and to provide alternative plots as new ways to perceive their careers, and in the process new possibilities for how to move forward.

For example, counseling clients who have recently lost their jobs in an organizational takeover often come to career counselors with "Tragedy" as the dominant plot by which they understand their recent experience. This may block their capacity to see new opportunities. However, if they can be assisted to see this in terms, for example, of

"Overcoming the Monster" this would allow them to see that unemployment is a challenge to be met rather than a fate to be helplessly acceded to.

Forensic or Cognitive Interviewing (CI)

In the CTC, it is acknowledged that individuals socially construct their world views and that this extends to their memories. However, in our formulation (Pryor & Bright, 2003b) meaning is not entirely just constructed. Realism is also acknowledged. For instance, reality testing is an important aspect of the CTC. The CI is an attempt to minimize the impact of post hoc social construction of memories. The CI aims to garner an accurate recollection of events by reinstating the context of the original events. Tulving and Thompson (1973) originally developed the "encoding specificity hypothesis"—that retrieval cues to memory are successful as a function of the degree to which they overlap with the encoded information. So mentally re-creating as much detail as possible about some previous event will increase the chances of the accurate recall of that event. In career counseling terms, recalling the circumstances under which a previous career decision was made will serve to elucidate the dominant influences that were operating. This technique will reduce the tendency toward post hoc rationalization of events or overlooking subtle but important influences.

For instance, a series of poor career choices may have been due to the client experiencing financial exigencies at the time. Looking back, these issues might not be as salient for the individual, and career decisions that were actually financially driven are now recalled as being driven by interests or some other post hoc and rational view. Under some circumstances these constructions themselves are clinically relevant and worth pursuing with the client (e.g., Savickas, 1997). In career counseling terms, it is important for the client to recall details without filtering, to allow the counselor the opportunity to put together a pattern of influences. A client who "censors" out a recollection that his mother had been hassling him for the previous year to get a "respectable" job, but instead chooses to focus on his math ability and how it matched accountancy, may be withholding a critical clue as to his true career patterns of influence.

Finally, the CI recognizes non-linearity in the sense of multiple perspectives. The interview encourages the client to consider the events and influences from the perspective of significant others. This can be valuable in elucidating additional valuable insights.

Circles of Influence

The "Circles of Influence" technique (Bright & Pryor, 2003) represents a graphical approach to understanding the different influences that come to bear upon an individual's career decision making (see Figure 8.3). The circles of influence are represented by three major concentric circles that represent three key factors of career influence: Unplanned Events, Family and Friends, and Teachers, Advisors and the Media, derived from Bright, Pryor, Wilkenfeld, and Earl (2005).

Clients are given the circles and asked to consider either their current situation, or a time in the past when they had to make a career decision. They are encouraged to write down the names or positions of people or things that they felt had an influence on the decision they made, or are in the process of making.

The graphical nature of the task provides a ready structure to consider different patterns of influence. With more adult clients, several circles can be constructed that detail the influences at work across a number of key decisions. From these multiple circles, patterns or emergent themes can be discerned and analyzed.

The circles of influence technique benefits from being empirically derived, meaning that the categories or circles used are not arbitrarily present, or merely asserted vaguely from an untested theoretical

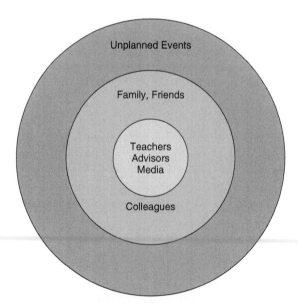

Figure 8.3 The "Circles of Influence" technique.

position. This increases the validity of such an approach to understanding the probabilities in a client's life from their perspective. It also orients the client toward an awareness of the unplanned and unexpected, and therefore provides avenues and openings for the client to consider the role of the unplanned in their lives.

POSSIBILITIES

We now turn to the Possibilities. The emergent perspective on career decision making focuses on seeking to explore possible outcomes. The aim is for thinking to emerge from current self-limiting structures to make use of processes that allow more room for creativity, intuition and openness, thus leading to new options that could be constructed or crafted into viable career choice alternatives (Amundson, 2003a). The emergent decision-making perspective focuses on possibilities and has the following characteristics:

- Assuming personal responsibility
- Making choices
- Refusing to let fear conquer action
- Maintaining positive action
- Looking to the future with optimism and excitement
- Searching for new and enlightening knowledge
- Adopting multiple descriptions of a situation simultaneously
- Recognizing and welcoming uncertainty
- Working with incomplete knowledge and recognizing it will always be so
- Following your curiosity
- Taking risks
- Learning from failure
- Pursuing your passion
- Listening to your intuitive self.

(from Pryor, Amundson & Bright, 2008)

A total of 10 techniques will be adumbrated, further organized into card sorts, games and parables, and techniques derived from the arts.

Card Sort Techniques

Sometimes Magic: A Card Sort

Chaos theory emphasizes that meaning, insight, inspiration, creativity and opportunity awareness are emergent properties from human experience (Pryor & Bright, 2003a). Since chance is a parameter of our lives, rather than deny it we could consider ways to embrace and utilize it positively (for a complete outline of the procedures for using this technique refer Pryor & Bright, 2006). This exercise derives closely from the Sometimes Magic: Celebrating the Magic of Everyday Learning card sort (Vallence & Deal, 2001a,b). The procedures described represent an adaptation of the original material for career counseling purposes. This adaptation was undertaken with the permission of the original authors. Each card has a colorful drawing of an Australian animal with the words "Sometimes Magic HAPPENS WHEN ... [for example] I have a good teacher."

Hand out the Sometimes Magic cards. Ask the person to sort through the cards and to separate those that may suggest special experiences that they have had. Then invite the person to consider each card and to think of a particular event or experience that relates to this card's description. When the person has decided on an experience for a particular card, invite the person to describe it. Then ask the person how the experience relates to the description. Further questions can then be asked to help the person consider the magical aspect of the experience, what was learned, how did the person reacted, what actions he or she took, what worked and what did not. Such reflections encourage individuals to start thinking more divergently about the unusual, the unique, the possibilities that situations may present, and how they may be able to take action to open up opportunities.

Congruence Interest Sort

The Congruence Interest Sort (CIS; Pryor, 1995) is a 64-item card sort assessing the eight dimensions of Roe's (1956, 1972) classification of vocational interests. The items were developed using standard psychometric item analysis techniques. On each card is an activity statement, and the test taker is requested to sort each card according to how attractive the activity is to her or him. After the test taker has sorted the cards into up to five stacks, the cards are then scored for the eight interest dimensions (eight cards per dimension). Up to this point the CIS functions directly analogously with a standard vocational interest inventory such as those developed through matching models, including the Self Directed Search (Holland, 1999).

In Chapter 7 the themes exercise, the personal constructs exercise, the "other activities" exercise and the contingency exercise were briefly described. Full accounts of these exercises can be found in Pryor

(2007). What these exercises demonstrate is the ways in which assessment can go beyond the normative to the idiographic with the one technique, and then combine both. The flexibility of card sorts enables further exploration of an individual's interests, enabling a more complex and individualized approach to assessment. Thus individuals can be asked to consider the extremely attractive card stack and look for themes more specific to each person's preferences than the generalized interest categories based on the original work of Roe (1956). This also allows for the emergence of new patterns in line with chaos theory expectations. The procedure can be repeated with the extremely unattractive cards. Further, adapting personal construct theory, individuals can be asked to compare subsets of attractive and unattractive cards to derive additional constructs, giving insight into the uniqueness of each individuals' perceptions.

In addition, traditional inventory measures are virtually always limited in content validity as a direct consequence of having a restricted number of items. This is simply a practical necessity. However, considering the multifactorial nature of potential influences on individuals' career thinking, another way in which the CIS can be used is to allow individuals to supplement the sorted cards with additional activities that they are invited to articulate (Pryor, 2007). These additional activities may be either things they love or things they loathe doing. Not only does this involve the person in the assessment process—assessment has developed from being "done to" to "doing myself"—it also provides further insights into the specific and unique impacts that individuals experience on their career thinking and behavior.

Moreover, since the CTC points to the potential impact of contingency on careers, the CIS cards can be re-sorted on the basis of various "what if …" conditions. For example, Mike's CIS results indicated that he is not very interested in any of the activities covered by the cards with the exception of a weak preference for clerical activities (Organizing scale). However, Mike's parents have had a very major impact on his career thinking—telling him to find a secure job such as accounts work because "You will always have a job in accounts." Mike's CIS results appear to reflect this. Mike's career counselor invited Mike to re-sort the cards as if his parents were not correct—"What if you sorted the cards, not according to just finding a secure job but according to your own preferences?" When Mike did the re-sort it was found that this time he scored higher on the Culture scale than any other because, as he subsequently explained, "I have always been interested in history." Now Mike has a choice, he may still choose to do what his parents want or he can choose to make decisions more specifically in line with his own personal preferences. He may even look for some kind of compromise such as librarian, which is likely to be reasonably secure and also likely to provide opportunities to be involved in history at some level.

Mike now is less certain, he is probably less decisive, and he has to think more deeply and creatively about how he can resolve such issues. As we saw in Chapter 7, from a matching theory strategy the assessment of Mike has failed—a congruent match between the person and the occupation has not been found. However, from a CTC perspective Mike's uncertainty and indecision now are productive outcomes since they are the result of a preparedness to think in open systems terms: that is, to recognize and confront the challenges of the complexity, change, chance and interconnectedness of career development reality. Of course, the career counselor may go on, should Mike request it, to assist Mike further to explore options either in terms of specific occupations or by creatively looking at work possibilities that help Mike to explore further the ways in which he wants to work and to what matters he wishes to give his priority.

Other Card Sorts to Explore Possibilities

There are very many different card sorts that have been designed for use in career development. Typically these have focused on the "traditional" areas such as interests, strengths and motivation. There are, however, a range of card sorts that have been developed for broader counseling applications that can be usefully employed within the CTC framework. We will briefly outline two further card sorts that address possibilities that we have found fit well within the CTC approach. Both can be seen as addressing hope (Pryor & Bright, 2009).

Optimism Boosters

Optimism Boosters (Byrne, 2004) are a set of 30 cards that are designed to increase optimism and mood. They are broadly inspired by ideas from the Positive Psychology movement (Seligman, 1992) that optimism can be learned. The cards are divided into three "'skill sets": Goals, Possibilities and Strategies. The Goal cards help people understand what they want to achieve. The Possibility cards help people to reframe the story they are telling themselves. The Strategies cards assist people to apply problem-solving techniques to work out how they will achieve their goal.

The potential of the cards within CTC terms is that they assist clients to understand the emergent patterns in their lives and to see different possibilities that emerge. The interactive nature of the card sort format encourages clients to explore a range of different possibilities by using different cards, rather than adopting a single perspective on a problem. They also are useful in understanding the fluid and ever changing nature of situations and problems.

Signposts Cards

Signpost cards (Deal & Masman, 2004) are a set of 48 cards designed to explore "Everyday spirituality." The cards are designed not to be specifically religious but to prompt reflection about meaning and significance. Each card contains an engaging photograph and an accompanying phrase such as "recognising possibilities" (with an image of chess pieces on a board) or "Embracing change" (differently colored leaves) or "standing in uncertainty" (a man standing on a train platform with a training rushing by).

These cards are a useful way to explore a clients' deeper values and from a CTC perspective help a client to understand the dimensions of an individual's strange attractor, the limiting forces that values have in shaping behavior and that may become particular strengths. The evocative nature of the cards tends to provoke clients to consider their careers in terms of emergent values, which in turn can create new possibilities and clarity.

One way of using these cards with clients presented itself serendipitously while planning to train a group of counselors in the use of these cards. Only one set of cards was available from the publisher for the session, which meant that training participants would be obliged to share. The presenter decided on the spot to deal the cards out in turn like a game of cards. The trainees were divided into pairs to play a game. They spread out their hand of cards on the table for the other person to see. Then each player took turns to request a card from the other player's hand that they particularly liked or identified with; however, the other player did not have to agree to the request. The result was quite animated "horse trading," and it was interesting to see how passionate the players were in their requests and refusals, as they developed a strong sense of ownership and identification with the values depicted.

This game approach provides an unthreatening way to encourage reflection on the bigger emergent values that both constrain behavior and provide possibilities. In the following section we consider further the use of games in careers.

Games and Parables

Games

There has been a lot of interest in the application of metaphors in career counseling (e.g., Amundson, 2003a; Inkson, 2007), but interestingly the metaphor of life as a game has been largely overlooked. In psychotherapy, several authors in the 1960s and 1970s promoted the use of this metaphor (e.g., Berne, 1964; Maccoby, 1976), but little else has been made of what is a popular metaphor in everyday life.

Games serve as potent metaphors because they provide a familiar context and one in which some of the key CTC concepts such as uncertainty, non-linearity, phase shift, and complexity can be introduced and utilized. Games, at least the non-trivial ones, are subject to a complex array of influences. For instance, player fitness, the weather, umpire or referee mistakes, the surface on which the game is played, the roll of dice, the cards dealt or the toss of a coin, along with myriad other influences can all affect the outcome of the game.

Games exhibit non-linear effects too. Often winning or losing (and even careers) can hang in the balance over a matter of fractions of an inch: the difference between the ball being in or going over the net, or being out and hitting the net. Such a "match point" metaphor was explored by Woody Allen in a film of the same name (Allen, 2005). In fact, a contingent view of life and reality is either explicit or implied in virtually every one of his films from *Stardust Memories* onwards.

Games must exhibit uncertainty to capture our long-term interest. Only the sadistic or chronically unimaginative would want to watch completely one-sided contests. The nature of a game can change dramatically and unpredictably, perhaps where one side scores a goal in soccer against the run of play, or an heroic tennis rally proves to be a tipping point in the balance of a match.

All of these points and many more can be profitably compared to the experience of careers. These ideas are explored further in Pryor and Bright (2009).

Parables

The use of myths such as that of Narcissus, iconic stories such as that of the Wizard of Oz (Amundson, 2006) and animal allegories such as "Who moved the Cheese?" (Johnson, 1999) are among the creative techniques that counselors are using as ways to stimulate clients' creativity, awareness and sense of exploration in career development. We have found that some of these existing techniques are too esoteric, too long or too unfamiliar to be effective with some of our clients. Instead, we sought to develop a more homely everyday example that could be concisely presented in verbal, written or pictorial form and discussed in a single counseling session. We call it the "Parable of the Ping-Pong Ball." The aim of the parable is to:

1. Illustrate how increasing complexity results inevitably in decreased predictability of outcomes.
2. Demonstrate that even though our ability to predict in a situation is limited, this does not mean that we cannot understand or explain what happened.
3. Indicate non-linearity of change.
4. Introduce the notion of the "phase shift."
5. Highlight human limitation of knowledge and control in the problem solving (decision making) situation and the necessity to make decisions without having total, or often even adequate, knowledge of influences and outcomes.
6. Point to the reality and the necessity to continue to make decisions and face challenges on an ongoing basis.

What follows is an abridged version of the parable; for a fuller treatment see Pryor and Bright (2006). In the parable there is a dog, let us call her Emma, the dog's owner, Ben, and another person, William. While William is waiting for Ben and Emma to arrive, he experiments dropping a ping-pong ball to see where it lands. He notices that the breeze coming through a window alters the path of the ball. Later, when Emma the dog arrives, she sometimes tries to catch the ball and is sometimes uninterested, making it even harder to predict where the ball will land. Then a pack of local dogs arrive, having detected Emma's scent, and Emma runs off with the ping-pong ball, with the other dogs in hot pursuit. Who would have predicted that?

The point of the parable is to point out how difficult it rapidly becomes to predict the trajectory of a humble ping-pong ball as more and more influences are added into the scene. This serves as a way of raising awareness about complexity and the limits of personal control.

Techniques Developed from the arts

The obvious place to look for inspiration when searching for techniques that promote creativity is in the arts. Art therapy is long established in psychiatry, having been used regularly since the 1940s. Techniques such as drawing (Amundson, 2009) and reference to movies (Pryor & Bright, 2006) and stories (Savickas, 1997) have been applied successfully in career counseling.

Collage (Adams, 2003; Loader, 2009) is a technique that has particular application within the CTC. Collage involves clients cutting, placing and pasting images onto paper (or a computer screen) to represent some aspect of their life, interests, values, aspirations or all of these. For instance, a technique commonly used by one of the authors is to ask a client to produce a collage of "Me Now" and then another of "Me in 5 or 10 Years."

Collage is a relatively free technique that requires little or no formal skill to produce attractive work (compared to painting, music or drawing). Second, collage encourages clients to express themselves in patterns, and some of these patterns emerge as meta-patterns owing to the synergy of the combinations of collage elements. Third, collage benefits from being one of the few techniques that allow clients to free themselves from the constraints of linear accounts of their lives. The current preoccupation of many writers in the career development field with narrative accounts implicitly or explicitly encourages linear thinking about careers. Stories have a beginning, a middle (or sometimes muddle!) and an end. They tend to tie up loose ends, which can be both a strength and a weakness (Pryor & Bright, 2008). Fourth, collage is one of relatively few techniques in career development that do not present significant hurdles in terms of verbal fluency or reading skills; nor does it require good interpersonal skills. Thus it is a technique that can be well suited to those who are not overly proficient in reading and/or speaking in the counselor's native tongue, or are perhaps shy.

The non-linear aspect of collage, combined with the natural emergent patterns that arise, provides immediate connections to two of the central tenets of the CTC. Figures 8.4 and 8.5 are an example of a client's collages for "Me Now" and "Me in 10 Years."

You can see in Figure 8.4 how the client has found key images and words that have personal meaning. The building in the bottom represents his workplace. The piece is well organized, obeying formalisms of vertical and horizontal layout. The images capture what is important beyond work such as sailing, gardening and family. There is a certain literalness or concreteness in the frequent use of words rather than pictures to capture key meaning. There is also a sense of pressure in the picture captured in words such as "meltdown," "control" and

Figure 8.4 Collage by a late middle age client depicting "Me Now."

Figure 8.5 Collage by a late middle age client depicting "Me in 10 Years."

"in the thick of it." There are also references to his work as a career advisor with a book and a reference to engagement. The phrase on the right-hand edge near "control" says "Unlock the power for brilliant results"—another reference to counseling work.

In contrast, Figure 8.5 presents a nearer to retirement image that shows relaxation, a sense of legacy ("he is a legend"). There is consistency between the images as well as change. The very strong outdoor theme is evident in both pictures (e.g., the boat, the garden), but this image is more expansive literally and figuratively as we see the references to international travel (Big Ben in London, the postcard) and the literal use of the word "freedom" and "now for the fun part." There is also imagery related to planning.

We might work with the client and identify Holland codes from these images. Good candidates to discuss would be Realistic (the outdoor theme) and Conventional (the organizing theme) as well as the more obvious Social theme that reflects his occupation as a teacher and careers advisor.

The arrangement is orderly in both images, and it is interesting to note that he felt such a strong need to identify his family on the second image that he was motivated to write the word into the collage, presumably because he was unable to find appropriate images or words to paste on.

Notice that these images provide a compelling emergent pattern that is complex and also non-linear. We see different facets of his life presented simultaneously rather than arranged according to some arbitrary linear formula. It is often interesting to get clients to complete a lifeline of their lives as a preliminary to this exercise. When they do this unprompted, it is not unusual for clients to focus upon the "milestone" events of transition in their lives, such as started school, finished school, first job, second job. The interesting question is what they have left out of their timelines, and generally it is the sort of material that appears in the collage. In other words, it is the values and the ongoing day-to-day things that rarely appear in the lifeline, but regularly appear in the collage. The collage then appears to tap into the more personal, more real strange attractor of the individual, rather than the public face, the more constrained torus attractor of a milestone life history.

Kinetic sculpture

Kinetic sculpture is a movement (figuratively and literally) in the arts that is closely associated with the Swiss artist Jean Tinguely. Tinguely's sculptures are immediately recognizable as they typically comprise a series of wheels, levers and pulleys sourced from a variety of different machines. The components are all interconnected, and most importantly they all move and articulate with each other. This moving, swinging, clanging system collectively produces a striking emergent pattern. Tinguely's own view of his art is perhaps best captured in his "manifesto" for "Statics" published in March 1959, which stated:

> Everything moves continuously. Immobility does not exist. Don't be subject to the influence of out-of-date concepts of time. Forget hours, seconds and minutes. Accept instability. Live in time. Be static—with movement. For a static of the present moment. Resist the anxious fear to fix the instantaneous, to kill that which is living. Stop insisting on "values" which cannot but break down. Be free, live.
>
> Stop painting time. Stop evoking movement and gesture. You are movement and gesture. Stop building cathedrals and pyramids which are doomed to fall in ruin. Live in the present; live once more in Time and by Time—for a wonderful and absolute reality …

In this statement, the parallels with the key notion of the inevitability of change that is central to the CTC are clear. Indeed, it is no coincidence that the artist went on to produce two installations called *Chaos 1* and *Chaos 2* in the 1970s.

Kinetic sculptures can be very potent tools to talk about the dynamics of change, and consequently introducing these sculptures through scale models, photographs and preferably short videos can be useful in promoting discussion of Tinguely's central tenets as set out in his manifesto, which are in many ways strikingly consistent with the CTC.

A simple practical exercise involves presenting clients with short film clips of Tinguely's installations in operation (these can be found by searching online video resources such as YouTube and Google videos). Then ask the client or group to consider the difference between this type of sculpture and a more conventional static one. The client or group is then asked to reflect on the nature of the movement presented: Was it smooth and predictable, or odd and unpredictable? How did things change over time in the sculpture? Were any of the movements lifelike? How could the sculpture presented relate to the client's own experience of their career?

More involved activities related to kinetic sculpture may involve encouraging the client to construct their own sculpture. This can be done using elastic bands, cardboard, springs and toy wheels.

Alternatively, more sophisticated models can be built using modeling toys such as Meccano® or motorized Lego®.

Films

Films provide an excellent resource to assist clients to illustrate aspects of their lives, and they also provide the counselor with a powerful way of making a point using a readily understood and engaging medium. Film can be used in many different ways in career counseling, but for our purposes we are interested in films that highlight pertinent aspects of the CTC. The authors have identified and used in their work a range of films that illustrate different parts of our theory and communicate some of the important career development implications of adopting the CTC perspective.

It is not possible within the constraints of this chapter to highlight all of the possible films and their application, but a few examples that utilize chaos ideas could be used with clients or in vocational education contexts such as high school career classes.

- *Sliding Doors*—this movie focuses on the notion of non-linearity. The main character's life is portrayed in two radically different stories contingent on whether she gets onto a train (the doors slide behind her) or whether she just misses it (the doors slide in front of her).
- *The Butterfly Effect* (three versions)—this also portrays the impact of non-linearity and how small acts can have immense consequences.
- *Melinda and Melinda*—this is another example of how a person's life story can be interpreted in multiple ways dependent upon which archetypal narrative is used to frame the facts. In this case Comedy and Tragedy are contrasted.
- *Chaos*—an action film relating to a bank holdup in which the criminal mastermind leaves chaos theory-based clues for the investigating police officer—illustrating the interplay of the predictable and the unpredictable.
- *Chaos Theory*—a man named Frank Allen who has a beautiful wife and daughter has his whole view of his life changed when his wife wrongly accuses him of having an affair and fathering a child with another woman. When he has a DNA test to confirm his innocence, the doctors discover that he's unable to produce children. In fact, he has never been able to father a child, at which point he realizes that his daughter is not his. The limits of

our control and knowledge are exemplified with the unintended consequences of such limitations.

PLANS

The previous section focused on a range of different techniques designed to assist the client recognize the possibilities of a life lived on the edge of chaos. However, as Janet Lenz (2008) from Florida State University reminds us, people have at some stage to make choices. Consequently, while recognizing the inevitability of change and uncertainty, and aware of the warning of Jean Tinguely to resist fixing the instantaneous, we need to convert the possibilities into viable plans of action. In this section four techniques that can assist in this process are highlighted.

Mind Mapping

Mind mapping is a technique originally developed by Buzan (1986, 1993) that was intended to use graphic techniques in information recall, brainstorming, personal organization, summarizing material and cueing for presentations. The fundamental aim of the technique is to represent a large amount of information on a single page through the use of connected key words and/or drawings. Pryor (2003) demonstrated how mind mapping could be used to incorporate complexity and change into the medico-legal report writing process. Full details of the technique's use can be found in that source. However, it can be noted that mind mapping can be used in career counseling as a method of pattern identification.

In stressing complexity and interconnectedness, the Chaos Theory of Careers presents the career counselor with the challenge of being able to assist counseling clients to recognize and to utilize such career development realities. The graphic presentation of individuals' personal and career histories can enable both counselor and client to perceive patterns of responding such as avoidance, impulsiveness, playing it safe, compromising, "chasing the bucks," conflicts with others and so on, that might not otherwise be obvious. Similarly, through mind mapping the emergence of preferences such as particular interests, desired rewards, task approach habits, relationships with others and so on, may become more evident. This technique can help individuals to acknowledge influences on their lives and careers that they are otherwise reluctant to acknowledge or find it difficult to recognize. A common example is the influence of other family members for good or ill. We often notice how young siblings frequently follow older ones into courses, industries, occupations and employing organizations and yet at the same time deny wanting to "live in the shadow" of an older brother or sister. Mind mapping can allow the person to appreciate such influence while at the same time throughout the rest of the map also reveal their individual uniqueness.

Butterflies and After Eights

One of the harder concepts to convey to some clients is the relationship between stability and instability, between pattern and surprise, the planned and the unplanned. Many clients will seek out your services precisely because they are experiencing uncertainty, which they do not like, or are feeling lost or stuck. It is understandable that people in those situations will inevitably tend to grasp for certainties and seek closed-systems solutions to problems. In CTC terms they look for solutions that are embodied in the Point, Periodic and torus attractors.

In some circumstances where the client is traumatized, unsophisticated or unsupported there is a rationale for limited solutions captured by closed-system approaches. Also if the problem is short term or trivial, or requiring a rapid and definite response, then simplistic goal setting (point attractor), simplifying to competing alternatives (periodic attractor), or implementing routines or advocating following the rules (torus attractor) may be the most sensible approach. However, most career counseling has a time horizon that projects a long way into the future; the presenting problems are usually complex and rarely thought of as trivial. In other words, more often than not it is necessary to work in more complex ways that embrace the strange attractor. This brings with it the challenge of conveying the notion of simultaneously considering both the planned and the unplanned.

The Butterfly model was originally conceived to capture the notions of planning and the unplanned by depicting a figure of eight shape on its side, like the infinity symbol. The left-hand loop represented Planning activities, and the right-hand loop represented unplanned activities. The authors when presented with this model saw immediately the resemblance to Lorenz's Attractor, which looks like a butterfly. Figure 8.6 depicts the Butterfly model in the abstract and Figure 8.7 shows a worked example.

The model shows the intimate and inevitable linkages between the planned and the unplanned. It shows that while you may spend periods circling around in planful activity, perhaps even to the extent of becoming complacent and over-confident in your predictions, eventually the system will phase shift into the unplanned region which will then necessitate further planning activities. It captures the essence of

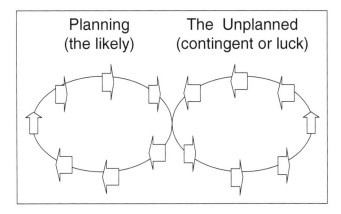

Figure 8.6 The Butterfly model.

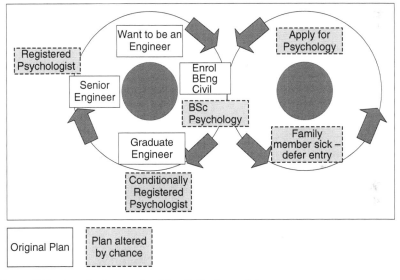

Figure 8.7 A worked example of the Butterfly model.

Dwight Eisenhower's point when he said, "In battle plans are useless, but planning is indispensable" (quoted in Richard Nixon, "Krushchev," in *Six Crises* (1962)). This serves as a reminder that we should not aim to produce a career plan; rather, we should foster the skills to assist the individual to learn how to plan and revise their plans.

Creative Thinking Strategies

When dealing with important problems, issues and even people, individuals often fail to find a workable solution because they have not understood the challenge appropriately or have only been able to look at the situation from one perspective. That is, they do not ask the most appropriate questions. Reformulating a challenge may provide new dimensions to the problem and unforeseen opportunities within it. New questions may expose how the way the issue was framed in the first place have excluded ways of perceiving the situation that would have assisted in resolving the problem or creatively meeting the challenge.

Fundamentally, this is the rationale underpinning the Creative Thinking Strategies technique. There are lots of books and techniques focusing on particular challenges such as workforce entry, outplacement, life transition, financial planning, retirement, personal adjustment and so on. Some of these are excellent but they tend to be quite specific in focus and content. It would be good, however, to be able to focus more generally on the process of strategic problem solving since such skills could be applicable over a wide range of issues and problems.

Creative Thinking Strategies (Pryor & Bright, 2009) focus on the process of generating new insights to challenges by asking questions that might not otherwise be considered and thereby generating new perspectives out of which original solutions can be generated. This is a card sort technique which, though directed generally toward work issues, asks questions that can open up problem-solving strategies that will have much broader applications and relevance. The Creative Thinking Strategies card sort is intended to help people with career decision making, innovative problem solving, and opportunity recognition and creation as well as constructive change responsiveness.

Creative Thinking Strategies originally arose out of thinking presented in Pryor, Amundson and Bright (2009). The cards are arranged into three strategy type categories: probability thinking (Probabilities), possibility thinking (Possibilities) and strategic action (Plans). There is a question on each card that reflects one of these three creative thinking strategies. However, the cards can also be classified into sets of three focusing on specific decision-making/problem-solving challenges. A total of 22 such challenges were identified for Creative Thinking Strategies and are also included as cards. Figure 8.8 provides an example of one set of four cards relating to the challenge of "Being influenced by others."

Creative Thinking Strategy cards are linked to the CTC perspective of emergent thinking (McKay, Bright, & Pryor 2005; Pryor & Bright,

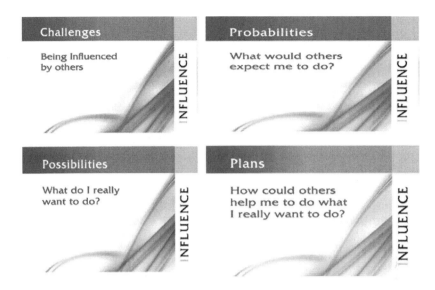

Figure 8.8 Example set of Creative Thinking Strategy cards.

2006). Order and stability are convergent perspectives, whereas chance and change are emergent perspectives. Convergent techniques identify probable outcomes. The aim is to converge, through processes of analysis, elimination and logic, to one or a few choice options that could most likely be implemented. In contrast, the emergent perspective emphasizes imagination, intuition, creativity and openness. The CTS cards therefore represent a tangible and practical method of employing a CTC framework in counseling.

Finally, the Counseling Quadrant (see Figure 8.9) assists the counselor in understanding the relationship between postmodern and positivist counseling techniques and how and why different approaches are useful and complimentary. People can be characterized in terms of their knowledge of their convergent and emergent qualities. Convergent qualities are those that are shared among many people, such as assessed vocational interests, intelligence quotient, skills and declarative knowledge. Convergent knowledge is common to people and circumstances. It is predictable and replicable. Emergent qualities arise from the complex interaction of the many and varied factors that influence career behavior (Bright, Pryor, Wilkenfeld & Earl, 2005). Emergent qualities cannot be predicted in advance but they can be clearly discerned once they have emerged. They are qualities that are unique to the individual and that set them apart from other people.

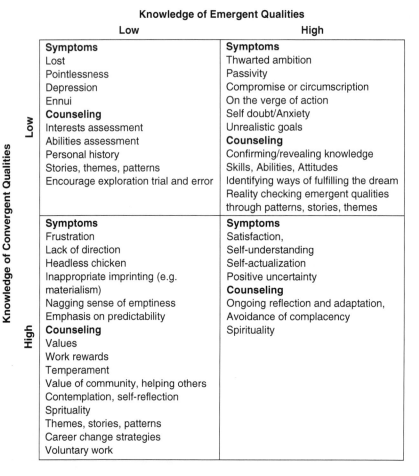

Figure 8.9 The Counseling Quadrant.

Emergent knowledge is neither predictable nor replicable. Emergent qualities are influential and sometimes determinative in the course of a person's career.

Convergent knowledge is about how people relate to the world around them. Emergent knowledge is about how people relate to themselves. Generally, convergent knowledge tends to be represented by simple metrics, whereas emergent qualities are best captured with more complex structures such as patterns and narratives.

The upper left-hand quadrant describes a client with low levels of knowledge about their convergent and emergent qualities. Such a person is unsure of their interests, abilities or strengths and weaknesses.

A combination of techniques designed to enhance knowledge of convergent and emergent techniques would be appropriate. For instance, a tool such as an interest inventory could be useful in providing insights to such clients about their vocational interests. Abilities testing could provide such clients with a better knowledge of their strengths and weaknesses. Such techniques are commonly used by counselors and may be thought of as being part and parcel of traditional career counseling.

If the counselor has been successful in increasing the client's knowledge of their convergent qualities then such a client may now be best characterized as being in the lower left-hand quadrant. However, this is not sufficient to help the client who seek personal meaning in their career choices, and who wants to pursue something that matters to them. Such a person may be experiencing a sense of frustration and feel as though they have lost their direction. They have a sound idea about their vocational interests and their own abilities in relation to most other people; however, such knowledge is insufficient. They may have a sense that they are different to other people but not yet have managed to identify what this nagging doubt is and what their true motivating life forces are. In Chaos Theory of Careers terms, they have failed to understand their strange attractor. For such clients, techniques that emphasize their individuality and take cognizance of their personal circumstances are more likely to prove successful in identifying their preoccupations (e.g., Savickas 1997), understanding their life stories or identifying their strange attractors (e.g., Bright & Pryor, 2007).

Clients who are identified as being predominantly in the top right-hand quadrant have a strong sense of their own identity yet may lack any sense of how they connect with other people in the community. For instance, they may not fully appreciate the actual performance levels of their abilities or how their interests relate to those of the workforce. They may feel that they are underachieving or that they have compromised or limited their career development. Equally, they may express unrealistic vocational goals in light of their personal circumstances. They often feel a strong sense of disconnection between where they would like to be and where they currently are. Such clients may be introduced to a variety of techniques that can help them appreciate the steps they need to take in order to get from their current situation to their vocational goals. Alternatively, techniques such as reality checking may be useful in realigning their vocational goals to some of the realities of the labor market. For instance, many children from deprived households express unrealistic vocational goals and have little idea of the educational implications of these expressed goals (Beavis, Curtis & Curtis 2005).

The Counseling Quadrant reminds counselors that the goal of counseling is to move clients toward a higher level of knowledge of their convergent and emergent qualities. In other words, the goal is to move clients toward the bottom right-hand quadrant.

The Chaos Theory of Careers reformulates and presents a new agenda for career counseling that needs to assist clients to recognize and utilize the challenges of complexity, change and interconnection in the world of work. A wide range of techniques and strategies have been outlined to assist both counselors and their clients to do this in creative ways. In doing so, no claim is made about not needing crucial other more traditional sources of information such as, among other things, personal background, education, work history, occupational information and labor market data. However, there is one other kind of exploration relevant to the Chaos Theory of Careers that needs to be addressed. At an even more fundamental level, the boundaries of the strange attractor are the values, ethics, personal visions and sense of meaning that people ascribe to their lives. Beyond the effectiveness of decision making there is a further dimension: what is the guiding reason behind the decisions, what is the purpose to which allegiance is deserved, and what is really significant (Covey, 2004). Ultimately these are matters of spirituality, and Chapter 9 deals with the ways in which the Chaos Theory of Careers can assist in understanding and addressing such issues of "ultimate concern" (Tillich, 1952).

CHAPTER 9

Practical Applications: Meaning, Purpose and Spirituality

Life is spiritual.

One of the most universal of all human characteristics is the impulse to consider personalities, forces or principles greater than, or at least in some sense beyond, ourselves. It manifests itself in virtually every continent, culture, race and tribe. From the most primitive and "untouched" village in the highlands of New Guinea to Manhattan, New York, evidence of this apprehension of "a greater than ourselves" can be clearly seen. In fact, it could be said that spirituality is about as universal in human communities as work. Therefore it is hardly surprising that the links between the two have been made at least since the time of the writing of the Book of Genesis. In Chapter 2 of Genesis, a picture is presented of the man tending the garden and naming the animals. That is, he was working. In Chapter 3, after human disobedience, one of the fundamental curses that descends on the man and woman is their work.

Subsequently, through the history of most faith traditions, thoughtful spiritual religious leaders for thousands of years have ruminated about the connection and integration of spirituality and work (e.g., Placher, 2005). However, the career development literature, which has an identifiable history of about 100 years, appears until comparatively recently and with a few rare exceptions (e.g., Minear, 1954), to have largely neglected the nexus between the two. It is also probably true to say that the rich tradition of thought from theologians, gurus and other spiritual thinkers of the past on the spiritual dimensions of work, remains to date largely neglected in the extant career development literature. In this chapter an attempt will be made to outline some of these neglected areas of spirituality as they may relate to work and to discuss how the Chaos Theory of Careers seeks to include them within its general explanatory ambit.

SPIRITUALITY AND CAREER DEVELOPMENT THEORY

One of the reasons for the failure to see the connections between spirituality and careers is that traditional career development theories such as Holland (1997), Gottfredson (1996), Krumboltz (1994) and Super (1980) tended to focus on decision making as process, and human abilities and traits as content. If spirituality was mentioned it was typically in the context of religious careers. The focus was on the content of the choice.

Postmodernist approaches to career development such as career construction theory (Savickas 1997) probably provide the most coherent integration of spirituality into career development. Career construction theory emphasizes individuals' desire to find/create meaning and purpose in and through work in the broader context of their life themes. While this theoretical account of the connection between spirituality and work is reasonable as far as it goes, the question that must be asked is does it go far enough to encompass adequately the dimensions of spirituality as they may potentially relate to work? While meaning and purpose are important to the conception of spirituality, it is doubtful that they can also adequately subsume other spiritual concepts such as transcendence, mystery, God, paradox, suffering, salvation, harmony, unity/oneness, eternity, calling, evil and wisdom. Of course, it might be that this is too big an order for any one theory of career development. However, in the rest of this chapter at least some of these fundamental dimensions of spirituality will be linked to the theoretical dimensions of chaos theory in general and the Chaos Theory of Careers (CTC) in particular. It is hoped by so doing to fulfill the promise made in Pryor and Bright (2004) that chaos theory would provide the most coherent conceptual integration of spirituality and career development of any modernist or postmodern theory. In doing so, new insights and linkages may become apparent to guide future theory, research and practice. But first, let us look a little more closely at the concept of spirituality.

THE NATURE OF SPIRITUALITY

Most contemporary discussions of spirituality begin with the distinction between its institutional expression in term of religious activity and its personal expression as typified in the self improvement literature (Burke, Chauvin & Miranti, 2005). Spirituality encompasses both and it should also be noted that the religious and the individual expressions of spirituality are, of course, not necessarily mutually exclusive. Thus religious people often seek spiritual development as individuals and those without religious institutional attachments will often seek like-minded interest, therapy and self-help groups with which to associate. However, notwithstanding such overlap there do tend to be significant distinctions that can be identified in the two forms of spiritual expression. These distinctions are:

1. Religious activity is corporate in expression whereas individuals frequently are "finding their own path."
2. Religious expression typically emphasizes teaching, tradition and revelation as truth whereas spiritual individualism eschews dogma in favor of self-understanding and the uniqueness of the person's journey.
3. Religious spirituality tends to encourage commitment to beliefs and values as encompassing standards whereas individualized spirituality is more likely to stress the exploration of beliefs and values and often only to the extent that they encourage or promote each person's evolution of their appreciation of such beliefs and values.

Precise definitions of "spirituality" can be found in the literature (e.g., Kinjerski & Skrypnek, 2008), however it may be better to simply characterize some of the salient dimensions of such a numinous concept, particularly in terms of its relevance to work. Bloch's (2006) summary of the current literature on spirituality and work identified five consistently emerging dimensions.

Connection

Spiritually is typically characterized by a sense of the interconnected nature of reality. All things are linked to one another in some way. This stresses the interdependent character of the natural world of which humans constitute only a small part. Spiritual approaches such as Gaia, pantheism and immanence are instances of this kind of thinking. Briggs and Peat (1999) observe that in many native cultures this idea is fundamental to their survival and care for their environment. Modern ecological perspectives in science have rediscovered the importance of the interconnections between different components of the environment, as illustrated in attempts to address issues such as climate change, pollution and global warming. Spiritual thinking causes us to consider the perceptions and implications of our part in the human community, our world and the universe as a whole. Such a dimension draws attention to the embedded nature of work in human life and experience and the resultant challenges of integration and balance.

Purpose

Spirituality also typically entails humans' sense of meaning, purpose and significance. Human self-consciousness enables is, and perhaps compels us, to ask self-defining questions such as: Who am I? What should I do with my life? How should I behave in one situation or another? What really matters in life? Such questions and issues and the responses each of us makes, either explicitly (by commitment) or implicitly (by our thinking and actions), become the basis for how meaningful and fulfilled our lives have been, are and will be. Some forms of spirituality seek to address such challenges by searching within to seek a deeper self-understanding. Other forms of spirituality look to the traditions and teachings of others, past or present, to be guided into the path it is believed we were created to take (Warren, 2002)

Transcendence

Spiritual thinking typically draws humans to the conclusion that there is something and/or someone more than what we immediately perceive, understand or know. This idea or intuition of "a greater than ourselves" may take the form, among others, of a personal God, a ground of Being, a transcendent power such as grace or love, destiny or some sort of "spirit of things." Transcendence is the term most frequently associated with ideas of accessible power beyond normal human capability to enable some task to be completed, an apprehension of responsibility to a Higher Power or some sense of assurance that "in the end everything will be alright," even if at present it does not appear to be.

Harmony

This notion links the three previous concepts relating to spirituality. Harmony typically involves a concern for coherence: how everything fits together into an intelligible whole. Spiritual thinkers will talk about the Oneness, the unity in diversity, the One, the Om, unity of creation and so on. This is more than just connection since it implies transcendent purpose and the obligation to contribute to, and to promote, greater peace and harmony in one's own life, those of others and in the universe as a whole. In fact, for many spiritual thinkers this represents a meaning and sense of worth that could be identified as a calling.

Calling

It is fairly common from a spiritual perspective for individuals to identify what they are doing with their lives, and in their work, with the idea of "being called" (Guinness, 2003). It may be expressed as a sense of vocation, a mission to be pursued, a cause to be supported, an idea to be promulgated, a role to be fulfilled, "what I was meant to do" or a job that "fits me like a glove." Being called is sometimes understood as God telling the person what the Deity wants them to do (Smith, 1999), or it can be a discovered call relating to individuals' skills, values and interests finding appropriate expression in a task (Bissonnette, 1994).

How do these dimensions of spirituality—connection, purpose, transcendence, harmony and calling—find expression in humans' life and work?

SPIRITUALITY AND WORK

One of the current limitations for the study of spirituality and work is that there is comparatively little empirical data. Lips-Wiersma's (2002) study concluded that:

> spirituality is one of the determinants of career behavior. Spirituality influences the individual's beliefs of what are worthwhile purposes and these purposes in turn influence career behavior. (p. 514)

In reviewing the available literature on spirituality, working and leadership, Duchon and Plowman (2005) similarly concluded that spirituality does impact on worker performance, productivity and retention and that the new challenge for leadership is to create more meaningful work for employees in organizations. In the following section, seven areas in which spirituality has the potential to influence work are outlined.

Meaningful Work

Originally, work was primarily about survival. People grew crops, collected fruit and husbanded animals for food. While "survival" remains a major motivation for individuals to work, in richer countries, where individuals have the opportunity to choose between types of work, other criteria for decisions become more salient. These criteria may be practical, such as knowing others who work there or that the worksite is close to home. However, it is also the case that some of these criteria will be more spiritual in nature. Among the most common of these is the search for meaning in life and work. In viewing work as an arena in which individuals may implement their self-concept in the public context Super (1953, 1980) linked the quest for meaning and fulfillment with work. Savickas (1997) consciously built on this idea in viewing work as individuals opportunity for "self-development" and "self-completion" through the search for meaning. This is, according to Savickas, a creative and often lifelong process of exploration discovery, action and change through which we "share our unique contribution by joining spirit with other people in celebrating life through work, love, friendship and worship" (p. 3).

A lack of meaning in their work is often the complaint of disengaged and dissatisfied workers (Fox, 1994). Writers such as Frankl (1984) view the search for meaning as the fundamental drive or motivation of human effort and behavior. The increasingly mobile and fragmented nature of twenty-first-century work, in which individuals are more often required to change their occupations, renders the quest for meaning amid the change and confusion ever more urgent (Savickas, 2006).

Guidance and Calling

Colozzi and Colozzi (2000) identify the spiritual discovery of a sense of meaning and purpose through work as synonymous with "discovering one's calling." Typically this involves a sense that individuals have about the appropriateness of their work for the expression of their deepest skills, needs values and aspirations. They talk about the work they were meant to do, have to do and in which they find a sense of fulfillment.

People may have multiple callings, of which work is only one (Guiness, 2003; Smith, 1999). Usually work is a calling to express in a particular context a broader and more encompassing calling. Thus for a Christian the fundamental calling may be to serving Christ in the world, and work would be one of the potentially many contexts in which that calling might find expression, such as being called to become a medical missionary (Schuurman, 2004).

If a calling is perceived as personally commanded or invited by God then career decisions are likely construed as being guided. This may occur through some form of inner conviction or through a series of apparently serendipitous experiences interpreted as "open doors" leading to a particular training, occupation or job. For others, the call may be more in terms of personal passion, an intuitive sense of the rightness of one career choice over another, a quest for development, change and even adventure through one's career, a desire to find one's place in the world (of work) or just plain "something to believe in" (Richmond, 1997).

Ethics and Values

Most expressions of spirituality are in some way concerned with "right conduct." A spiritual perspective usually entails a moral perspective. Among the great faith traditions of the world, much of this morality appears remarkably similar in its individual and community expression. As Covey (2004) illustrates, for example, the Golden Rule of Christianity (treat others as you would like to be treated) can be identified across a wide range of apparently diverse religious faiths.

The desire and/or obligation to act rightly from a spiritual perspective typically derives from a perceived sense of responsibility. This responsibility may be to a Higher Power who has revealed the divine will to the community of which individuals are part, or simply to oneself in the form of personal integrity. The values individuals espouse are (ideally) the translation into action in the world of the morality of their spiritual perspective. Values as qualities and rewards from work have long been identified as influential on career decision making (Pryor 1979; Zytowski, 1970). Individuals will often prefer one occupation over another on the basis of the differences in the opportunities they provide for remuneration, independence, leadership, physical activity or personal development. However, the spiritual perspective on values frequently focuses on broader principles that can affect career decision making. Some career counseling clients will refuse to consider working for companies they perceive to be acting unethically, such as those that manufacture cigarettes, conduct mining operations in developing countries or are identified with doubtful financial practices.

Conversely, some individuals from various spiritual perspectives will seek out employment with organizations they perceive to be promulgating values in which they believe. Thus Catholics may want to work for the Catholic Church, vegans may seek employment in a health food store and "greenies" may seek a position with an environmental group. In fact, some research indicates that those whose values are closely aligned to those of their employing organization are likely to be more productive in their work and less likely to leave the organization than those whose values are not as congruent with their employer (Mitroff & Denton, 1999).

Human Limitations

Almost all forms of spirituality affirm the value of life and especially human life. They also affirm the potential of individuals to be righteous and to act nobly, even though the precise terms used may vary from one perspective to another. However, spiritual thinkers also tend to identify the limitations of humans in terms of knowledge, influence and control. Many faith traditions inveigh, for example, against the arrogant, the proud and the self-important. Some kind of humility before the immensity and mystery of God, the Universe or Being is typically enjoined. This derives directly from a sense of the transcendent since faith is an expression of trust in a greater than ourselves, who knows more and is more powerful and more efficacious in impacting our lives and the history of our race and our world.

One of the great myths of the last 200 years of scientific endeavor has been that of the extent of human power, knowledge and control (Peat, 2002). Despite its monumental achievements, the limitations of science itself are becoming increasingly clear (Dewdney, 2004). Increasingly, also, these limitations do not look like restrictions due to insufficient equipment or techniques that will one day be redressed. What is now evident is that a number of the limitations identified, such as Poincare's three body problem (Briggs & Peat, 1989), are actually intrinsically unsolvable (Prigogine, 1997).

The limits of science are actually only part of the domain of human limitations to which spiritual perspectives often point. Another is ethical. We either cannot discern what the right action is in a situation or, even if it is clear, we sometimes fail to do it. Such failures are often viewed as part of our finitude and our moral frailty. The aspiration to the ideal, or to be perfect or complete or whole or in harmony, can be found across a broad range of spiritual traditions. Indeed, often such traditions have their origins in one who is or is closest to this Ideal—Buddha, Mohammed, Christ and so on.

The limitations of individuals when negotiating the challenges of their career development is a surprising omission in the careers literature. For example, in the comprehensive and authoritative *Encyclopedia of Career Development* (Greenhaus & Callanan, 2006) there is not a single citing in the index for "mistake," failure," "limitation" or "error." There is a single citing of "career problems"; however, on the same page "career success" is cited 21 times. Spiritual traditions typically do not focus on human limitations and failures in order to encourage us "to wallow in our misery." Limitations and failures are viewed as inevitable but not irredeemable. Limitations and failures teach us instead to be humble, adaptable, cautious, resilient and brave in the face of life's uncertainties (Smith, 1999). As change becomes increasingly endemic to contemporary employment, individuals are likely to need to recognize the inevitability of failures in their career development (Chen, 2005; Ormerod, 2005): moreover, not only to recognize the possibility of failure but also to be able to learn from and use failures as strategies for exploring and eventually overcoming career development barriers and challenges (see Chapter 7).

Relationships

Although some spiritual traditions contain segments that withdraw from "the world" such as hermits, mystics and monks, the bulk of their adherents value relationships. Those with a personal God, such as Christianity, view relationships as the ultimate reality—thus in John's Gospel Jesus is reported to have identified eternal life with knowing Him. However, most spirituality finds some form of expression in the ways we treat each other. Words like love, peace, gentleness, kindness, forgiveness, compassion, understanding and defending are often used to express the ways in which the spiritual person "acts rightly" toward others. In general, spirituality seeks to encourage unity and understanding among people, and most faith traditions have long histories of caring for the vulnerable, the sick, the poor and the downtrodden in their societies. However, as human history amply testifies, these aspirations are by no means easy to realize even within the faith traditions themselves. Notwithstanding the not infrequent failure of spiritually minded people, it remains the case that in general a spiritual perspective views individuals as valuable and relationships as precious.

Super (1980) originally drew attention to the importance of viewing work in the broader context of the life roles that humans take up and relinquish over their life span. Out of this theoretical work came a literature exploring issues of "work–life balance," role conflict, role balancing, workplace childcare, flexible working hours, job splitting, working from home and so on.

Roles are significant, additionally, because they often define individuals' social and even personal identity. Almost inevitably, people compare themselves to one another and are influenced by, as well as seeking to influence, one another. People's occupations often reveal much about them, or others infer accurately or inaccurately a lot from this single piece of information, such as education level, socio-economic status, intelligence, interests, probable acquaintances and how much this person is likely to be like me. Hence in most new social situations people keep asking each other: "So what is it you do for a living?" Identity is a fundamental spiritual notion that has its links to those outlined earlier in this chapter including connection, harmony and calling. Further, some research (Duchon & Plowman, 2005) and opinion (Dutton, 2003) have indicated that a further spiritual dimension to relationships, in a more community or societal sense, is that of "making a contribution." In particular, in large organizations with large bureaucracies it is often hard for people to see how their work really means much more than a way to earn money (Conger, 1994). Such workers often want to believe that their work is actually "making a difference," "creating something worthwhile," "providing a service that others really need" and other such expressions of a desire for their work to have value beyond the mere performance of a set of duties. Most people have the spiritual urge to be part of something bigger than themselves, something important, some grand project or a kind of crusade.

The penchant for organizational "mission statements," championed by Covey (1989) for many years, represents one way in which companies have sought to respond to this need. When organizations actually allow workers genuine input into the mission statement process and then follow through at all levels of the firm, such statements do have power to be able to inspire the spiritual aspirations of employees. However, when there is no collaboration at the formative stage and no ongoing attempt to implement the noble sentiments enunciated in the "statement," employee cynicism rather than motivation is the more likely outcome. Moreover, this highlights why some are reluctant to the point of skepticism about spiritual asseverations. That reason is hypocrisy. The grander and more ambitious a person's spiritual aspirations, the greater the perceived fall and hypocrisy when that individual fails or at least is seen by others as not living up to the level of spiritual achievement espoused. For example, consider the media glee at exposing the adultery of any popular television evangelist.

THE CHAOS THEORY OF CAREERS AND SPIRITUALITY

One of the questions posed at the beginning of this chapter was: Can any theory of career development provide a comprehensive and coherent integration of the linkage between spirituality and careers? What follows is an attempt to answer this question in the affirmative through the application of the fundamental concepts of the Chaos Theory of Careers. In this endeavor it is hoped to demonstrate how further spiritual concepts at present overlooked in the career development literature may also provide crucial insights into the spiritual dimensions of careers.

The Chaos Theory of Careers construes the reality in terms of complex dynamical systems. These systems are open and therefore have a wide range of potential influences on them. The consequence of such influences is to cause these systems to develop and aggregate into coherent wholes that interact both endogenously and exogenously. These systems, however, as well aggregating into coherence are also capable at the same time of changing into turbulence. It is the sensitivity to change as a result of additions and interactions within such systems that makes them characteristically "chaotic." Thus such systems function contingently and aperiodically under the twin potentials for order and disorder. These systems can be conceptualized as "inhabiting" a phase space. Phase space is composed of as many dimensions (or variables) as an observer requires to describe a system's movement; the characteristic nature of this movement is called the system's attractor. The ways of interpreting attractors were outlined in Chapter 4 and the characteristic trace of an attractor, its fractal, was elaborated in Chapter 5.

For the purposes of the present discussion about spirituality and work, four major CTC concepts—complexity, change, connections and attractors (including fractals)—will be used as general headings under which to identify relevant spiritual concerns and concepts.

Complexity

Mystery—Transcendence

From the preceding it should be apparent that it is quite simply impossible to even identify and enumerate anything like the possible number of complex dynamical systems that currently exist. No one can and no one ever does. We usually focus our attention on those that become, or are likely to become, part of our human experience—thought, word and action. Thus Gelatt (1991) is correct in observing that virtually all career decision making (and indeed decision making in general in the real world) is carried out with incomplete knowledge and uncertainty about subsequent outcomes of such decisions. Dewdney (2004) quotes Einstein as saying, "Not only is the universe stranger than we think, it is stranger than we can think" (p. 83).

An inescapable implication of the level of complexity envisaged in the CTC is the limitation of human knowledge and control. In discussing personal spirituality, Peck (1997) noted that events and actions are virtually always "over determined"—the result of the interaction of multiple causes.

These considerations help us to recognize that in its complexity, life is a mystery. We never have all the answers. Peat (2002) goes so far as to suggest that complexity may imply that ultimate explanations may not even exist. St Augustine, in considering the transcendent nature of God, said that if you have a god you can fully understand then what you in fact have is an idol (St Augustine, 2005). Thus complexity also implies transcendence as we contemplate how little any of us really know. It remains true that the greatest fool may ask more than the wisest man can answer. In fact, science more generally is confronted with mystery in the form of quantum mechanics and the uncertainty principle to such an extent that no lesser figure in physics than Richard Feynman can conclude, "I think I can safely say that nobody understands quantum mechanics" (quoted in Chown, 2007, p. 72).

In fact, complexity is so embedded in reality, and as a consequence exposes our limitations, that Peck (1993) observed that in acknowledging mystery we must learn to delight in solving problems and in not solving them. In career development terms, these considerations suggest the need for humility and the need to avoid overconfidence in our capacities. Peck (1997) talked of a "crusade against simplism." In career thinking there is a need to avoid the equivalent of simplism, identified earlier as "closed systems thinking," which implies that it is possible to put every factor in its place and that what we purpose must eventuate. Insofar as complexity exposes our human limitations, it challenges all us to be able to tolerate ambiguity (Peat, 2002) and to face the challenge to envision and experience career decision making as an ongoing process of evaluation, adaptation and change.

Paradox

However, the mystery of living emerging from its complexity will also lead us to paradox, one of the neglected spiritual terms in the career development literature. Gelatt (1991) is one of the few writers in career development to address the need for paradox in order to negotiate a complex, changing world—paradoxically characterizing the approach needed as being "positively uncertain." The four major paradoxes that Gelatt (1991) identified were:

1. Be focused and flexible about what you want.
2. Be aware and wary about what you know.
3. Be objective and optimistic about what you believe.
4. Be practical and magical about what you do.

Spiritual teachers throughout the ages have frequently communicated in terms of paradox, such as "in giving, you receive," "the leader is the servant," "in losing your life, you gain it," "the greatest among you must be the least" and so on. Paradox is the blending of apparent opposites, not to negate but to complement one another. In chaos terms, it is a way of pointing to the nuanced complexity of human experience that frequently finds its expression in artistic creation. Positivist science typically struggles with paradox and tends to dismiss it as obfuscation. However, in the wave/particle nature of light and aspects of quantum mechanics, "hard" sciences themselves are becoming increasingly confronted with apparent paradoxes that appear intrinsic to reality rather than a consequence of our limitations to measure and explain it (Chown, 2007; Dewdney, 2004). The CTC's insistence on avoiding dichotomizing opposite concepts such as order and disorder, stability and change, predictability and chance and so on illustrates not only its capacity to accept paradox but, moreover, the necessity of paradox to account for the functioning of complex dynamical systems.

Identity

Spirituality is often about personal identity. Ashmos and Duchon (2000) drew attention to the inner life at work. Duchon and Donde

(2005) related this to identity in the workplace; their review of identity at work and their own research led them to conclude that it could be understood in terms of a person identity and a social identity. The social identity of workers is embedded in their work unit connection. The individual's personal identity can be differentiated as instrumental on one hand and expressive on the other (Shamir, 1991). The CTC's emphasis on the contingency of the functioning of complex dynamical systems illustrates the inevitability of uniqueness of each individual and therefore of the particular identity of each individual.

Uncertainty

Since complexity renders us limited in our ability to comprehend the world and even ourselves, the result is that we live in an uncertain world. Peat (2002) concluded from his overview of twentieth-century science that humans can no longer see themselves as the objective observers of the universe but instead see themselves as participants in the universe. The price for this change of perspective is to acknowledge our uncertainty. Peck (1993) expressed the view that the only security we can have in this inherently uncertain life is the realization of life's insecurity. Tiedeman's (1997) Life-Career Theory perspective had as a major tenet that life provides no guaranteed outcomes. As early as 1978, Peck had stated: "Most people most of the time make decisions with little awareness of what they are doing. They take action with little understanding of their own motives and without beginning to know the ramifications of their choices" (p. 306).

Some of the spiritual implications of uncertainty are the following:

Failing

If, as the CTC states, we are limited and uncertainty is the parameter of our existence, then it follows that all humans will almost inevitably fail at some things (Ormerod, 2005). Failure in career development is probably at least as common as career success, but this is certainly not reflected in the career development literature. For example, Inkson (2007), in a recent career development textbook, has five indexed references to career success but career failure or its equivalents do not get a single mention. Ortberg (2007) concluded "to live is to lose," and that failure should not define our identity but should instead lead us to humility.

This is in part the reason Moore (1997) suggested we should "pray for failure." Smith (1999) calls on people to accept themselves with all their limitations and in doing so to embrace and celebrate the ordinariness of human life. He goes on to say: "The genius of truth and freedom is found in accepting our limitations without overstating their significance. It is found in accepting with grace that we live our lives with limits, but also in keeping an eye on the possibilities without being heroic, grandiose or naïve" (p. 107).

Particularly in the field of vocational rehabilitation, clients may have special difficulty in accepting their limitations. Such limitations may have been imposed through accident, injury or sudden misadventure. Frequently, such individuals will express anger, frustration and depression at the loss of capabilities so quickly perceived to be imposed on them by either the willfulness or the negligence of others.

Doubt

Since the CTC emphasizes the challenges of uncertainty at a spiritual level, it directs individuals to the value of doubt. Peck (1997) echoes the same idea when he writes "a tolerance for uncertainty is crucial in the process of questioning our assumptions" (p. 46). Religious fundamentalism, in its extreme forms such as cults and terrorists networks, espouses a certainty that quickly leads to fanaticism and then to some form of self-destruction or the destruction of others. Since chaos theory involves an integration of what dichotomous thinkers see as opposites, faith and doubt are both components of a spiritual attractor in the same way that stability and change are in all complex dynamical systems (Guiness, 1976). "Fanatical" career counseling clients usually cannot be told anything, do not want to learn anything, refuse to question their current thinking and disparage all attempts to introduce them to new ideas. Consider the example of the 17-year-old male student who is doing poorly at school, whose numerical skills are at sixth-grade level, and who will not consider the possibility that he might not qualify for entry into any tertiary institution's engineering course when he leaves school. The counselor who is trying to introduce such an idea will be seen as pessimistic, sowing seeds of doubt to undermine his resolve and not to be taken seriously.

Counseling approaches based on the CTC encourage clients to be open-minded and questioning of what they might otherwise take for granted. Typically, counseling clients underestimate the contingent nature of reality. Usually, individuals think that the way events have been in the past is the way they will be in the future. Chaos-based career counseling encourages clients to question such an assumption, at least to the extent of investigating contingency planning, and sometimes further to consider creative new ways to think about work, occupations and careers through some of the techniques outlined in Chapter 8.

Courage

The uncertainty that the CTC highlights also demands courage to face the risks that are the inevitable consequences of creative engagement with life and careers. Peck (1978) noted that the development of individuals' capacity for loving for the spiritual benefit of others necessarily entails greater and greater risk taking. He went on to say that without risk taking individuals never grow up and assume responsibility for their own destinies. Smith (1999) wrote that confronting the risks of life requires courage. Tillich (1952), in a famous book, identified courage with the necessity of facing life's existential demands authentically. To date in the career counseling literature, there appears to be precious little about the need to encourage clients to be courageous in the face of the risks that enfold in uncertainty. While this reluctance may be a function of the grandiose romanticism sometimes associated with the word "courage," it still represents a major spiritual quality that many clients will require to develop and exercise in order to achieve meaningful outcomes in a world in which certainty cannot be guaranteed.

Change

Personal Development

Pryor and Bright (2007a) indicated that the Chaos Theory of Careers had the capacity to incorporate one of the great paradoxes of human experience. Since the time of the ancient Greeks it has been noted that human behavior involved both being (the stable characteristics of individuals by which we typically describe them) and becoming (the potential of individuals to develop, change and transform themselves). Complex dynamical systems demonstrate both "robustness" (the stability of being) with vulnerability (the likelihood of becoming) (Barbarasi, 2003). Using CTC principles, Pryor (2007) demonstrated in the context of assessing complexity how both being and becoming could be integrated into the evaluation of vocational interests (see also Chapter 8).

Spirituality is often concerned with personal development. Peck (1978) wrote, "the path of spiritual growth is a path of lifelong learning" (p. 306). Bolles (2008) identified links between spirituality and job hunting in terms of what we should learn and unlearn. Weiler and Schoonover (2001) saw part of the first step to the appreciation of spirituality in career development as deconstructing myths such as:

1) I am not responsible for my actions.
2) Others have the answers to my life.
3) Meeting an organization's goals is the same as fulfilling my needs.
4) Others can and should understand me.

Lips-Wiersma's (2002) research found that developing and becoming oneself was one of the most potent spiritual influences on career behavior according to her research participants. Mitroff and Denton (1999) provide empirical data to the effect that individuals found purpose in their jobs through, among other things, "realizing one's potential."

Without the capacity to incorporate personal development into a career development theoretical framework, it seems hard to justify the practical imperative of change through career counseling. This has always been a conceptual blind spot of all exclusively matching career paradigms such as the Theory of Work Adjustment (Davis & Lofquist, 1984) and Holland's Hexagon approach (Holland, 1997). That is, if counseling is simply about attaining the best correspondence of an individual's characteristics (abilities, interests, values) with the demands and regards of occupations, there seems no conceptual room to consider that counseling might be about more than increased self- and occupational awareness. This represents an overemphasis on "being" at the expense of "becoming." Dominant recent theories of career development such as Career Construction Theory (Savickas, 2005) place so much emphasis on the process dimension of counseling that the content can be neglected. That is, such approaches may emphasize "becoming" at the expense of "being." It is contended, therefore, that only the Chaos Theory of Careers adequately incorporates "being and becoming" into a coherent theoretical framework since it conceptualizes both as part of the functioning of dynamical systems.

Creativity

Briggs and Peat (1999) described chaos as "nature's creativity." Natural systems change and evolve often through turbulence in systems such as earthquakes, eruptions, hurricanes and bushfires. These are obvious and often dramatic; however, natural systems may also change slowly, such as glaciers retreating, erosion or germ infestation. Closed systems thinking, as outlined in Chapter 4, becomes obsessed with power and control, and in the process closes out creativity (Bright & Pryor, 2005a). In such thinking creativity is a threat, "a disturber of the peace," a maverick that must be driven out of town. Yet confronting a world and in particular a world of work that is changing rapidly and extensively without creativity is an attempt to meet tomorrow's challenges with yesterday's techniques. This is evident in the diversification in the ways in which people now work, such as portfolio careers (Handy, 1989), protean workers (Hall, 2002), global careers (Inkson, Lazarova & Thomas, 2005), seasonal employment, job splitting, job sharing, home businesses, boundaryless careers (Arthur & Rousseau, 1996), telecommuting and self-employment. Amundson (2009) referred to a "crisis of imagination" for individuals trying to develop their careers in the twenty-first century. The CTC's emphasis on change integrates creativity as proactive behavior initiating action and as reactive behavior adapting to exogenous change.

Non-Linearity

Non-linearity is one of the defining characteristics of chaotic systems. If susceptibility to change in initial conditions is uniquely an attribute of chaos, the nature of such change is potentially disproportionate or non-linear. In chaotic systems small changes may iterate through such systems, resulting in enormous and sometimes even system-transforming effects. A minor bite from a disease-carrying insect may later, as the infection multiplies and spreads, result in a person's major illness or even death. A single lightning strike in a eucalypt forest can be enough to set off a bushfire capable of burning out thousands of acres of forest or destroying villages or towns, killing hundreds of people.

The non-linearity of complex dynamical systems provides an account of some spiritual phenomena that career development thinking typically finds difficult to deal with. For example, the most complete text dealing with spirituality and work, Bloch and Richmond's *Connections between Spirit and Work in Career Development*, has no citation in the index for either miracles or synchronicity. The same is also true for the extensive *Encyclopedia of Career Development* (Greenhaus & Callanan, 2006). Yet religious people, in particular, invoke the notion of "miracle" to describe events in their lives and they see in synchronous events a sense of being led in a particular career direction. When the authors surveyed 670 university students (Bright et al., 2005), we received many written comments that indicated that the perceived influence of the supernatural was crucial in some respondents' career decision making.

Of course, much depends on how a concept such as "miracle" is defined. Miracles are typically defined as contraventions of the laws of nature. However, from a chaos perspective the "laws of nature" are actually statements of probability, not immutable essences of reality (Prigogine, 1997). It would actually be more accurate to define miracles in terms of out-of-the-ordinary events that could be attributable to divine origin. While the latter part of this explanation—divine origin—may be beyond the capacity of science or any human knowledge to fully comprehend, the first part is not. Chaos theory, as a form of science, is full of exceptional events that follow causatively but are unpredictable. It is the stochastic and contingent nature of reality to which chaos theory points, which illustrates that simply because, to quote a famous example, all the swans ever observed were white, that does not mean there are no black swans (Taleb, 2007). At this point no particular claim is being made about the veracity of any specific miracle or miracles in general. However, what is being contended is:

1. Some people claim a form of miraculous intervention led them to their current career or otherwise informed their career decision making.
2. All current attempts to link spirituality and work in the career development literature ignore this fact.
3. No current theory of career development other than the CTC has tried or is able to account coherently for this possibility.

Individuals who view their lives from a spiritual perspective seek and reportedly find meaningful underlying patterns in their own experience and in the experiences of others. Such patterns are interpreted in terms of the particular beliefs and expectations of each individual. The typical response of scientists to such interpretations is to dismiss them as unnecessary imposed order on what are essentially contingent phenomena. However, no less a figure in the history of psychology than Carl Jung not only took such reports seriously but also believed that they had the potential to provide major insights, not only into how individuals think, feel and behave, but also into the fundamental nature of reality. Jung's name for such phenomena was "synchronicity," which he defined as "the coincidence in time of two or more causally unrelated events which have the same meaning" (Jung, 1973, quoted in Peat, 1987, p. 35). He noted that synchronicities were particularly apparent to individuals in their times of anxiety and crisis. Moreover, they were also often associated with dreams or visions, which provide insights into the meaningfulness of each individual's life situation. Peat (1987) made out a case for the relevance of "synchronicity" to contemporary science. He did it on the basis of the limitations of the traditional scientific notion of linear causality. Peat invoked chaos notions including "dissipative structures," "implicate order" and "formative fields" to argue for an explanation of synchronicity in terms of emergent order from non-linear dynamics.

Despite Jung's repeated asseverations in his voluminous writings of the frequency of incidences of synchronicity, there is one fundamental weakness with the concept as he conceived it in terms of "causal parallelism." That weakness is as, Strogatz (2003) observes, that there is no rigorous evidence to support it. However, all is not lost since Strogatz himself redeems the general idea with the concept of "synchrony." Peat (1987) had argued for synchronicity on the basis of "the essential connectedness" of all things—an idea that has (as we shall later see in this chapter) become more popular in contemporary physics (Barabasi, 2003) and constitutes an essential part of the Chaos Theory of Careers. Strogatz (2003), explicitly using the non-linear dynamics derived from chaos theory, recognized that "the tendency to synchronize is one of the most pervasive drives in the universe, extending from atoms to animals, from people to planets" (p. 4). The capacity of chaos systems to form strange attractors constitutes one example of such synchrony. Strogatz (2003) cites an example of the synchronization of chaotic systems without close connections with each other. He writes:

> the more lasting legacy of synchronized chaos may be the way it has deepened our understanding of synchrony itself. From now on, sync will no longer be associated with rhythmicity alone, with loops and cycles and repetition. Synchronized chaos brings us face-to-face with a dazzling new kind of order in the universe, or at least one never recognized before. (pp. 204–5)

However, it should not be concluded that this necessarily "explains away" the perspective of the religious person perceiving a meaningful pattern in the events of their lives. Indeed, to a significant extent it supports the idea of identifying order that is meaningful underlying what often looks like the jumble of experiences we identify as our lives and careers. Chaos theorists often talk in terms of "hidden order" (Holland, 1995) and "order for free" (Kaufman, 1995). Thus while Jung's notion of acausal coincidence may be too mystical to be interpretable in empirical scientific terms, his idea of some form of linked order beyond immediate apprehension does appear to find some support in the concept of synchrony. So also does the potential application of the idea of meaningful coincidence to personal and career counseling. As Peat (2002) has written:

> Our rational, waking, reasoning life is only a small part of our total experience. Likewise, individual, personal experience is only a small part of what is available to us. At the collective level we all dip into what has been called the zeitgeist of the times. We have access to a dimly felt edge of where consciousness is moving. Some are more able to plug into it than others. (p. 111)

The CTC points to a complexity of reality as evidenced in non-linear change, which includes order and meaning beyond human capacity to comprehend fully. The meaning individuals seek to induce from such mystery provides insights for both individuals and their counselors into crucial vocational issues such as personal identity, ultimate concern, perception of worth and conceptions of success—all of which contribute inextricably to their career development.

Conversion

Religious belief can develop in a range of ways, the most dramatic of which is the "conversion experience." Typically, this involves an individual (it can happen to groups, but for the sake of presentation the focus here is on the single person), usually without much background in a specific religion, not infrequently from an anti-religious background in thought and/or behavior being challenged to change their lives radically and suddenly. For example, the prisoner with a history of criminal activity hears a religions message, reads a Bible or is ministered to by a loving and caring chaplain, and as a consequence "turns to God" and begins a transformation of character, values and behavior. Major faith traditions cite millions of examples of such changes throughout their centuries of history: not only conversions of convicted criminals but the less dramatic but no less profound conversions of others.

Upon the belief system to which individuals are converted will depend the nature of the impact of the conversion experience and the consequent effects on their career development. Some examples of such vocational implications could be:

- An unwillingness to work for a cigarette company
- A desire to avoid alcohol-oriented hospitality jobs
- Seeking out evangelistic or missionary occupations
- Joining a church-based organization
- Seeking work in an environmental or pacifist organization
- Refusing to work in gambling-based industries such as horse racing
- Changing from a profit-based to a charity-based company
- Eschewing "black market" employment.

Contemporary theories of career development do not address the conversion phenomenon in any explicit way. However, the Chaos Theory of Careers incorporates the notion of the "phase shift," which does provide an account for the conversion experience. As chaotic systems function dynamically between stability and change, the relative strength of the change influence and their non-linear dynamics become disproportionate to those of stability through the process of positive and negative feedback. At a particular point, arising from the internal dynamics of the system or impacted by an outside influence such as a life threatening experience, crisis or religious message or experience, such systems reach "tipping points" (Gladwell, 2000) and transform their configurations of influences into new patterns in the same way that ice transforms to water and water to steam. A new order emerges in both the configuration and the consequent functioning of the system, which is usually what happens in conversion when structures change (values, ethics and identity), resulting in changes in process (speech, behavior and emotionality) (Laszlo, 1991).

Connection

Chaos theory in general, and the Chaos Theory of Careers in particular, places emphasis on the essential integration of reality. Through the perspective of complex dynamical systems, nature is conceptualized holistically as multitudinous systems variously overlapping and interlocking. The notion of systems also draws attention to the need to focus on the links between existents as influences on a system's functioning as well as the impacts of components of a system on each other.

Chaos theory also directs attention to the interactive effects of components of systems that are fundamentally overlooked in a purely positivist approach: in particular, the importance of viewing systems as wholes, rather than just as agglomerations of components, out of which derives the phenomenon of emergence (Holland, 1998; Morowitz, 2002). Emergence is a property of systems acting as systems that derives from a system's functioning and cannot be identified merely as part of the system. For example, a choir of singers manifests musical qualities such as harmony that each singer separately cannot induce. The harmony only emerges (if you like, exists) when the choir is assembled and singing as a choir. It is this emphasis on interconnections, holistic thinking and emergence that allows the CTC to be able to account for a number of important spiritual concepts with significant implications for career development.

Coherence

There is a long tradition of religious thinking across faith traditions which emphasises the essential unity of creation. Eastern religious traditions refer to the "the Oneness" of all things. This is sometimes referred to as pantheism. However, in the Judeo–Christian–Islamic perspective all things are understood as emanating from the creative action of a single source, God. Influential religious individuals such as St Francis of Assisi have frequently taught about the unity of all things. Indeed, in his life and teaching St Francis identified natural objects, such as the sun and the moon as well as animals, as his brothers and sisters (Goudge, 1959). At its most basic level, coherence is the connection or linking of things into broader conceptions of meaning and harmony.

Meaning

Guinness (2003) presents spirituality in terms of coherence and continuity. Duchon and Plowman's (2005) empirical work drew attention to meaning as a major impact on work performance. Lips-Wiersma (2002) identified meaning, as an influence on career behavior, as being composed of three concepts, one of which was coherence; this related to integrated frameworks and perceptions of ordering outside the individual. Weilter and Schoonover (2001) link career success to the enhancement of spiritual growth. Spiritual growth, in turn, they conceive as "the most powerful and enduring way to meaning" (p. 83).

In the CTC meaning is an emergent property from the functioning of complex dynamical systems perceived holistically. It derives from the interactive interconnections of the often complex set of constituents of systems.

Harmony

Bloch (1997) linked meaning and harmony as spiritual dimensions of work. In doing so, she identified the importance of mindfulness as a technique to aid the quest for meaning and harmony and anticipated by more than a decade the more recent interest in mindfulness as a counseling approach. Bloch (2006) defined harmony as "working in a setting that harmonizes with your talents, interests and values" (p. 764). Lips-Wiersma (2002) also identified harmony as a core component of meaning in work. Peat (2002) captures the connection between harmony and chaos theory when he writes:

> Each of us today realizes our connection to the society in which we live through countless feedback loops. Each of us helps to generate and sustain the meaning by which that society functions. What's more, chaos is no longer something to be afraid of; it is an expression of the deep richness that lies within the order of the cosmos and our very lives. (p. 153)

Relationships

Repeatedly in religious literature and thinking in general, the notion of "love," and in particular "loving others," is found. Smith (1999) envisions a Christian perspective of work as being called to serving others. Guinness (2003) cites talents and skills as gifts given for the benefit of others. Colozzi (2007) suggests something similar in identifying work with opportunities to contribute to others, family and community. Covey's (1989) notion of leaving a legacy also captures a spiritual dimension of work in terms of making a difference in people's lives. Bloch (2006) wrote about community as an important spiritual dimension of work.

Most often such ideas focus around the concept of connection through shared responsibility. When Cain said "Am I my brother's keeper?" the implied answer in the text of Genesis is affirmative. This is premised on notions of equality and mutual responsibility through the connections of our common humanity. As noted earlier in this chapter, relationships are encapsulated in the CTC's emphasis on connectivity.

Attractors

One further concept from the Chaos Theory of Careers that provided explanatory power for incorporating spiritual concepts into career development is "attractors". Chapters 3 and 4 dealt with the concept in detail. For the current purposes, attractors can just be thought of as descriptive accounts of how complex dynamical systems function.

Morality

Earlier, attractors were identified with desired end states, ordered boundedness and visions of reality. The boundaries of an attractor are the limits within which a system functions. For humans, such an attractor's boundaries represent the limits of acceptable functioning or behavior. This is equivalent to identifying individuals' morality in terms of ethics and values.

Ethics and values are typically central to much religious thinking. Universal codes of conduct such as the Ten Commandments are evident in many religious traditions. Ethics and values frequently impact on individuals' career decision making in either positive or negative ways. Positively, people will seek out occupations and institutions in which to work that are aligned with what is considered valuable and worthy to them. Negatively, they will avoid occupations and institutions that contravene individuals' sense of right and wrong. Of course, for some individuals ethics and values may not be clearly articulated or thought through. As a result, they may engage in exploratory career development trying out different occupations and institutions as working options. For example, the university graduate who starts working for a multinational company may find the corporate demands of effort, time, travel and organizational commitment too onerous and too sacrificial of other priorities such as family and friends. The graduate may then try private practice as a sole practitioner but find that the freedom of working for oneself requires too much personal discipline in order to make enough money to support self and dependents. Eventually, the graduate may decide to join a group consultancy practice in which work is generally focused around a small group of local companies, with the work undertaken in teams. Now the graduate does not have the commitment demands of the large corporate or the insecurity of income of the sole practice. The graduate has come to realize that what is valuable are time with and support for friends and family, in a way that would have never been fully realized without the varying experiences of work.

In CTC terms, the graduate has gained greater insight into personal priorities through active exploration of career as a strange attractor. In the development of a stronger sense of personal valuing, the graduate has made firmer the boundaries of the fractal of that attractor. It is now clearer for this person what he or she is prepared to do (what is within the ambit of the attractor) and what is not acceptable (what has been located beyond the attractor's boundary).

Wisdom

Smith (1999) noted that "perhaps nothing matters vocationally as much as becoming wise" (p. 138). He goes on to envision wisdom in terms of the capacity to respond creatively and with emotional maturity to the changes, challenges and setbacks that constitute human experiences, especially career development. Briggs and Peat (1999) appropriately identify that many of the significant spiritual teachers in human history relate living wisely with the embracing of paradox. Pryor and Bright (2007a) identified wisdom in CTC terms as "living on the edge of chaos": that is, the interaction between stability and instability, being and becoming, and what can be known and controlled and what cannot. In essence, "wisdom is to live responsibly and responsively in light of the contingency of our lives recognizing our potential and utilizing our potential" (Pryor & Bright, 2007a, p. 392).

Purpose

As conceptualized in the Chaos Theory of Careers, purpose is one way of understanding the driving force that gives shape to each individual's life as a strange attractor. It is a sense of purpose, conscious or unconscious, that drives the movement of the strange attractor aperiodically, deterministically and boundedly. Ortberg (2007) observed that "one of the most devastating experiences in life is a sense that what I do does not matter" (p. 77). That is, when there is no purpose to human life and work, individuals are at a place of deep spiritual barrenness.

A component of a sense of purpose is hope. Weiler and Schoonover (2001) quote Kierft, stating that hope is the forgotten virtue. It has been identified as a longing for or trace of God in our being. Such a conception links it with the CTC attractor concept of the fractal which is the trace of the strange attractors' movement or functioning. Smith (1999) observes that in our lives and careers setbacks and disappointment are inevitable. He identifies vocational maturity with the capacity to endure such hurtful outcomes with hope. The CTC openly acknowledges that uncertainty may include negative as well as positive outcomes for individuals in their lives and career development. Hope is the spiritual dignity that individuals with a perspective bigger than their own immediate felicity bring to the pain and disappointment of barriers, limitations, obstacles and stumbling blocks.

A second dimension of purpose is commitment. Those with a sense of purpose are not only hopeful, but are also committed to the worth or importance of the purpose that impels them. While joy and fulfillment are very real and desirable consequences of persistence and strategy, it is the spiritual reality of suffering for one's commitments that rarely if ever rates a mention in the career development literature. However, many teachers and faith traditions embrace suffering as an essential aspect of human experience. In Buddhism, life in this world is identified with the experience of suffering. Peck (1978) states that a full life is a life full of suffering. Jung (1974) viewed neurosis as a way to avoid facing the "legitimate" existential suffering of human experience. Frankl (1984) identified spiritual meaning with the experience of suffering. Smith (1999) concluded that "in some form a cross will mark every vocation; there will be some way in which the pain of a broken world intersects our call" (p. 152).

It is when humans face and accept the pain and suffering that derive from their commitments that they can rise above self-pity to a deeper sense of grace in purposes beyond themselves. Typically, it is at such times that religious faith is deepened with a renewed sense of divine presence, or faith is jettisoned in the despair of a sense of abandonment and bitterness. The CTC's emphasis on human limitations in the face of complexity and change as experienced by all of us and in our world entails that the experience of suffering will be an essential component of human experience. It is simply part of being human, the alternative to which we would find hopelessly intolerable. As Rescher (1995) indicates in his discussion of luck—good and bad: "the acceptance of luck … is consequent upon the limitations of our knowledge and is part of the inevitable price we have to pay for existence as the sort of creatures we actually are" (p. 197).

After all, without indeterminacy, despite its sometimes realized capacity to expose our vulnerability to suffering, the human freedom to respond bravely and to redeem creatively the worst of situations would not be possible. To lose such freedom in a trade-off with a totally predictable closed system existence would in reality be to lose one's humanity.

This was exemplified in the vocational setting for us most poignantly. A client comes to mind who had experienced a major work accident. His injuries had left him in considerable and perpetual pain, day and night. He sought help in finding new employment. The issue of medication to ease his pain levels and increase his functionality was discussed since such outcomes would significantly improve his vocational potential. The young man responded that the medication, if strong enough, did take the edge of his pain. However, he reported that the price he paid for taking such medication was a series of side effects that so dulled his mind and his responsiveness to his surroundings that he resolved not to persist will such strong pain tablets. He characterized his decision in the following terms: "I dislike the pain and wish it could be removed or lessened further, but at least while I have it, I know that I am alive!"

This client's choice to endure the suffering of his pain rather than dull it and himself out of existence is an inspiring affirmation of what it is to be human and to face the contingencies of life with courage, commitment, hope and purpose. He eventually resumed work, this time as a bookkeeper for a company on a part-time basis, and subsequently supplemented his income by starting his own small business providing accounts support to other small businesses.

Calling

As work becomes less closely linked with organizations and occupations, individuals are often seeking new ways to create meaning and significance for their careers (Wrzesniewski & Tosti, 2005). One way is to integrate their working lives more closely with their lives in general. Typically, this leads to a desire to link the meaning and goals of work with their broader sense of meaning and aspiration. This broader sense is often referred to as a calling or "the reason I am here."

Traditionally, career as calling was associated with religious occupations such as clergy or missionaries or with professions of a helping nature such as medicine, nursing and social work. Such callings were frequently viewed as "vocations," which derives from the Latin "to call." The Puritans, for example, saw work as part of being called by God, being called to God and being called for God. Work was linked to the broader spiritual calling to serve and obey God in the world. Smith (1999) identifies three calls for a Christian as a general call to the obedience of faith; a specific call to mission or vocation in the world; and a call to act in the immediate moment. In such a perspective, all work is potentially sacred. Weiler and Schoonover (2001) identify calling in the context of career as unique to each individual as part of individuals' linking to meaning beyond themselves.

Colozzi (2007) views calling as similar in process but broader in perspective. Calling is part of the process of construction and/or finding meaning for one's life. It is, according to Colozzi, like being drawn to certain activities and contexts in which one's skills and talents are developed and used; in which one's passion is evoked; in which one experiences balance across life goals; which contributes to the broader community and which promotes one's own health and well-being. Wrzesniewski and Tosti (2005) summarized research relevant to a sense of calling in work by suggesting that those who work in a career to which they feel called are likely to:

- Report higher job and life satisfaction
- Be seen by employers as having higher work motivation
- Indicate higher occupational commitment
- Be more creative in their task approach
- Be less likely to regret their choice of occupations.

The CTC concept of the attractor encapsulates the notion of calling through the twin ideas of being drawn and end states. Gharajedaghe (1999) characterized attractors as accounts of how systems move or are attracted to ultimate end states. These end states for individuals can be the sense of meaning and purpose that they want to realize. When individuals are able to enunciate explicitly such "end states," they are likely at such a point to identify their attraction to these "end states" as a sense of calling.

SOME CONCLUSIONS

Insofar as it is possible for us to know, spiritual experience is a uniquely human characteristic. There is something mysterious and even ironic about this. As we became throughout our prehistory more self-conscious, it appears we also became more conscious of something or someone who is beyond us. The more we have come to realize how incomprehensible both our world and we, ourselves, actually are, the more we have apprehended a sense of the numinous in the universe. At various times humans have thought they had almost found all the answers, as in the early part of the twentieth century (Peat, 2002). However, the theories of relativity, quantum mechanics, and chaos and complexity in the last 100 years have exposed how hubristic such earlier claims to certainty and the finality of human knowledge and control really were.

Nevertheless, it appears that our yearning for "the sacred" is no less compelling in modern times than it has ever been in human history (Kaufman, 1995). Individuals today are seeking purpose, hope and solace in diverse places. One of the most influential writers about contemporary spirituality is Peck (1993), who wrote:

> Our unique human capacity for change and transformation is reflected in our human spirituality. Throughout the ages, deep-thinking people looking at themselves have come to discern that we are not all at the same place spiritually or religiously. (p. 119)

Since working constitutes such a major component of the lives of most of us, it is understandable that increasingly the search for spiritual values and fulfillment would find its expression in work. There has been a changing spiritual perspective in modern times which is also reflected in a changing view of reality in general. Chaos theory is one of the manifestations of these changes.

With respect to work, the Chaos Theory of Careers seeks to identify, integrate and illuminate the nature and implications of this renewed spiritual perspective. In its emphasis on the complexity and the overdetermined nature of reality and human behavior, the spiritual dimensions of mystery, uniqueness, human limitations and the inevitability of uncertainty can be rendered more intelligible through the coherence of a single perspective about the essential nature of reality. In the CTC's focus on the dynamical nature of systems, especially human functioning, we can appreciate our quest for personal development and creativity, and our experience of non-linearity, synchrony and radical change such as conversion and the miraculous. In the CTC's perspective on the interconnections within and between systems, the spiritual ideas of coherence, meaning, harmony and relationships can be encompassed. Finally, with the CTC's use of the chaos concept of "attractor" we can more readily incorporate into career development thinking spiritual notions including morality, hope, purpose, suffering and calling.

While some of these spiritual dimensions, such as meaning, purpose and calling, have been discussed and researched by others, many dimensions of spirituality have not even been mentioned in the career development literature to our knowledge. The CTC draws attention to these neglected spiritual notions and illustrates how they can coherently be integrated into a single theory of career development. As the more nihilistic dimensions of postmodernism come to be seen as essentially effete as a basis for understanding the world and our existence, individuals are increasingly seeking to interpret and live their lives with a respect for the numinous and the sacred. Their careers, therefore, are becoming an essential dimension of the expression of such aspirations. For this reason, the need for careers counselors to be sensitive to and able to recognize the spiritual implications of career transitions and decision making is likely to become correspondingly more important. The Chaos Theory of Careers provides the most comprehensive and inclusive theoretical perspective in the career development field for the incorporation, integration and elaboration of this relationship between spirituality and working.

CHAPTER 10

Practical Applications: Organizational Development

Life is organized.

Without organization, systems have neither characteristic ways of behaving nor boundaries to delineate them. Therefore it should not be surprising that as people interconnect through work they form organizations. Organizations are connections. If, as Drafke (2006) contends, organizations consist of two or more people with some mutual interest, then connections are at the heart of an organization. Career development in organizations can therefore be understood in terms of developing those connections. Even in the simplest organizations, those connections can become exceedingly complex very rapidly. Suppose an organization consisted of two sales staff and that each of those staff had four different clients to sell to. At any time there could be 16 different connections between sales staff and clients. If the company became successful and increased its sales force to eight staff, each with four clients, there could be 65,536 different patterns of connection. According to 2002 US census figures there was an average of 20 employees per organization. If in such an average organization each employee was limited to only interacting with four other people, the average organization could have 1.09 trillion (a 1 with 12 zeros after it) patterns of connection.

Given these staggering figures, it is perhaps understandable that organizational analysis and interventions historically have been based upon highly simplified, reductionist and logical models in an effort to overcome such combinatorial explosions (Senge, 1990). Undoubtedly, simplified models have been useful in understanding how organizations operate. As organizations have become increasingly complex and subject to ever faster changes as a result of the usual suspects of technology, competition and globalization, it is questionable how valuable or relevant these simple linear models continue to be. However, the developments in chaos and complexity theory over the last 20 years hold out promise of a more powerful and realistic approach to organizational analysis that does not ignore the complex nature of organizations, and it is in that context that the Chaos Theory of Careers can be applied to career development within organizations.

Modern working environments are inescapably complex, rapidly changing and increasingly global, bringing into question traditional static "exact fit" models of career development (Dawis & Lofquist, 1984). Models that are centrally focused on the fit of the person to the job underestimate the degree of complexity, the extent and complexity of change, and the frequency of unplanned events that both the person and the job are subject to. What is required is a conceptual model that embraces complexity, change and interconnection. The Chaos Theory of Careers (Pryor & Bright, 2007a) is proposed as such a theory for a new understanding of organizations and individuals' career development within them.

TRADITIONAL MODELS

For much of the last century, the goal of many managers was to get their organizations "running like clockwork." Each process, each person could be thought of as a different cog in the mechanism (Whyte, 1956). Managers oiled the cogs, and replaced the worn out, broken or missing cogs and, if they had ambitions, perhaps added new and bigger cogs that provided more power or functions.

Such an approach resembles the ideas of some of the early leaders in organizational behavior such as Frank Taylor, Henry Gantt and Lillian Gilbraith and the so-called Scientific Management movement (Drafke, 2006). Such figures were rightly criticized by Elton Mayo and later by the Human Relations Movement more generally as privileging rationality above emotion (Drafke, 2006). This, too, is reflected in Frank Parsons' (1909) notion of "true reasoning" to fit an individual's aptitudes, abilities and interests to a job's requirements, constraints and opportunities.

One of the earliest applications of systems thinking applied to organizations (and a lot of other phenomena too) can be found in Boulding (1956). He delineated nine different applications of systems thinking, which in order of complexity are Frameworks, Clockworks, Thermostats, Cells, Plants, Animals, Human Beings, Social Organizations and Transcendental Systems. Presciently, Boulding concludes;

> Finally, the above scheme might serve as a mild word of warning even to Management Science. This new discipline represents an important breakaway from overly simple mechanical models in the theory of organization and control. Its emphasis on communication systems and organizational structure, on principles of homeostasis and growth, on decision processes under uncertainty, is carrying us far beyond the simple models of maximizing behavior of even ten years ago. This advance in the level of theoretical analysis is bound to lead to more powerful and fruitful systems. Nevertheless we must never quite forget that even these advances do not carry us much beyond the third and fourth levels, and that in dealing with human personalities and organizations we are dealing with systems in the empirical world far beyond our ability to formulate. We should not be wholly surprised, therefore, if our simpler systems, for all their importance and validity, occasionally let us down. (p. 208)

It was a decade later when Katz and Kahn (1966) expanded on the notion of the organization as a system. However, the current dominant view of an organization as an "open system" (Wood et al., 2004) still appears to be highly mechanistic in nature. Indeed, Baruch (2004) states that "although outdated, [Whyte's 1956 *Organization Man*] is still relevant for both men and women" (p. 79). Wood et al. (2004), in the opening to their textbook, describe organizations in these terms:

> many organizational scholars believe that organizations can be best understood as open systems that transform human and material resource "inputs" received from their environment into product "outputs" in the form of finished goods and/or services. The outputs are then offered to the environment for consumption. If everything works, the environment accepts these outputs and allows the organization to obtain the resource inputs it needs to continue operating into the future. (p. 6)

In this model, "People" are lumped together with Information, Materials, Equipment, Facilities and Money to form the "Input Resources." It is clear what the term Human Resources means in this context—labor is merely one input alongside materials and other inputs. So the Human Resource process is the transformation of that human input into useful outputs, and those responsible for these human inputs are typically found in the occupation of "Human Resources." The "Organization" brings together these human and physical resources in a transformative process to produce the "Product Outputs" of goods or services. The model is a simple linear progression from Inputs via Transformation to Outputs with a linear feedback mechanism feeding back into the Inputs.

Thus although the language has changed in the last 100 years, the dominant description of how organizations run still has a markedly mechanistic feel to it. The model describes a clear linear logical function. The path from one part of the model to another is clearly set out and the outcomes are predictable. Indeed, one of the striking aspects of such a model is, as the authors point out, that things only go wrong for an organization if they fail to satisfy "environmental demands" (Wood et al., p. 6).

What is striking in this updated model is the implied assumption (or perhaps hope) that "everything works." The model is based on the premise of keeping things "ticking over." Furthermore, this model appears to imply a reactive attitude to change. Change is only necessary if the environment changes. There is no imperative to innovate unless the environment dictates it. In addition, there is no consideration of how the elements within the organization might create change in the absence of environmental forces.

In such a model, career development is a straightforward proposition. Individuals can be matched to the blueprint to see if and where the cog belongs in the machine. Identifying career paths generally involves a consideration of the adjoining cogs in the mechanism and a climb up the organizational structure ladder.

The mechanistic view of an organization also lends itself well to motivational techniques such as goal setting which are predicated on the notion that the future is (reasonably) predictable and unchanging. Thus in such a framework, pathways are clear and goals can be set. It is possible to work out a route from one cog to another one in a different part of the mechanism. It is also possible to work out how the movement of performance of any one cog influences another and the machine as a whole.

As a consequence, most organizational interventions, including career development interventions, have emphasized the benefits of control, clarity, predictability, transparency and accountability. Interventions are often aimed squarely at reducing or eliminating ambiguity, uncertainty, lack of transparency and lack of accountability. The current orthodoxy in organizational career development is still centered on notions of control and predictability. The human or individual element is often characterized as a source of error variance that leads to sub-optimal outcomes. Its mantra is PLAN, ORGANISE, CONTROL. As Baruch (2004) points out, "Acute problems concern the ambiguity and complexity of the issue of managing people. And people are the most difficult asset to manage—they are unpredictable (at least to some extent), they have their own will and plans (which do not necessarily fit with those of the organization) ... these issues affect how career management can be dealt with, and limit what executives can expect from organizational career management systems" (p. 131).

It is perhaps not surprising, therefore, that in reaction to the inherent unpredictability of individuals, and the perception that the work landscape continues to experience unprecedented change, a major theme of career planning in organizations is effectively to outsource responsibility for these tasks to the individual. This is reflected both in practice and in the career development literature that is quite starkly divided into theories and interventions that privilege the individual, and theories and processes that privilege the organization. For instance, theories such as Holland (1997), Lent, Brown and Hackett (1994), Patton and McMahon (2006), Reardon, Lenz, Sampson and Peterson (2000) and Savickas (1995) emphasize the individual and their concerns as central. Environmental factors are characterized as surrounding the individual, or that into which the individual attempts to fit. Theories privileging the organization include Baruch (2004), Herriot and Pemberton (1966) and Gutteridge, Leibowitz and Shore (1993). In these approaches organizational concerns such as business strategy, human resource management practices and market conditions are considered relevant and important.

Too often these approaches clash in organizations. The popular mantra aimed at individuals, to "follow one's passion," does not sit readily with a career management perspective of training, hot-housing, controlling and managing careers. As Drafke (2006) points out, "not everyone is convinced of the usefulness of a positive approach to human behavior—after all fear does motivate. Many still believe that if you don't like a workplace, just leave; don't expect the workplace to change just to make you happy. The OB [organizational behavior] theory that happy workers are productive workers has not been established absolutely" (p. 7).

When attempting to understand the behavior of individuals or collections of them, simplifying assumptions such as the mechanistic models of Whyte's *Organization Man* or the systems theories of Wood et al. (2004) can be very useful for narrowly defined problems and in the short term. Wood et al. (2004) contend that so-called systems goals are "so important to firms because they provide a road map to assist in the linking together [of] various units of an organization to assure its survival. Well-defined systems goals are practical and easy to understand: they focus the manager's attention on what needs to be done"(p. 355). However, most career development issues are neither simple nor short term. As Stacey, Griffin and Shaw (2003) argue, "systems thinking about organizations, while it may be very useful for understanding and controlling behaviour of a repetitive kind, cannot deal with the question of novelty" (p. 104).

Taleb (2007) addresses this issue of novelty in a broader manner. Novelty derives from the old French "novelte" from novel, meaning new or fresh. Fresh or new is not commonplace, it is not the norm: it is *rare*. For Taleb, "the rare event *equals* uncertainty" (pp. xxiv). He argues that "almost everything" (pp. xxiv) that involves social interaction is produced by rare but significant jumps. Uncertainty and its implications are not easily captured or considered when reality is reduced to the well-defined and practical.

The tendency to focus on the "foreseeable" future (a not very clear term in itself) means almost by definition making the explicit choice to focus on what we know we know, and what we know we don't know. As Taleb argues, it is most often "what we don't know we don't know" that is the most influential factor, yet this factor is excluded from notions of system goals. Indeed, the way systems theoretical thinking has been applied to organizations has been to promote a view of a predictable machine. Such thinking is clearly evident in the dominant theories of organizational change. For example, Wood et al. (2004) devote three sentences in a textbook of 736 pages to unplanned change. This indicates the underestimation of the incidence and impact of unplanned events within organizations. Even when the unplanned is addressed, it is in terms of a reactive attitude and as a minor disturbance to the ongoing stability and predictability of the system as a whole. Thus they state:

> The appropriate goal in managing unplanned change is to act immediately once the change is recognised, to minimise any negative consequences and maximise any possible benefits. (p. 635)
> Systems thinking approaches to change very often still adopt the

three-phase rational model of change proposed by Kurt Lewin (1951) of unfreezing, change and re-freezing. Lewin argues that before change can occur we must identify and act against forces holding us back from change; then we do the changing, and then we attempt to reinforce the change by marshalling new or existing force fields to freeze or bed down the change. This approach echoes the systems theorists' approach and sees change following a logical and predictable path.

Building on Lewin's work, Edgar Schein's (1968, 1987, 1988, 1996) Process Consultation is an example of a more sophisticated approach to change that places greater emphasis upon the dynamic and interactive nature of personal interactions and organizational interventions. Schein's ideas predicted much of the contemporary career development thinking about the counselor-client relationship. He states:

> Process consultation as a philosophy acknowledges that the consultant is not an expert on anything but how to be helpful, and starts with total ignorance of what is actually going on in the client system. One of the skills, then, of process consulting is to "access one's ignorance," to let go of the expert or doctor role, and get attuned to the client system as much as possible. Only when one has genuinely understood the problem and what kind of help is needed, can one even begin to think about recommendations and prescriptions, and even then it is likely that they will not fit the client system's culture and will, therefore, not be refrozen even if initially adopted. Instead, a better model of help is to start out with the intention of creating an insider/outsider team that is responsible for diagnostic interventions and all subsequent interventions. When the consultant and the client have joint ownership of the change process, both the validity of the diagnostic interventions and the subsequent change interventions will be greatly enhanced. (p. 36)

Notwithstanding Schein's acknowledgement of the dynamics of change, his process consultation model is ultimately a stage model of change that is driven, or at least guided, by setting initial specific goals. Ultimately, the model characterizes change as something that can be clearly conceptualized and captured in a goal, and something that can be worked towards by moving through a pre-defined set of stages.

In a similar vein, Hultman (1998) characterizes change as an essentially rational and logical choice. "Before they become willing to change, people weigh the costs, relying on facts (actual costs) and beliefs (anticipated costs), and the values (benefits). Once a decision to change has been made it is implemented through action" (p. 63). Probably the most extensive organizational application of systems approaches can be found in Senge (1990). His influential work does point to the need to address complexity in terms of holistic thinking and his approach to change represents a significant development in systems thinking about organizations and how they function and impact the individuals who work in them. He identifies five disciplines of what he terms "Learning Organizations." These disciplines are systems thinking, personal mastery, mental models, building shared vision and team learning. Senge explicitly addresses the notion of complexity, dividing it into dynamic and detail complexity: the former focusing on process and the later on content. Despite the acknowledgement of complexity, it is clear that Senge is interested in characterizing systems in closed terms: "Living systems have integrity. Their character depends on the whole. The same is true for organizations; to understand the most challenging managerial issues requires seeing the whole system that generates the issues" (p. 66). Openness as a quality is more closely linked in Senge's work to understanding the limits of rationality as a tool for discovering the world, and the links to spiritual belief that flow from this. The influence of openness on the organization as a system is only tangentially explored. There is no consideration of limits of predictability, chance and randomness, but he does acknowledge non-linearity (labeled leverage) and also the need to move beyond simple cause and effect chains. Ultimately, however, Senge leans toward the application of systems thinking to derive "laws" and "archetypes" and micro-worlds as methods for accurately predicting organizational behavior.

While it is undoubtedly true that some personal and organizational change does occur as the result of careful consideration and rational evaluation, as a model for organizational or personal change Senge's approach neglects to consider a number of important factors that derive from complexity in systems including emergence, non-linear change, phase-shifts, fractals and attractors. In sum, traditional models of organizations, organizational change and career development neglect chaos and complexity.

THE CHAOS THEORY OF CAREERS

An approach to career development in organizations is required that overcomes the simplifications of characterizing people and organizations in mechanistic, or closed systems terms, that can accommodate notions of freedom and purpose, stability and change, predictability and chance, being and becoming, while at the same time providing a principled account of structure and limitation. We propose that the Chaos Theory of Careers can provide a conceptual structure and set of processes to support career development for individuals in organizations.

The Chaos Theory of Careers represents an advance on traditional notions of organizational career development, because unlike most traditional models the CTC utilizes complexity, change, chance and uncertainty as its most central concepts. The key elements of the Chaos Theory of Careers state that both people and organizations can be seen as comprising systems that are:

- Complex: i.e., subject to many different influences
- Changing continually: sometimes gradually or even trivially, and at other times suddenly and non-linearly
- Highly interconnected: all elements in the system are connected to every other element
- Emergent: a feature of the system is that over time a clear pattern emerges that can be seen at every level of the system: it is called Fractal Behavior
- Open: the system is open to external influences that generally serve to modify the overall pattern in minor ways, but have the potential to have a sudden and dramatic influence
- Inherently unpredictable: containing both pattern and surprise.

Within organizations as systems, there are any number of other systems that are formally recognized—such as the Sales Department, Finance, Human Resources, Administration, Marketing and Senior Management—and informal systems—such as the "grapevine," cliques of employees, the "old boys' network" and incidental friendships. Individuals' career development and progress may be influenced by both formally recognized systems and informally functioning systems. Networking within such systems is one of the career development skills within bureaucracies that tend to receive comparatively little attention in the career development literature as a whole (Darling, 2005). In the rest of this chapter, two important issues of career development for those in organizations are addressed to illustrate the contribution that the Chaos Theory of Careers perspective can make to a new understanding of the nature of such work.

CHAOS AND GOAL SETTING

It has been argued in this book that most extant models of organizational change and career development are highly rational and usually depend upon goal setting to establish a motivational mechanism for change. However, goal setting rests on the assumption that the goal posts (the environment) and the goal setter are not subject to any dramatic change beyond that expected to occur as a result of setting the goal. This is usually accompanied by a requirement that any change or career plan that cannot be articulated in every detail has not been "thought through" or is the product of fuzzy thinking. It is commonly accepted that successful goals can be characterized as Specific, Measurable, Achievable, Realistic and Time-based—the so-called SMART goals. However, if the premises of change, chance and uncertainty that underpin the CTC are acknowledged and embraced, they have the potential to undermine goal setting as described in SMART terms.

This requirement for predictability as a necessary condition for goal attainment is reflected in the work of Mark Tubbs (Tubbs, 1986), who examined 87 separate studies on goal setting, and found a clear pattern of results: under laboratory conditions goals worked; in real-life settings, they were far less effective. The reason they were far less effective was essentially due to complexity. Career development is a continually developing series of planned actions which are impacted by unplanned events, which in turn lead to revisions or new plans, which in turn are impacted by the unexpected, and so on (Borg, Bright, & Pryor, 2006). There is an ongoing and inevitable relationship between the predictable and the unpredictable, between pattern and surprise, and between composition and improvisation. As Stacey, Griffin and Shaw (2003) point out, "If a system's specific long-term behaviour is unpredictable, then setting specific goals for it is a questionable activity" (p. 91).

One of the central ideas in goal setting is goal commitment. It is usually believed that goal setting will only be effective if you truly want to achieve your goals. So maybe this explains why goals can be less effective in real-life settings because commitment may wane over time. Unfortunately, that does not seem to be the case. Donovan and Radosovich (1998) conducted an examination of goal commitment and performance across 12 studies over 20 years, involving 2,000 participants, and found that goal commitment had very little effect on the levels of performance of the individuals studied.

At the heart of complex systems is feedback (Briggs & Peat, 1989). Feedback acts to accelerate or moderate the complex processes, and is itself complex. The timing of feedback is sufficient to alter the effectiveness and nature of the feedback. Feedback that is out of time can have the exact opposite effect to feedback that is timely. An alternative approach is to be committed to feedback rather than to goals per se. So instead of being committed to winning a gold medal, be committed to monitoring your time to complete a lap. This means being committed to establishing feedback mechanisms and attending to them.

Feedback mechanisms need to be both positive and negative, and continuous and intermittent. For instance, when seeking to increase sales of a product, the continuous feedback mechanisms might be the number of calls the sales representative makes every hour to prospective customers; positive feedback measures might include the number of new leads that they discover every day, and the negative feedback measures might include the number of rejections they receive each day. Intermittent measures might include comparing their monthly results to a colleague's sales figures.

Notice in this example that both positive and negative feedback measures were used because relying solely on the positive news about the number of new leads being discovered may be quite misleading, especially if the number of rejections being received is increasing dramatically. Having a range of feedback processes increases the chances of getting a better picture of what is happening. Having both continuous and interval measures of performance is also an important element here. In the example of the sales representative, if the number of new leads was very low and the number of rejections quite high, we might conclude that the sales representative was doing poorly. However, the intermittent measure—the monthly comparison to a colleague's figures—might indicate that our sales representative is doing a good job under difficult circumstances because they are outselling their colleague.

Within the CTC, if goal setting is to escape the rigid confines of the point attractor, the SMART formulation needs to be modified in a manner that challenges much conventional change management wisdom regarding the importance of the clarity of goals, and their precise measurability. Furthermore there exists empirical evidence to support such a move toward fuzzier, less measurable, less immediately achievable, less apparently realistic and less time-based and more revisable goals (e.g., Abrahamson & Freedman, 2006; Shapiro, 2006; Tubbs, 1986; Donovan & Radovisch, 1998).

STRATEGIC PLANNING, CAREER PATHS AND SUCCESSION PLANNING

An emergent theme of this book is the limitation of our ability to plan and control the future. This is a consequence of the inherent dynamic complexity of people and organizations. It may have profound implications for how to manage people in organizations. From a career development perspective, a major aspect of management that can have a far-reaching impact upon organizations and their employees' careers is strategic planning.

Strategic planning is an essential dimension of organizational management and has a direct bearing on the design and development of career paths within an organization. It is an area of management that typically emphasizes rationality and the power of prediction more than most others with the possible exception of financial management (e.g., Drafke, 2006).

Despite the obvious intuitive appeal of strategic planning, rarely are the costs or even the assumptions of strategic planning thoroughly considered. Taleb (2007) contends that much of the analysis (upon which most plans are based) is woefully inadequate and overconfident because it fails to appreciate the scalability (or non-linearity) of many economic phenomena. Abrahamson and Freedman (2006) provide many examples of organizations that appear to thrive on a lack of strategic planning. Their analysis leads them to conclude that Flexibility, Completeness, Resonance, Invention, Efficiency and Robustness are the dividends of adopting a "messy" approach to organization. Flexibility arises because there is no imperative to stick to a predetermined plan, and thus organizations (and individuals) have the freedom to be contingent. Completeness is achieved by not focusing (and thereby filtering) information. In CTC terms, this allows for emergence of a pattern or multiple patterns. Completeness complements flexibility because the system retains more possibilities with which to respond. For example, the more chord progressions a jazz musician can play, the greater the compositional and improvisational possibilities. Resonance refers to the interface between one system and another—where the systems are open to mutual influence, there is a possibility of resonance occurring; where the systems are closed, resonance cannot occur. Resonance is beneficial to organizations because it promotes the development of symbiotic and synergistic relationships within organizations and between organizations. Further, Abrahamson and Freedman (2006) point to the story of Fleming's serendipitous discovery of penicillin as an example of resonance. In CTC terms they are describing the difference between a closed system attractor (e.g., point, pendulum or most likely torus) and the open strange attractor. Invention is permitted in a messy system because there is a greater potential for apparently unrelated components to be brought together, thus allowing new connections (and hence invention) to occur. Duggan (2007) makes a similar argument about intuition. Efficiency gains can be achieved by outsourcing tasks to other systems, which increases the overall mess. Finally, Robustness is a feature of messy systems. It can provide redundancy (back-ups) and also resilience (e.g., cross-bred dogs tend to succumb to fewer maladies than pure breeds).

Strategic planning rests on the notion of predictability, but as Starbuck (1992) argues:

> formal strategizing often focuses on big issues involving large sums and many people. These are nearly always long-term issues, yet the long term never unfolds as expected. Thus, planners expend effort countering threats that never turn into actual problems, and on dreams that never become real opportunities. (p. 80)

Evidence to support the idea that there are financial benefits associated with engaging in strategic planning in organizations is actually very difficult to find (Abrahamson & Freedman, 2006; Grinyer & Norburn, 1975; Starbuck, 1992).

Classical strategic planning is excellently captured in Porter (1980). In developing a strategy, Porter recommends three stages with nine steps in total. First, identify what the organization is currently doing and the assumptions behind current strategy. Second, analyze the environment—the market sector, competitors, society and their strengths and weaknesses. Finally, evaluate the existing strategy against the results of the analysis, generate alternative strategies, evaluate the alternatives and implement.

From this outline it should be plain that Porter's processes emphasize the rational and the logical. However, his outline fails to specifically address the issue of how alternative strategies are developed. Yet this appears to be a fundamental challenge for all those seeking to develop their careers through crucial decision making. Porter fails to address this because he does not appear to have a suitably rational and replicable explanation of how people generate these strategies. Experienced career counselors will be able to point to a long list of clients who had tremendous personal insight and labor market knowledge (analogues of Porter's first two steps) but who flail about uninspired and unable to find a meaningful direction. In terms of Bright and Pryor's (2007) Counseling Quadrant, it appears that the client had a lot of convergent knowledge, but little in the way of emergent knowledge. The CTC recognizes the value of specific knowledge in the process of decision but it also draws attention to the need for imagination and creativity since careers are not only discovered but are also created.

Duggan (2007) identified the missing link in strategic planning as "strategic intuition." He argues that intuition arrives like a flash or strike to the eye, "trompe d'oeil." Interestingly, Duggan's proposed mechanism for intuition relies upon instance-based models of memory such as Douglas Hintzman's (1990) Minerva model. He argues that intuition occurs when two or more previously stored experiences are brought to mind and linked to create a new and novel insight. The insight provides a solution to a problem, and once it emerges the pathway to the desired state is generally straightforward. The approach implies that planning ultimately is about following intuitions, which are the product of the combined knowledge of those who have input to the problem combined with a degree of luck and experience in seeing the connections. Such a notion is consistent with Medawar's (1967) *Art of the Soluble*, which provided insights into which problems in science are most likely to be fruitful to research at any time. In CTC terms, this refers to the complex interaction of elements to form unpredictable and novel emergent patterns.

Thus it appears that strategic planning actually relies fundamentally on processes that are complex, unpredictable and ultimately irrational. Such a mechanism explains why good strategy is not simply a case of deciding upon a desired goal and then simply marching toward it (Duggan provides compelling examples from military history of the failures that result from literally adopting this approach to strategy). Rather, an effective strategy is contingent upon where the person or organization currently is and involves discovering a solution that will move either the person or the organization from where they are to some other desirable point. Duggan relates the story of Emperor Napoleon at the siege of Toulon. Napoleon's generals insisted on directly storming the fort of Toulon and failed miserably owing to the overwhelming British force. Napoleon had argued that if, instead, they took the smaller fort of l'Aguilette, the British would be cut off from their supply chain and would be forced to abandon the fort of Toulon. After Paris fired the first general for his failure, the next one adopted Napoleon's plan, which worked perfectly. Napoleon did not simply set strategic objectives and then march towards them; rather, he did what he could at the time. Furthermore, Napoleon was a keen student of military history and was aware that the Americans had used a similar strategy of separating the British from their supply chain in Yorktown 12 years earlier. His strategic planning was based not upon goal setting, but upon doing what you can as a situation emerges. For Duggan, Strategic Intuition is synonymous with creativity, as strategy can be seen as being created from the combination of elements of the current situation with past experience to literally create the strategy.

Duggan's analysis provides a clue to why traditional goal setting fares so poorly in motivation and career planning because of its tendency to encourage people to engage in wishful thinking rather than creative thinking. It encourages a mentality of identifying a goal and marching toward it, rather than identifying a solution to a problem and following that. The former involves assumptions of rationality and predictability, and the latter involves complexity, non-linearity, creativity and emergent patterns.

Sanders (1998) also sought to apply chaos perspectives to strategic management and identified seven general principles that derive from non-linear dynamics. Her principles are:

1. Look at organizations, situations and challenges holistically; otherwise you will miss the emergent patterns.
2. Focus on the interplay of order and disorder with complex systems and how self-organizing change functions within them.
3. Be aware of the potential non-linearity of change and how to utilize it beneficially or restrain its negative effects.
4. Direct attention to the connections, relationships and patterns of interaction within systems.
5. Scan across disciplines and industries to find new trends and opportunities.
6. Think non-linearly.
7. Recognize the importance of perspective in order to detect fractal phenomena in societies, industries, organizations and individuals.

Sanders' (1998) approach to the application of chaos theory to strategic planning is summarized as: "The present is the future in its most creative state" (p. 143).

Savickas (1995) characterizes career behavior as solutions to personal problems, and career paths and strategic succession planning in organizations can also been seen in these terms. Within this framework, career paths in organizations are not set in stone but continually change and emerge as different problems and solutions emerge. Consequently, Strategic Planning can also be seen as the Art of the Soluble.

A PRACTICAL MODEL OF CREATIVITY

If career and organizational behavior can be seen in Savickas' (1995) terms as solutions to problems, then having a clear sense of how to generate creative solutions is likely to be a useful tool for counselors, coaches, individuals and managers. The Beyond Personal Mastery® and Beyond Corporate Mastery® model of change (Bright, 2009a,b) was developed to provide a practical evidence-based framework for personal and organizational creativity. Figure 10.1 illustrates the Beyond Personal Mastery® framework (the Beyond Corporate Mastery® Framework is identical, but applies to groups not individuals).

The model comprises Action Steps and Mind Steps required for creativity.

There are two fundamental and complementary ways of achieving personal change: you can take action and you can change your mind. Taking action can change your mind and changing your mind facilitates action. Thus my model that I call Beyond Personal Mastery™ involves seven Action and seven Mind steps.

The seven action steps are: Inspiration, Patterning, Learning, Emulating, Combining and Adding, Strategizing, and Doing. Many people make the mistake of starting out on a change process by setting objectives and strategizing (cf. Duggan, 2007). You'll notice that comes towards the end of this process, in line with the idea of doing what you can at the time rather than committing too soon to a course of action that events will conspire to undermine.

1. Inspiration. This literally means to inhale, suggesting a link between action and inspiration. The more you move, the more you need to inhale; and the more you move, the more chances for inspiration. In practical terms, this may involve seeking out others' ideas through meetings, conversations and invitations

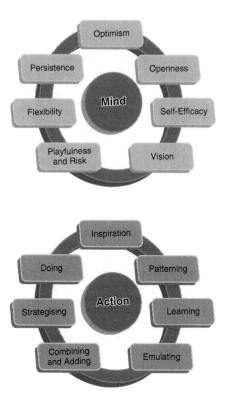

Figure 10.1 The Beyond Personal Mastery® model of change and creativity.

or exposing yourself to new ideas via other mediums such as books, classes, training, newspapers, magazines and television, internet, theatre, galleries and museums. Choosing things that are novel and breaking the routine are other ways of achieving this. The aim here is not directly to "get a job," solution or even direction. Simply, the idea is to be exposed to many different experiences.

2. Patterning. As new experiences are gained, the idea is to look for the structures, the hidden meanings, the ideas contained within them. How is the experience presented and structured? What does it mean to you? What are the common elements that occur frequently throughout the experience, and what are the essential aspects of it? What could be taken away from the experience without it marring your enjoyment?

3. Learning. Which experiences did you like and which did you not like? Why? What do all the things you like have in

common? What do all the things you didn't like have in common? What do you know now that you didn't know before you embarked on step 1? How does the new pattern of experience challenge your pre-existing categories, scripts and schemas? How could that learning be useful to you?

4. Emulating. In this step you practice copying and reproducing an activity that you liked. Often, trying to do something is a great way of getting a deeper insight into an activity and a good way of testing whether you really are interested in it or not. In business and the arts, many successful people never get beyond this stage. For instance, in Bangladesh they've just built an exact copy of the Taj Mahal, and Melbourne has a wheel like the London Eye. An apprenticeship can be seen as successfully being concluded when the apprentice is about to emulate the tradesman and can reproduce the techniques necessary for the trade.

5. Combining, Adding and Emerging. At this stage you go beyond copying and create something original and uniquely suited to you or your circumstances. This happens when you make links between things you have learned—your experiences—and other stored experiences to create something new. It is about combining pieces of your jigsaw in a new way to produce a new pattern that you know will work. The more pieces of the jigsaw you collect through experience and learning, the more patterns you can create. This is consistent with Duggan's (2006) notion of strategic intuition. Napoleon can be seen to have combined his knowledge of American military tactics with the situation he confronted at Toulon, and added to it by adapting the American tactic to a different military environment.

6. Strategizing. Once you see the new pattern and possibilities, you can work on how you are going to get from where you are to where to need to be. This is where a lot of the traditional and rational ideas about evaluating alternatives and planning goals fit in. Strategizing deliberately is towards the end of the process, because it allows for the path to be set by past experience (inspirations) and by the solution to the problem generated in the combining and adding stage. In this way it reflects Anygal's (1941) observation that the path one is already on determines what choices can be made; the goal does not set the direction, the direction determines what can be a goal.

7. Doing. Finally, you need to act and at the same time go back to step 1 and cycle through the steps. The model is a dynamic one that is based on the premise that we are continually in a state of both being and becoming.

The seven Mind steps that complement and support the Action steps are: Optimism, Openness, Self-Efficacy, Vision, Playfulness, Flexibility and Persistence.

1. Optimism. If you do not believe that some things can get better, you will have no reason to try wholeheartedly. The recent resurgence of interest in Positive Psychology (e.g., Seligman, 1998, 2002; Gillham, 2000) highlights the importance of optimism in change programs.
2. Openness. The curse of clever people is that they too readily analyze new information and categorize it (i.e., dismiss it) into their existing schemas and frameworks. In this way they can be blind to nuances and nuggets that can change their lives. The curse of stupid people is that don't bother analyzing new information in the first place. The result in both cases is a kind of content and complacent maintenance of the status quo. The result of this is no movement, no change and no hope. Note that this is not an invitation to fall for asinine schemes and behavior. As Harold T. Stone (n.d.) said, "I try to keep an open mind, but not so open that my brains fall out."
3. Self-Efficacy. This is a concept pioneered by psychologist Albert Bandura (1994), and relates to the belief that you can do something or achieve something. People who believe they can successfully complete a training course or diet are more likely to do so than those without this self-belief. Self-efficacy is not just about positive self-talk (though this can help), but also about engaging in the action steps, to provide the proof to yourself that you really can do it. This is why the Emulating action step is so important. Once you can master a task you can go beyond mastery of it.
4. Vision. Vision has got a bad press because it has been overused and devalued in numerous vision statements. However, what is meant by vision is creating something akin to a mental movie in which you can see yourself doing whatever it is you are seeking to do. In many ways it is consistent with Ibarra's (2003) notion of working identity. Can you see yourself acting

and interacting with the other people in this desired domain? Do you feel comfortable, are you succeeding? The idea here is not dissimilar to imagery exercises that sports psychologists may use with sportsmen and sportswomen, or indeed the way some musicians approach learning new instruments or pieces. The purpose of envisaging is to create some active engagement that may lead to other opportunities as you act on the world. Vision here also encapsulates a much bigger sense of purpose, of how the individual or organization fits into a bigger interconnected universe.

5. Playfulness and Risk. Children will often test their toys to destruction, or use them in "inappropriate" ways. It means coming to an idea without pre-conceptions, to see it for what it is. It is a bit like throwing away the instruction manual. The Zen Buddhist term for this is Shoshin.

6. Flexibility. This is perhaps best summed-up by Groucho Marx's quote, "These are my principles and if you don't like them, don't worry I've got others!" It means most diamonds have flaws as well as brilliance, and it depends how you hold them up to the light. The flexible mind will see the possibilities.

7. Persistence. Often the most important things we do in life have involved a degree of risk and meet resistance from some quarters. It is amazing how many people fail simply because they lose the courage of their convictions. Recognize that giving in is ultimately your choice and yours alone.

CHAOTIC LEADERSHIP

Characterizing organizations as complex and dynamical presents a challenge to the traditional notions of leadership. As Plowman et al. (2007) observe:

A central principal of complexity theory is emergent self-organization, whereby systems achieve order because multiple local agents interact and those interactions produce unintended outcomes without the intervention of a central controller ... Thus, organizations take on properties and structures that are unexpected ... because people and groups interact and the results of those interactions produce perpetual novelty. What, then, is the role of leadership in complex organizations? If leaders cannot predict and control the organization's future, what do leaders do? (p. 342)

Stacey, Griffen and Shaw (2003) point out that "most managers continue to believe that their role is essentially one of designing an organisation and controlling its activities" (p. 18). However, Plowman et al. (2007) offer evidence that successful leadership is not so much about control but instead about providing the conditions for change to occur and provoking change in others. They conclude: "Our findings show that as enablers, leaders disrupt existing patterns of behavior, encourage novelty, and make sense of emerging events for others" (p. 354). This description of complexity leadership is very similar to the way we have characterized CTC counseling in Chapter 7 and is also consistent with Wheatley's (1991) distinction between control and order within organizations. The leader's role is to control not by imposing order but rather by encouraging the emergence of new forms of order.

For example, in analyzing the transformation in the fortunes of a large but previously shrinking church congregation, Plowman et al. (2007) analyzed protocols taken from 22 interview transcripts containing 167 quotations about leadership that were agreed upon by two separate data encoders. These revealed three key elements: disrupting existing patterns, encouraging novelty and sensemaking. These were identified as the leadership basis for the church's transformation. The leaders did not seek to perpetuate the stable structures of the established organization and try to make them more efficient. Instead, they embarked on a program of destabilization using conflict and uncertainty to encourage questioning of previously accepted functional certitudes. The church did this by being controversial, for instance welcoming marginalized groups into their congregation, changing the music and styles of worship, and unlocking the doors of the church during the week to make it accessible to all. They also acknowledged uncertainty openly and encouraged discussions and suggestions about how to address their predicament. They encouraged novelty and created conditions whereby a small group of younger people came up with an idea to provide breakfasts to the homeless. This idea was openly accepted and created a radical change in direction for the church. The congregation was encouraged to experiment and to try out new ideas rather than try to fit their ministry within the well-worn but apparently increasing sterile internal and external service conventions. Underlying these endeavors were simple rules that were described as a "tenacious rigidity about the principle and complete flexibility about how to go about carrying out the principle"(p. 350).

Another aspect of leadership that they noted in these situations they termed "swarms." Like ants all seemingly working without direction, but ultimately cooperating extensively to achieve more than the sum of the individual ants, these swarms of people created the conditions for ideas to emerge such as the Sunday breakfasts for the homeless, and later on, spontaneously, for a doctor to establish a medical screening service at the breakfasts. Leadership from the pulpit, it was observed, consisted of reminding people of the principles and then encouraging people to respond with both integrity and creativity.

Finally, the leadership role involves making sense of what is happening and identifying what is important in the change and how it relates to the principles. In so doing, they are capturing and authoring the history and identity of the organization, effectively serving the organization as leaders, rather than the organization serving the leader. There are now many documented examples of different aspects of chaos and complexity approaches to organizations available (e.g. Holman, 2010; Priesmeyer, 1992; Sertl & Huberman, 2010; Stacey, 1992). McMillan (2008) provides an extensive range of "vignettes" that highlight different aspects of complexity in practice in various different organizations.

Inevitably, with "new science" approaches to high-stakes situations like changing or leading an organization, there will be misinterpretations of what is being attempted by people who are steeped in traditional command and control and mechanistic model approaches to people and organizations. This is a very real challenge that not only affects the large numbers of managers who continue to receive a diet of training and education based on the premise of a knowable future, but also is inherent in industrial relations and its accompanying legislation that privileges certainties of outcomes and seeks to enshrine and delimit practices. While anyone who has been employed has reason to be both frustrated by legally enshrined work practices and also thankful for their presence, these practices are unlikely to be repealed or simplified to a small set of key principles anytime soon.

Complexity approaches to organizations also face the challenge of misapplication of the key ideas. In particular, approaches that disregard the fact that any structure, including the chaotic strange attractor that we argue best describes organizations, must have limitations (i.e., principles, rules or parameters) or it can no longer be described in those terms. Thus the notion of a complete and extreme form or organizational anarchy is not a desirable or useful one and has no place in chaos approaches to organizations. In applying Chaos Theory to organizations, we have no wish to re-create the conditions that allegedly obtained at the Beatles Apple Corporation:

> the owners' hopelessness in managing their own creation: Out of his depth, a Beatle might commandeer a room at Savile Row, stick to conventional office hours and play company director until the novelty wore off. Initially, he'd look away from the disgusting realities of the half-eaten steak sandwich in a litter bin; the employee rolling a spliff of best Afghan hash; the typist who span out a single letter (in the house style, with no exclamation marks!) all morning before "popping out" and not returning until the next day. A great light dawned. "We had, like, a thousand people that weren't needed," snarled Ringo, "but they all enjoyed it. They were all getting paid for sitting around. We had a guy there just to read the tarot cards, the I Ching. It was craziness." (Clayson & Leigh, 2003, p. 256)

In summary, chaotic leadership, like all other aspects of chaos theory, is a combination and interplay of structure and experimentation, of stability and change, of developing strategies and being open to change, of recognizing responsibility and that much of what happens is no one's particular fault. Without structure and stability organizations have no basis for operating, no culture, no reputation for quality, and little trust and loyalty from their clients, customers and even employees. However, it is becoming increasingly clear that deterministic thinking has been overemphasized in organizational operations and development and that, as a consequence, the belief in planning, controlling and organizing has been correspondingly exaggerated (Mlodinow, 2009; Sanders, 1998). From the perspective of the CTC, leadership is increasingly about creating an organizational environment in which creativity, flexibility, sensitivity to non-linear change, opportunity awareness and adaptability are valued, encouraged and rewarded and which at the same time is tolerant of unusual ideas, seeking out emergent patterns and trends, questioning accepted approaches and appreciative of "noble failure" (as distinct from recklessness).

CONCLUSION

Traditional models of organizations persist in the framework of the machine metaphor with individual career development being reduced to the movement of cogs within its components. Attempts to "modern-ize" this framework by substituting "systems" concepts represent pre-dominantly, to date, a change in nomenclature rather than substance. The essential failure of such endeavors is the fundamental weakness of general systems theory as whole. It lacks a dynamic to account for the motivational drive of systems' functioning toward change and trans-formation (Butz, 1997).

The Chaos Theory of Careers (CTC) provides a new way of con-sidering organizational performance and organizational career devel-opment issues that encapsulates complexity, change, chance, stability, pattern and emergent culture. Within this framework, both individuals and their organizations can be reconceptualized as complex dynami-cal systems whose behavior produces emergent order, which in turn reproduces itself as fractal patterns of functioning over different times and contexts.

The fractal nature of organizations means that if vision, feedback, ongoing learning, creativity and experimentation are encouraged and rewarded then ideas, possibilities, trial and error, and small projects of discovery are likely to occur at varying levels within the company as ways to respond to competition, change and growth. This becomes an organizational culture that employees imbue and participate in, if they wish to remain in the company. Successful enterprises have such fractal qualities. Such a perspective demands a radical rethinking of fundamental organizational career development challenges including goal setting, strategic planning and leadership.

CHAPTER 11

Where Are We Going and Where We Have Been

The future is now, not then.

It is probably true to say that most of us most of the time view the future as a long way and a long way off. Such thinking reflects the vestiges of a deterministic perspective that current conditions (fully understood) are in the process of inescapably causing a subsequent and ultimately predetermined reality, and therefore to the extent that we can fully understand the present, we can predict that stable reality before its inexorable manifestation. Indeed, we develop courses in our universities and find institutes to address "future studies and developments." Our media are apparently endlessly replete with any number of experts prognosticating about financial markets, political actions, technological advances, social change, globalization, the environment, the weather and so on. In particular, we pay attention to those who reputedly predicted the current situation before it emerged, which in turn appears to give their current forecasts so much greater credibility. Alternatively, we pay close attention to those who analyze past events so cogently that we now seem to understand how obvious it was that what has happened just had to happen.

In our own working experience, both authors have been employed by large organizations in which the management repeatedly developed future plans to provide direction and inspiration. Structures were developed, major infrastructural and technological investments were made, new systems put in place, additional expertise recruited and budgets forecasted with five- to ten-year horizons. We would be involved in seemingly endless rounds of meetings, writing submissions, estimating costs, developing proposals and formulating policies as well as reviewing and responding to others' meeting minutes, submissions, estimates, proposals and policies. Then, not long after all these actions were initiated to bring about the grand new future we were all looking forward to experiencing and enjoying, some unanticipated event or series of events would intervene and effectively subvert all our plans and efforts. This would then occasion new efforts to respond to this new situation with reformulated grand plans. And so it would go on— planning for futures that never came. Taleb (2007) provides numerous examples of such unforeseen events and of the futility of long-term predictions and plans. Therefore the future we can actually influence is in the present and not some far off horizon that metamorphoses before we ever arrive there. This is the chaos perspective of career planning as part of the process of career development. It makes us wary of making sweeping predictions about future developments.

Paul Valery, the French novelist, was reputed to have once said that the problem for us now is that the future is not what it used to be. From a chaos theory perspective, the nature of this change is from a predetermined singular causal outcome from its preceding necessary and sufficient conditions to a future that is being formed in the present and that is inherently and intractably uncertain. Most people have no great difficulty in accepting that the future is uncertain, but it is the inherent and intractable nature of that uncertainty that most either fail to acknowledge or refuse to accept. A similar debate about quantum mechanics and the "uncertainty principle" took place in the rarefied atmosphere of theoretical physics (Lindley, 2008) and it now has become relevant in the field of career development and counseling.

Thus it is one of the themes of this book that the predominance of narrative approaches to understanding, either on a large scale such as history or on a personal scale such as the use of story in counseling, beguile us with post hoc causal explanations that suggest the inevitability of what happened. Consider, for example, major, usually adverse, events such as the 1941 bombing of Pearl Harbor. After the event, a plethora of historians' accounts seek to demonstrate how warning signs were neglected, how alternative strategies were neglected, how the leadership was complacent and so on, and that as a consequence it should have been clear that the military and naval disaster that did occur, would occur. However, as Mlodinow (2007) demonstrates, there were quite reasonable alternative scenarios that could have played out, and the actual outcome would not have been especially evident even if all the subsequent preconditions had been known and verified. As humans, we want to cling to the determinist illusion that we can, in principle, know and therefore control the future, or at least our own future. Regrettably, it is not only our politicians, media commentators and future experts of all kinds who perpetuate this myth; it not infrequently can be career counselors who exaggerate their claims about their own capacities to know and be able to predict aspects of the future. In contrast, much of this book has been ultimately devoted to addressing the career development challenges of all of us confronting an inherently and intractably uncertain future.

If confronting uncertainty is one of the major unmet challenges of contemporary thinking and practice in career development at present, so too is the issue of complexity. One of the great revelations of twentieth-century science is that the world is far more complicated, complex and diverse than most scientists at the beginning of that century could have even imagined (Peat, 2002). Some have even suggested that reality may be more complicated than the human mind can ever comprehend (Lindley, 2008). In this book, much attention has been devoted to the implications of complexity for the career development practice of counselors and the careers of their clients. Attention was drawn to the ultimate inadequacy of closed systems thinking in the face of complexity and the need for open systems thinking characterized in chaos theory terms as the strange attractor: that is, thinking and acting in light of the constant interplay of stability and change, order and disorder, plans and chance. The necessity of thinking paradoxically, of seeking out the connections between logic and creativity, the acknowledgement of mystery and transcendence, and the value of humility and luck readiness were highlighted as integral to all our responses to the implications of complexity for career development. Contemporary thinking in the career development field, it has been contended, has barely scratched the surface of such issues and, further, that the Chaos Theory of Careers is the only conceptual framework in which they can be cogently and coherently integrated.

Einstein reputedly observed that, in science, things should be kept as simple as possible but not simpler. What the career development field as a whole is beginning to acknowledge is that the range and number of influences on individuals' careers has been significantly unappreciated. The first genuinely contextual account of career development was offered by Vondracek, Lerner and Schulenberg (1986). Systems theory (McMahon & Patton, 1995) followed, along with the contextual formulation of Collin and Young (1992). However, these approaches simply lack the conceptual infrastructure to come to terms with the implications of complexity that chaos theory in general has to offer. Some of this conceptual infrastructure is scattered through the career development literature, but these invocations of concepts such as non-linearity, feedback and emergence have not been integrated into coherent theoretical perspectives.

In this book we have endeavored to demonstrate the explanatory power and theoretical promise in addressing complexity in career development of chaos theory concepts such as fractals, phase shift, emergence, non-linearity, attractors, feedback mechanisms, interconnection, the edge of chaos, self-similarity, luck readiness, the integration of convergent and emergent perspectives, the interplay of order and disorder, and sensitivity to change. The authors are also conscious that other chaos theory concepts, such as synchrony and resonance in systems, have not been applied coherently to career development to date. There is so much more to be done.

NEW DIRECTIONS AND FURTHER DEVELOPMENTS OF THE CTC

The Chaos Theory of Careers indicates new directions for the ongoing exploration of career development of individuals, specific groups, communities, organizations and even nations. The theoretical, research, counseling and consulting implications outlined below have the potential to open up new possibilities for our understanding of career development and for new ways in which we may be able to enhance the career development of individuals and the corporations in which they are employed:

- Cultural diversity is an increasingly discussed topic in career development. Global perspectives are part of the complex vision that is shaping personal aspirations and corporate enterprise. The CTC notion of attractors recursively influencing one another is a new way to understand and navigate the challenges of such diversity and globalization.
- Fractality as an explanatory device for individual career development and the functioning of community groups and organizations deserves elucidation.
- Resonance is the coalition of influences "lining up" to reinforce one another in terms of their impact. Synchronicity is a term that Carl Jung introduced which has largely escaped coherent theoretical explanation but for which the idea of resonance across influences and attractors may account.
- Spirituality in career development requires further investigation,

especially the issues of similarities across faith traditions and differences in spiritual perspectives as influences on careers. The CTC's emphasis on meaning, purpose and fulfillment in terms of the strange attractor provides a new conceptual framework for such analysis.

- Complexification of thinking is a counseling perspective that requires further development in terms of both strategy and techniques.
- Further empirical development of the Complexity Perception Index and the Luck Readiness Index is required.
- Research into understanding uncertainty and its role in career development, future planning and current adjustment is needed.
- Further explication and application of the "career wisdom" concept in counseling is also needed. How might the spiritual dimensions of the strange attractor be applied to life transitions? How do "complexity perception" strategies relate to dimensions of luck readiness for counselors and their clients?
- In theoretical terms, the conceptualization of the attractors needs to be further refined and explored to yield more powerful applications of these concepts. The relationship between each of the closed system attractors and the strange attractor needs to be explored further. What (if any) are the transformation conditions governing how and when one attractor evolves or regresses to another form of attractor? How do attractors relate to traits and states? Is attractor thinking domain specific? That is, if you have a tendency to think in terms of the torus attractor in your career, do you think likewise in your home life? How can we measure the attractors more accurately? Can different forms of strange attractors be identified within or across people, and what implications does this have for career behavior? Is there any variation in the tendency to be "stuck" within one attractor—that is, are we more likely to fall into thinking in terms of the point, pendulum, torus or strange attractors? What are the dynamics of the operation of different attractors within the one system (or individual) at the same time?

In the last century there were three revolutions in science as a whole: Einstein's relativity, quantum mechanics and chaos theory. Being the most recent, chaos theory remains the least developed theoretically, empirically researched and practically applied. In this sense it constitutes the most promising domain for new ideas, techniques and applications. Chaos theory presents a new understanding of reality and of our responsiveness to that reality. Its applications continue to be expanded across a wide range of human activity well beyond its origins in mathematics and physics. Its relevance to career development now is being increasingly appreciated. The possibilities for the future appear as uncertain to predict as in any other area of human endeavor. However, we take this to mean that in its application there are exciting possibilities for the future of career development, psychology, science and knowledge in general.

Notwithstanding the potential of the Chaos Theory of Careers for the future of career development theory, research and practice, it must also be recognized that such an approach does have limitations and challenges.

SOME LIMITATIONS AND CHALLENGES FOR THE APPLICATION OF CHAOS THEORY TO CAREER DEVELOPMENT

One of the problems of postmodernism as we have experienced it, particularly at career development conferences, is a general unwillingness, or lack of confidence, among those in the field to engage critically in debate about the strengths and limitations of ideas, concepts and theories that are variously developed and propounded. In this book we have tried to point to some such limitations in an effort to promote such constructive discourse. However, in doing so, it must of course be acknowledged that our own approach has both limitations and challenges which are yet to be overcome.

Green and Newth (2000) set out a series of "grand challenges" for complexity theory in the area of informatics, many of which apply to the CTC. Thus it is a useful place to start our considerations of limitations.

Self-Organization and Emergence

Green and Newth point out that we still understand relatively little about how patterns and structures emerge out of the interactions of components within a system. How can we get a system to reliably produce a desired emergent pattern, if indeed we can?

Non-Linearity

Capturing non-linear effects in human behavior has proved very difficult. Generally when confronted by a set of data, scientists will look for the simplest model to explain that data. This is almost always a straight line, and very often this is all that is required for the data set. However, this presupposes that the data set is truly representative, which it rarely turns out to be. Samples in studies are often opportunistically collected, for example from course credit or "volunteer" student participants. There are few longitudinal studies in the career development literature, and lifelong longitudinal studies with a representative sample are non-existent.

Data sets are thus limited in their composition and then further limited by the limited set of measurements taken using the sample. As Green and Newth (2000) point out, feedback and external constraints will act to restrict samples and measurement that act to keep processes within limited ranges, and hence the results can end up looking linear. Minbashian, Bright and Bird (2009) considered linear and non-linear modeling of datasets containing personality and job performance ratings and found that although non-linear relationships were evident, linear methods such as multiple regression were remarkably robust in mapping these relationships. Sample size and the quality of measurements were identified as general problems in establishing the presence of non-linear relationships.

These may seem like somewhat abstruse statistical concerns; however, given the centrality of the notion of non-linearity in the CTC, being able to demonstrate the presence of non-linear effects would be very valuable. It also sounds a cautionary warning to those who envisage that we may be able to use mathematical non-linear models to predict career behavior in the same manner as such models are beginning to be to used in weather forecasting.

Narrow Measures

Green and Newth (2000) argue that we may have to re-think what we mean by measurement if we are to progress our understanding of chaos and complexity approaches. In particular, they argue that the reductionist notion of restricting measurement to numerical data immediately creates problems for analyzing complex structures. They propose that we extend the definition of measurement to any procedures for data collection that satisfy criteria:

- Values are expressed within a well-defined formal language.
- Relationships between different values are defined by a model.
- A set of standards defines meaning of terms and constants in the language.

- Values are obtained by following a well-defined formal procedure.

Thus, using these criteria, "behavioral strings entered in an event recorder" and DNA sequences become measurement. Instead of then trying to apply numbers to what is normally seen as "raw data," we work with these new measures instead. In so doing, pattern recognition in many phenomena could be reinterpreted in terms of measurement. Such an approach would potentially admit new measures into our vocabulary. For instance, narrative could be construed as a measure. This move to broaden measurement opens up interesting possibilities for exploring the CTC.

Predictive Validity

As Savickas et al. (2009) point out, counselors are still attached to linear causal models of behavior and therefore continue to demand career theories that hold out the promise of predicting the future. Despite the evidence of the modest ability of traditional theories and their associated measurement tools to predict the future, nonetheless this criterion is likely to be applied to chaos theory. They point out that attempts to model fractal behavior exist in many disciplines such as meteorology, economics, mathematics and indeed within psychology. Savickas et al. (2009) argue that part of their Life Designing manifesto is to begin to model career behavior with the aim of producing "forecasts." For the very reasons that we believe career behavior is chaotic and sometimes fractal, such forecasting endeavors are fraught with problems. For instance, the lack of any rigorous formal language capturing the key concepts in the field, or indeed any agreement on what these concepts are, presents formidable barriers. However, perhaps the potentially insuperable drawback for forecasting models is the issue of sensitivity to change in initial conditions. Even supposing we can get any reasonable grasp on which variables to include in our models, we still have the problem of estimating the initial conditions. If career behavior is chaotic then sensitivity to initial conditions is one of its fundamental properties, and yet our attempts to estimate these may often amount to little more than informed or practical guessing.

Second, we believe that attempts at forecasting are likely to be more successful at the sociological rather than the individual level. While weather forecasting has greatly improved in accuracy and employs chaos-related modeling, it is still relatively inaccurate in two respects:

1. The accuracy degrades dramatically over time periods of much more than three days, and it fails completely to capture local weather effects. These failings are important, especially in careers work, because we tend to want forecasts over periods significantly longer than three days, indeed more like five years.
2. While knowing about general trends is interesting, the weather that generally matters to us is that localized to our current situation. In the same way, career forecasts that really matter to us concern us, and not some abstract general situation.

Research Methodologies

Attempts to research phenomena that are complex, interconnected and changing all at the same time continue to present challenges for chaos proponents. Reductionist models of research, characteristically indicated by the controlled environment of the laboratory, remain the most accepted and the most published research in science generally. In career development research, modified forms of reductionism continue this tradition. However, such methodologies are likely to have the effect of controlling out of the research the very essence of what it is trying to investigate. Some aspects of chaos theory are susceptible to objective measures using traditional linear statistics and psychometrics. However, those researching in the field need to begin exploring less rigorously controlled paradigms of data collection, analysis and presentation. Case studies have had a significant influence in the history of psychology and are sometimes included in volumes outlining various career development theories. However, their purpose is almost always to exemplify the counseling application of a particular theory—rather than a research investigation of its central tenets.

Elliot (2005) outlines qualitative and quantitative approaches to researching narrative in the social sciences. Since narrative has the potential to capture more of the complexity and connections within individuals' career development (notwithstanding its limitations), the methodologies she outlines may constitute a way in which research in career development could be further broadened in the quest to explore more aspects of the Chaos Theory of Careers.

FINAL COMMENTS

If the Chaos Theory of Careers as presented in this book is to assume a significant place in contemporary thinking about career development, it should be able to contribute to the career development field in those terms in which all theories in applied sciences do. What should a good theory do to contribute to its field?

- Be relevant to the major emerging challenges in the field—see Chapters 1, 9 and 10.
- Critique current perspectives in the field—see Chapters 2, 4, 5 and 10.
- Integrate existing ideas, concepts and findings—see Chapters 2, 3, 6 and 7.
- Indicate practical applications of its concepts—Chapters 7 and 8.
- Suggest new directions for research—see Chapters 6 and 11.
- Introduce new concepts and perspectives—see Chapters 4, 5, 9 and 10.
- Identify and account for concepts neglected by existing theories—see Chapters 5 and 9.

It is understandable that most people feel threatened by uncertainty, disoriented by change and overwhelmed by complexity. Human efforts to try to deal with such realities include, among other things, insurance, personal or national savings, future planning, laws and regulations, and probability theory. However valiant and useful, these measures ameliorate rather than obviate the effects of such realities. On a personal level, the human mind and the human spirit have grappled with these effects, which all of us inevitably experience, for as long as humans have been able to record their thoughts and feelings. The stories of Amanda Jones and Wang Guiying that we presented in Chapter 1 illustrate that change and complexity are ever present in all lives. The singular greatest contribution that chaos theory has made to human thinking as a whole has been to expose our human limitations in the face of these realities and their effects, and in light of such a realization to indicate ways in which we all can still live productively and meaningfully on the edge of such chaos.

Reality Checking Exercise

See Chapter 8 for a brief summary of this technique.

Aims:

- To have participants consider the nature of the decision-making context in which they make decisions by reflecting on their own experience.
- To expose some of the shortcomings of the assumptions constituting the basis for traditional matching approaches to decision making.
- To suggest that the principles of chaos theory are already in common practice but often just not recognised.

Materials: Reality Checking Checklist—hand-out and overhead of the checklist.

Procedure: Hand out the checklist.

Allow people time to complete the checklist by putting a Y or N after the question mark for each question. With a show of hands, ask participants to indicate who put Y or N for each question. Record answers on a checklist overhead with the questions on it. Focus on questions with high levels of agreement, i.e., the most Y responses. Ask participants how such agreement for a particular question might undermine the traditional matching model or what such agreement might tell you about the reality of our decision making. "Yes" responses indicate agreement with propositions derived from, or consistent with, a chaotic approach to career decision making.

Focus on questions where there is some dispute, i.e., the most number of N responses. Invite a discussion by those from "both sides" as a way to understand what the differing perspectives actually are and whether they can be reconciled. Invite those who gave Y or N responses to such questions to give an example to illustrate how they see this aspect of decision-making reality.

Invite participants to add up their Y's. From these answers, ask participants what the responses overall tell us about the realities of career decision making in our time. Invite a show of hands for the Y scores. Suggest that if their score exceeds 12 (i.e., two thirds) then they are probably chaos theorists without knowing it.

Have you ever made a decision which then had some outcomes you had never thought of at the time of deciding?	YES	NO
Has fear of taking a risk ever prevented you from doing something important in your life?	YES	NO
Have you ever wanted something, obtained it, and found out you preferred something else?	YES	NO
Have you ever had the experience of seeing a situation one way and finding out someone else sees it in a totally different way?	YES	NO
Have you ever experienced an unplanned event that had a big impact on your life?	YES	NO
When making a decision, do you sometimes just choose an option without worrying about whether it is the very best choice or not?	YES	NO
Have you ever found it an advantage not to know something?	YES	NO
Have you ever had a crisis or conversion experience that changed your life in some significant way?	YES	NO
Have you ever had the experience of being in either the right or wrong place at the right or wrong time?	YES	NO
When taking action, do you ever just follow your instincts or your intuition?	YES	NO
Have you ever relied on information when making a		

decision only to discover later that it was incorrect?	YES	NO
Have you ever distorted the truth either to yourself or to others?	YES	NO
Have you ever set a clear goal or a precise objective and discovered a better one along the way to the original goal?	YES	NO
Have any major decisions in your life been made on a basis that was not totally rational?	YES	NO
Have you ever had the experience of being told something personal about yourself, of which you were completely unaware?	YES	NO
Do you ever act before you think as a way to investigate a situation or to make a decision?	YES	NO
Have you ever experienced a "self-fulfilling prophecy"?	YES	NO
Have you ever made a small mistake that resulted in a big problem later on down the line?	YES	NO
Have you ever found wishful thinking to be an advantage?	YES	NO
Have things occurred in your life that you never thought would have been possible?	YES	NO

Signature Exercise

PROCEDURE

Ask the person or group to take a piece of paper and, when the counselor indicates, to write their signature as many times as they can in 30 seconds. Usually it is easier for them to go down the page; if they get to the bottom of the page, suggest they start another column on the same page.

At this point do not explain exactly what you, the counselor, are trying to illustrate. If clients question the relevance of the task, tell them just to trust you and that the whole task is going to take less than a minute to perform. If a client will not trust you for a minute then, as a counselor, you have major trust and empathy problems on your hands that would need to be addressed before any further counseling could proceed.

When the person is ready, show them that you will be timing them and then say "Go." Sometimes, if dealing with lower ability clients, it may be a good idea to check that they accurately understand the task.

After 30 seconds invite the client to stop. Then encourage the person to look at the pattern of signatures on the page, not for similarities in each but for the differences in some of them. Ask them to mark differences or variations in letters, capitals, spacing, size of writing, slope or overall levelness of the signatures. Most clients have no difficulty recognizing variations in the writing of their signatures. Invite them to enumerate and illustrate some of them to you. Then ask them if, at the same time, each name written is recognizably their signature. They will inevitably respond affirmatively.

Conclude by saying that the page of signatures therefore has a clear pattern of order (all the signatures are recognizably similar) but at the same time they indicate random variations (the subtle differences of graphology between some of the signatures).

This exercise could be conducted as a group task. In fact, the authors have done this at professional conferences. Very little adaptation is required. Group participants are usually invited to exchange their paper with another for the purpose of identifying the subtle changes before the paper is returned to its owner. This gives a level of independent validation of chance variations in the total array of signatures. For participants who do not know each other or for some other reason might be reluctant to divulge their signature to others, the task can be modified so that they can write the name of their employing organization, a well known product or icon name, or the name of a famous historical figure.

We try to write our signatures the same way each time for practical reasons of identification, authentication and commerce. However, because we are not photocopy machines, we cannot exactly reproduce in every detail even something as simple as our own name. Moreover, for any practical purpose we do not need to because those who want us to sign something are also aware (often unconsciously) that a signature can have variations of graphology without being a forgery. All of us recognize that signatures have a recognizable pattern while at the same time may contain chance variations in appearance. We could try to control our writing so that our signature looked identical every time by being very careful and paying close attention to detail. We might get very close to one signature being very similar to the previous one but, even if we bothered to do this, close inspection of such a signature written over time would again reveal subtle variations insinuating themselves. There are limits to our levels of control even over the writing of our own name. Why? It is the nature of reality: order and chance, predictability and unpredictability, pattern and random variation. Once accepted, this may become a mindset for career development counseling focusing on what can be ordered, predicted and controlled, and what can not.

In counseling quadrant terms (see Bright & Pryor, 2007), the signature exercise helps the client move from the left-hand quadrants associated with low emergent knowledge to higher levels of emergent knowledge. By illustrating that we are more than endless repetitions of behavior, the exercise helps a client to move away from self-descriptions solely in terms of convergent qualities.

The Limitations of Knowledge in Decision-Making Exercise

PRINCIPLE

Chaos theory emphasizes the complexity of the range of influences on career development and the incompleteness of our knowledge always at the point of decision making.

LEARNING MESSAGE

We make decisions often with incomplete knowledge; we learn as we experience or live out the implications of such decisions and adapt as well as can as we go along.

ACTIVITY

1. Ask participants to bring to mind two or three important decisions that they have made in the past. (They do not have to be work related but they can be.) Some examples could include a change of residence, an exotic holiday destination, a choice of partner, a change of job/employer/career and so on.
2. Ask participants to write down these important decisions, and for each decision to write answers these four questions:

   a) What did you know about the alternatives you had at the time of your decision?
   b) How did you find out more information before choosing? (What strategies if any, did you use?)

    c) What did you find out, that you did not know before you made the decision, after you had made the decision?

    d) What changes did this new knowledge cause you to make? (Allow 5–10 mins.)

3. Invite participants to pair up to share and discuss their answers to one decision each. (Allow 5–10 mins.)
4. Plenary session: Invite participants to provide general answers to the four questions. Focus attention on the initial incompleteness of their knowledge and on "the surprises" that they discovered after choosing.

WRAP-UP

\# Most important decisions we make in our lives are made with incomplete and not infrequently inaccurate knowledge.

\# Inevitably, this means that our decision making cannot be rigorously logical or totally rational.

\# As a consequence, virtually all our important decisions have a degree of uncertainty, which we tend to disregard or suppress.

\# We often think we know more and are more in control of our decision making than we actually are.

\# To continue this "illusion," we often rationalize the benefits of a decision after we have made it to make what we have decided seem more reasonable and logical—psychologists call this the process of "cognitive dissonance."

\# We learn from our decisions as we "live with them"—of course, this learning may be correct or incorrect, helpful or destructive.

\# As a consequence of this learning, we adopt strategies of adaptation—we may change ourselves, we may influence others and/or we may change our circumstances, situation, environment.

\# The direction of such adaptation is likely to be in order to contribute to the overall goal we had at the beginning of the decision-making process. This is what some chaos theorists refer to as a fractal pattern of the strange attractor.

\# But not necessarily, since the experience of decision making, learning and adaptation and change may have been radical enough to cause us to redefine or even jettison one or more of our goals. Chaos theorists usually designate such radical changes as "phase shifts."

\# These experiences and processes then become the bases on which the next decision or series of decisions will be made.

BIBLIOGRAPHY

Abraham, F. & Gilgen, A. (eds.). (1995). *Chaos theory in psychology*. Westport, CT: Praeger.

Abrahamson, E. & Freedman, D. H. (2007). *A perfect mess: The hidden benefits of disorder*. New York: Little, Brown, & Co.

Adams, M. (2003). Creating a personal collage to assist with career development. In M. McMahon & W. Patton (eds.), *Ideas for career practitioners: Celebrating excellence in Australian career practice* (pp. 4–7). Brisbane, Qld: Australian Academic Press.

Allen, W. (Director), Wiley, G. (Producer), Tennebaum, S. (Producer). (2005). *Match Point*. [Motion Picture]. United States. Dreamworks.

Amundson, N. (2003a). *Active engagement: Enhancing the career counseling process*. Richmond, BC: Ergon Communications.

Amundson, N. (2003b). *The physics of living*. Richmond, BC: Ergon Communications.

Amundson, N. (2005). The potential impact of global changes in work for career theory and practice. *International Journal for Educational and Vocational Guidance, 5*, 91–99.

Amundson, N. E. (2006). Walking the yellow brick road. *Journal of Employment Counseling, 43*, 31–38.

Amundson, N. (2009). *Active engagement: Enhancing the career counseling process* (3rd ed.). Richmond, BC: Ergon Communications.

Amundson, N. E., Harris-Bowlsbey, J. A. & Niles, S. G. (2005). *Essential elements of career counseling: Processes and techniques*. Upper Saddle River, NJ: Pearson.

Amundson, N., Poehnell, G. & Pattern, N. (2005). *Careerscope: Looking in, looking out, looking around*. Richmond: BC. Ergon Communications.

Anygal, A. (1941). *Foundations for a science of personality*. New York, NY: The Commonwealth Fund.

Ariely, D. (2008). *Predictability irrational: The hidden forces that shape our decisions*. New York, NY: Harper.

Arnold, J. (2004) The congruence problem in John Holland's theory of vocational decisions. *Journal of Occupational and Organizational Psychology, 77*, 95–1.

Arthur, M. B. & Rousseau, D. M. (eds.). (1996) *The boundaryless career: A new employment principle for a new organizational era*. New York, NY: Oxford University Press.

Ashmos, B. E. & Duchon, D. (2000). Spirituality at work. *Journal of Managerial Inquiry, 9*, 134–145.

Assouline, M. & Meir, E. I. (1987). Meta-analysis of the relationship between congruence and well-being measures. *Journal of Vocational Behavior, 31*, 319–332.

Athanasou, J A. (1999). Judgements of interest in vocational education subjects. *Australian and New Zealand Journal of Vocational Education Research, 7(1)*, 60–76.

Australian Bureau of Statistics (2008) Report 4719.0 – Overweight and Obesity in Adults, Australia, 2004–05.

Baker, D. B. (2009). Choosing a vocation at 100: Time change, and context. *Career Development Quarterly, 57(3)*, 199–206.

Bandura, A. (1994). Self-efficacy. In V. S. Ramachaudran (ed.), *Encyclopedia of human behavior* (Vol. 4, pp. 71–81). New York, NY: Academic Press.

Barabasi, A.-L. (2003). *Linked: How everything is connected to everything else and what it means for business, science, and everyday life*. New York, NY: Penguin.

Baruch, Y. (2004). *Managing careers: Theory and practice*. Edinburgh: Pearson.

Beavis, A., Curtis, D., & Curtis, N. (2005). *Junior secondary school students' perceptions of the world of work: A report prepared for The Smith Family*. Camberwell, Australia: Australian Council for Educational Research.

Bergmann, P. G. (1976). *Introduction to relativity*. New York, NY: Dover.

Berne, E. (1964). *Games people play: The psychology of human relationships*. New York, NY: Grove Press.

Betsworth, D. G. & Hanson, J. C. (1996). The categorization of serendipitous career development events. *Journal of Career Assessment, 4*, 91–98.

Betz, E. L. (1984). A study of career patterns of college graduates. *Journal of Vocational Behaviour, 24*, 249–264.

Betz, N. E. (2004). Contributions of self-efficacy theory to career counseling: A personal perspective. *The Career Development Quarterly, 52(4)*, 340–354.

Betz, N. E. &. Klein, K. (1997). Efficacy and outcome expectations influence career exploration and decidedness. *The Career Development Quarterly, 46(2)*, 179–189.

Bissonnette, D. (1994). *Beyond traditional job development: The art of creating opportunity*. Chatsworth, CA: Mill Wright and Associates.

Bloch, D. P. (2005). Complexity, chaos, and nonlinear dynamics: A new perspective on career development theory. *Career Development Quarterly, 53(3)*, 194–207.

Bloch, D. P. & Richmond, L. J. (eds.). (1997). *Connections between spirit & work in career development*. Palo Alto, CA: Davies-Black.

Bloch, D. P. (1997). Spirituality, intentionality and career success: The quest for meaning. In D. P. Bloch & L. J. Richmond (eds.). *Connections between spirit & work in career development* (pp. 25–208). Palo Alto, CA: Davies-Black.

Bloch, D. P. (2006). Spirituality and careers. In J. H. Greenhaus & G. A. Callanan (eds.), *Encyclopedia of career development* (Vols. 1 & 2, pp. 762–764). Thousand Oaks, CA: Sage.

Bloch & L. J. Richmond (eds.), *Connections between spirit & work in career development* (pp. 85–208). Palo Alto, CA: Davies-Black.

Blustein, D. L. (1989). The role of goal instability and career self-efficacy in the career exploration process. *Journal of Vocational Behavior, 35(2)*, 194–203.

Blustein, D. L., Pauling, M. L., Delvlania, M. E. & Faye, M. (1994). Relation between exploratory and choice factors and decisional progress. *Journal of Vocational Behavior, 44(1)*, 75–90.

Bolles, R. (2008). *What color is your parachute.* Berkley, CA: Ten Speed.

Booker, C. (2004). *The seven basic plots. Why we tell stories.* London, UK: Continuum Press.

Borg, T., Bright, J. E. H. & Pryor, R. G. L. (2006). The Butterfly Model of careers: Illustrating how planning and chance can be integrated in the careers of high school students. *Australian Journal of Career Development, 15(3)*, 53–58.

Boulding, K. (1956). General systems theory: The skeleton of science. *Management Science, 2(3)*, 197–208.

Briddick, W. C. (2009). Frank findings: Frank Parsons and the Parson family. *Career Development Quarterly, 57(3)*, 207–214.

Briggs, J. (1992). *Fractals the patterns of chaos: Discovering a new aesthetic of art, science and nature.* New York, NY: Simon & Schuster.

Briggs, J. & Peat, F. D. (1989). *Turbulent mirror: An illustrated guide to chaos theory and the science of wholeness.* Grand Rapids, NY: Harper & Row.

Briggs, J. & Peat, F. D. (1999). *Seven lessons of chaos: Spiritual wisdom from the science of change.* New York, NY: Harper Collins.

Bright, J. E. H. (2003). *Should I stay or should I go: How to make that crucial job move decision.* Edinburgh, UK: Pearson.

Bright, J. E. H. (2008a). Shift happens. *Australian Career Practitioner, 19(2)*, 18–20.

Bright, J. E. H. (2008b). The Factory Podcast. [Podcast]. Retrieved July 2, 2008, from www.brightandassociates.com.au/wordpress/.

Bright, J. E. H. (2009a). Beyond Personal Mastery®. Retrieved January 1, 2010 from www.beyondpersonalmastery.com.

Bright, J. E. H. (2009b). Beyond Corporate Mastery®. Retrieved January 1, 2010 from www.beyondcorporatemastery.com.

Bright, J. E. H. & Burton, A. M. (1994). Past midnight: Semantic processing in an implicit learning task. *Quarterly Journal of Experimental Psychology, 47(1)*, 71–89.

Bright, J. E. H. & Burton, A. M. (1998). Ringing the changes: Where abstraction occurs in implicit learning. *European Journal of Cognitive Psychology, 10(2)*, 113–130.

Bright, J. E. H. & Pryor, R. G. L. (2003). The exploring influences on career development technique. In M. McMahon & W. Patton (eds.), *Celebrating excellence in Australian career practice: Ideas for career practitioners* (pp. 49–53). Brisbane: Australian Academic Press.

Bright, J. E. H. & Pryor, R. G. L. (2005a). The chaos theory of careers: A user's guide. *Career Development Quarterly, 53(4)*, 291–305.

Bright, J. E. H. & Pryor, R. G. L. (2005b). *The Complexity Perception Index.* Sydney, NSW: Bright and Associates/Congruence Pty Ltd.

Bright, J. E. H. & Pryor, R. G. L. (2005c). *The Complexity Perception Index: Manual.* Sydney, NSW: Bright and Associates/Congruence Pty Ltd.

Bright, J. E. H. & Pryor, R. G. L. (2007). Chaotic careers assessment: How constructivist and psychometric techniques can be integrated into work and life decision making. *Career Planning and Adult Development Journal, 23(2),* 30–45.

Bright, J. E. H. & Pryor, R. G. L. (2008). Shiftwork: A Chaos Theory of Careers agenda for change in career counselling. *Australian Journal of Career Development, 17(3),* 63–72.

Bright, J. E. H., Pryor, R. G. L. & Harpham, L. (2005). The role of chance events in career decision making. *Journal of Vocational Behavior, 66,* 561–576.

Bright, J. E. H., Pryor, R. G. L., Wilkenfeld, S & Earl, J. (2005). Influence of social context on career decision-making. *International Journal for Educational and Vocational Guidance, 5(1),* 19–36.

Bright, J. E. H., Pryor, R. G. L., Chan, E. & Rijanto, J. (2009). The dimensions of chance career episodes. *Journal of Vocational Behavior, 75(1),* 14–25.

Brooks, L. (1978). Non-analytic concept formation and memory for instances. In E. Rosch & B. Lloyd (eds.). *Cognition and categorisation* (pp. 169–211). Hillsdale, NJ: Erlbaum.

Bronfenbrenner, U. (1979). *The ecology of human development.* Cambridge, MA: Harvard University Press.

Bronfenbrenner, U. (1989). Ecological systems theory. In R. Vasta (ed.). *Annals of Child Development, 6,* 185–251. Greenwich, CN: JAI Press.

Brott, P. (2001). The storied approach: A postmodern perspective for career counseling. *Career Development Quarterly, 49,* 304–313.

Brown, C., Glastetter-Fender, C. & Shelton, M. (2000). Psychosocial identity and career control in college student-athletes. *Journal of Vocational Behavior, 56(1),* 53–62.

Brown, D. &. Brooks, L. (eds.). (1996). *Career choice and development.* San Francisco, CA: Jossey-Bass.

Brown, D. (2007). *Career information, career counseling and career development* (9th ed.). Boston, MA: Pearson.

Bujold, C. (2004). Constructing career through narrative. *Journal of Vocational Behavior, 64,* 470–484.

Burke, M. T., Chauvin, J. C. & Miranti, J. C. (2005). *Religious and spiritual issues in counseling: Applications across diverse populations.* New York, NY: Brunner-Routledge.

Butz, M. R. (1995). Chaos theory: Philosophically old, scientifically new. *Counseling and Values, 39,* 84–98.

Butz, M. R. (1997). *Chaos and complexity: Implications for psychological theory and practice.* Washington, DC: Taylor & Francis.

Buzan, A. (1986). *Use your memory.* London: BBC Publications.

Buzan, A. (1993). *The mind map book.* London, UK: Penguin.

Byrne, S. (2001). *Optimism boosters.* Bendigo, Vic: Innovative Resources

Cabral, A. C. & Salomone, P. R. (1990). Chance and careers: Normative versus contextual development. *Career Development Quarterly, 39(1),* 5–17.

Caplow, T. (1954). *The sociology of work.* Minneapolis, MN: Minnesota University Press.

Chen, C. P. (2005). Understanding career chance. *International Journal for Educational and Vocational Guidance, 5*, 251–270.

Chester, A. & Glass, C. A. (2006). Online counselling: A descriptive analysis of therapy services on the internet. *British Journal of Guidance and Counselling, 34(2)*, 145–160.

Chiles, Meyer & Hench (2004), as cited in Plowman, D. Solanksy, S. Beck, T. Baker, L, Kulkarni, M. & Travis, D. (2007). The role of leadership in emergent, self-organization. *Leadership Quarterly, 18*, 341–356.

Chown, M. (2007). *Quantum theory cannot hurt you: A guide to the universe.* London, UK: Faber & Faber.

Christensen, T. K. & Johnston, J. A. (2003). Incorporating the narrative in career planning. *Journal of Career Development, 29(3)*, 149–159.

Clayson, A. & Leigh, S. (2003). *The Walrus was Ringo: 101 Beatles myths debunked* (p. 256). New Malden, Surrey: Chrome Dreams.

Cochran, L. (1997). *Career counseling: A narrative approach.* Thousand Oaks, CA: Sage.

Collin, A. (1990). Mid-life career change research. In R. A. Young & W. A. Borgen (eds.), *Methodological approaches to the study of career* (pp. 197–220). New York, NY: Praeger Publishers.

Collin, A. & Young, R. A. (1992). Constructing career through narrative and context: An interpretive perspective. In R. A. Young & A. Collin (eds.), *Interpreting career: Hermeneutical studies of lives in context* (pp. 1–12). Westport, CT: Praeger.

Colozzi, E. A. (2007). Spirituality, career development and calling: Emergent phenomena. Paper presented at NCDA Global Conference, Seattle on July 8, 2007.

Colozzi, E. A. & Colozzi, L. C. (2000). College students' callings: An integrated values-oriented perspective. In D. A. Luzzo (ed.), *Career counseling of college students: An empirical guide to strategies that work* (pp. 63–91). Washington, DC: American Psychological Association.

Conger, J. A. (1994). *Spirit at work.* San Francisco, CA: Jossey-Bass.

Covey, S. R. (1989). *The seven habits of highly effective people: Restoring the character ethic.* Melbourne, Vic: The Business Library.

Covey, S. R. (2004). *The 8th habit: From effectiveness to greatness.* New York, NY: Free Press.

Crutchfield, J. P., Farmer, J. D., Packard, N. H. & Shaw, R. S. (1986). Chaos. *Scientific American, 255(6)*, 46–57.

Darling, D. (2005). *Networking for career success.* New York, NY: McGraw Hill.

Darwin, C. (1859). *The origin of the species.* London, UK: Murray.

Davey, R., Bright, J. E. H., Pryor, R. G. L. & Levin, K. (2005). Of never quite knowing what I might be: chaotic counselling with university students. *Australian Journal of Career Development, 14(2)*, 53–62.

Dawis, R. (1996). The theory of work adjustment and person-environment-correspondence counseling. In D. Brown, L. Brooks & Associates (eds.), *Career choice & development* (3rd ed.) (pp. 75–120). San Francisco, CA: Jossey-Bass.

Dawis, R. V. & Lofquist, L. H. (1984). *A psychological theory of work adjustment.* Minneapolis, MN: University of Minnesota Press.

Deal, R., Masman, K. (2004). *Signposts: Exploring everyday spirituality.* Bendigo, Vic: Innovative Resources.

Denga, D. I. (1984). Locus of control and its relationship to occupational choice behaviour. *International Review of Applied Psychology, 33(3),* 371–379.

Dewdney, A. K. (2004). *Beyond reason: Eight great problems that reveal the limits of science.* Hoboken, NJ: Wiley.

Donovan, J. J. & Radosovich, D. J. (1998). The moderating role of goal commitment on the goal difficulty–performance relationship: A meta-analytic review and critical reanalysis. *Journal of Applied Psychology, 83,* 308–315.

Drafke, M. (2006). *The human side of organizations* (9th ed.). Upper Saddle River, NJ: Pearson.

Duchon, D. & Plowman, D. A. (2005). Nurturing the spirit at work: Impact on work unit performance. *Leadership Quarterly, 16,* 807–833.

Duggan, W. (2007). *Strategic intuition: The creative spark in human achievement.* New York, NY: Columbia University Press.

Durschmied, E. (2000). *The hinge factor: How chance and stupidity have changed history.* New York: Arcade.

Dutton, J. E. (2003). *Energize your workplace.* San Francisco, CA: Jossey-Bass.

Edelman, S. (2002). *Change your thinking.* Sydney, NSW: ABC Books.

Elliot, J. (2005). *Using narrative in social research: Qualitative and quantitative approaches.* London, UK: Sage.

Ellis, A. (1969). A cognitive approach to behavior therapy. *International Journal of Psychiatry 8,* 896–900.

Fergle, J. (2007, July). Using metaphors, myths and fables in career development and job search. Paper presented at NCDA Global Conference, Seattle, WA.

Ford, D. H. (1987). Implications for counseling, psychotherapy, health, and human services of the living systems framework (LSF). In M. E. Ford & D. H. Ford (eds.), *Humans as self-constructing living systems: Putting the framework to work* (pp. 347–375). Hillsdale, NJ: Lawrence Erlbaum Associates.

Fox, M. (1994). *The reinvention of work.* San Francisco, CA: Harper.

Frankl, V. (1984) *Man's search of meaning.* New York, NY: Washington Square Press/Pocket Books.

Friedman, T. L. (2005). *The world is flat. A brief history of the twenty-first century.* New York, NY: Farrar, Straus and Giroux.

Gable, R. K., Thompson, D. L. & Glanstein, P. J. (1976). Perceptions of personal control and conformity of vocational choice as correlates of vocational development. *Journal of Vocational Behavior, 8(3),* 259–267.

Galassi, J. P., Crace, R. K., Martin, G. A., James, R. M. & Wallace, R. L. (1992). Client preferences and anticipations in career counseling: A preliminary investigation. *Journal of Counseling Psychology, 39,* 46–55.

Gelatt, H. B. (1989). Positive uncertainty: A new decision making framework for counseling. *Journal of Counseling Psychology, 36,* 252–256.

Gelatt, H. B. (1991). *Creative decision making: Using positive uncertainty.* Los Altos, CA: Crisp Publications.

Gell-Mann, M. (1994). *The quark and the jaguar: Adventures in the simple and the complexity.* New York, NY: Freeman.

Gharajedaghi, J. (1999). *System thinking: Managing chaos and complexity: A platform for designing business architecture*. Boston, MA: Butterworth-Heinemann.

Gillham, J. E. (ed.). (2000). *The science of optimism and hope: Research essays in honor of Martin E. P. Seligman*. Radnor, PA: Templeton Foundation Press.

Gladwell, M. (2000). *The tipping point: How little things can make a big difference*. New York, NY: Time Warner.

Gleick, J. (1987). *Chaos: The making of a new science*. London, UK: Heinemann.

Goldman, L. (1972). Tests and counseling: The marriage that failed. *Measurement and Evaluation in Guidance, 4*, 213–220.

Gottfredson, L. S. (1981). Circumscription and compromise: A developmental theory of occupational aspirations (Monograph). *Journal of Counseling Psychology, 28*, 545–579.

Gottfredson, L. S. (1996). Gottfredson's theory of circumscription and compromise. In D. Brown & L. Brooks (eds.), *Career choice and development* (3rd ed.) (pp. 179–232). San Francisco, CA: Jossey-Bass.

Gottfredson, L. S. (2006). Circumscription and compromise. In J. H. Greenhaus (ed.), *Encyclopedia of career development*. Thousand Oaks, CA: Sage.

Goudge, E. (1959). *Saint Francis of Assisi*. London, UK: Hodder and Stoughton.

Gould, S. J. (1991). *Ever since Darwin: Reflections in natural history*. New York, NY: W. H. Norton.

Gredge, R. (2008). Online counselling services at Australian universities. *Journal of the Australian and New Zealand Student Services, 31*, April, 4–22.

Green, D. G. & Newth, D. (2000) Towards a theory of everything? Grand challenges in complexity and informatics. *Complexity International (8)*. Retrieved www.complexity.orgu.au/vol08.green05, 6/3/2010

Green, L. & Sharman-Burke, J. (2000). *The mythic journey: The meaning of myth as a guide for life*. New York, NY: Fireside.

Greenberg, J. & Barron, R. A. (2000). *Behavior in organizations: Understanding and managing the human side of work*. Upper Saddle River, NJ: Prentice Hall.

Greene, B. (1999). *The elegant universe: Superstrings, hidden dimensions and the quest for the ultimate theory*. New York, NY: W. W. Norton.

Greenhaus, J. H. & Callanan, G. A. (2006). *Encyclopedia of career development* (Vols. 1 & 2). Thousand Oaks, CA: Sage.

Grinyer, P. H. & Norburn, D. (1975). Planning for existing markets: Perceptions of executives and financial performance. *Journal of the Royal Statistical Society, Series A, 138*, 70–97.

Guindon, M. H. & Hanna, F. J. (2002). Coincidence, happenstance, serendipity, fate, or the hand of god: Case studies in synchronicity. *Career Development Quarterly, 50*, 195–209.

Guiness, O. (1976). *Doubt: Faith in two minds*. Berkhamsted, UK: Lion.

Guiness, O. (2003). *The call: Finding and fulfilling the central purpose of your life*. Nashville, TN: Thomas Nelson.

Gutteridge, T. G., Leibowitz, Z. B. & Shore, J. E. (1993). *Organizational career development*. San Francisco, Jossey-Bass.

Gysbers, N. C. (2006). Using qualitative career assessments in career counselling with adults. *International Journal for Educational and Vocational Guidance, 6*, 95–108.

Hall, D. T. (2002). *Careers in and out of organizations*. Thousand Oaks, CA: Sage Publications.

Handy, C. (1989). *The age of unreason*. London, UK: Business Books.

Harkness, H. (1997). *The career chase: Taking creative control in a chaotic age*. Palo Alto, CA: Davies-Black.

Harren, V. A. (1979). A model of career decision making of college students. *Journal of Vocational Behavior, 14*, 119–133.

Harrington, T. & O'Shea, A. (1992). *Harrington-O'Shea Career Decision Making System*. Circle Pines, MN: American Guidance Service.

Hart, D. H., Rayner, K. & Christensen, E. R. (1971). Planning, preparation, and chance in occupational entry. *Journal of Vocational Behavior, 1(3)*, 279–285.

Harvey, C. S. & Harrild, B. E. (2005). *Comfortable chaos*. Bellingham, WA: Self-Counsel Press.

Heppner, M. J., Multon, K. & Johnston, J. A. (1994). Assessing psychological resources during career change: Development of the Career Transitions Inventory. *Journal of Vocational Behavior, 44*, 55–74.

Herriot, P. C. & Pemberton, C. (1966). Contracting careers. *Human Relations 49(6)*, 757–790.

Hintzman, D. L. (1990). Human learning and memory: Connections and dissociations. *Annual Review of Psychology, 41*, 109–139.

Holland, J. H. (1995). *Hidden order: How adaptation builds complexity*. Cambridge, MA: Perseus Books.

Holland, J. H. (1998). *Emergence: From chaos to order*. Reading, MA: Addison-Wesley.

Holland, J. L. (1959). A theory of vocational choice. *Journal of Counseling Psychology, 6*, 35–45.

Holland J. L. (1973). *Making vocational choices: A theory of careers*. Englewood Cliffs, NJ: Prentice Hall.

Holland, J. L. (1997). *Making vocational choices: A theory of vocational personalities and work environments* (3rd ed.). Odessa, FL: Psychological Assessment Resources.

Holland, J. L. (1999). *Self-directed search*. Lutz, FL: Psychological Assessment Resources, Inc.

Holman, P. (2010). *Engaging emergence: Turning upheaval into opportunity*. San Francisco, CA: Berret-Koehler.

Hultman, K. (1998). *Making change irresistible*. Palo Alto, CA: Davies-Black.

Ibarra, H. (2003). *Working identity: Unconventional strategies for reinventing your career*. Boston, MA: Harvard Business School Press.

Inkson, K. (2007). *Understanding careers: The metaphors of working lives*. Thousand Oaks, CA: Sage.

Inkson, K. & Amundson, N. (2002). Career metaphors and their application in theory and counseling practice. *Journal of Employment Counseling, 39*, 98–108.

Inkson, K., Lazarova, M. B. & Thomas, D. C. (2005). Global careers. *Journal of World Business, 44*, 349–440.

Isaacson, L.E. & Brown, D. (2000). *Career information, career counseling, and career development* (7th ed). Boston, MA : Allyn & Bacon.

James, C. (2006). *The north face of Soho*. London, UK: Picador.

Janis, I. L. & Mann, L. (1977). *Decision making*. New York, NY: Free Press.

Jantsch, E. (1980). *The self-organizing universe, scientific and human implications of the emerging paradigm of evolution*. New York, NY: Pergamon.

Jepsen, D. A. & Choudhuri, E. (2001). Stability and change in 25-year occupational career patterns. *Career Development Quarterly, 50,* 3–19.

Jones, F. & Bright, J. E. H. (2001). *Stress: Myth, theory and research*. London. UK: Prentice Hall.

Jones, F., Bright, J. E. H., Searle, B. & Cooper, L. (1999). Modelling occupational stress and health: The impact of the demand–control model on academic research and on workplace practice. *Stress Medicine, 14,* 231–236.

Johnson, S. (1999). *Who moved my cheese? An amazing way to deal with change in your work and in your life*. New York, NY: Putnam.

Johnston, G. (2000). *Aligning your work and purpose: Step out to an abundant life*. Melbourne, Vic: Information Australia.

Jung, C. G. (1974). *Dreams* (trans. R. F. C. Hull). Princeton, NY: Princeton University Press.

Katz, D. & Kahn, R. L. (1966). *The social psychology of organizations*. New York, NY: John Wiley.

Kauffman, S. A. (1995). *At home in the universe*. New York, NY: Oxford University.

Kellert, S. (1993). *In the wake of chaos: Unpredictable order in dynamical systems*. Chicago, IL: University of Chicago Press.

Kinjerski, V. & Skrypnek, B. J. (2008). Four paths to spirit at work: Journeys of personal meaning, fulfillment, well-being, and transcendence through work. *Career Development Quarterly, 56(4),* 319–329.

Kossman, M. R. & Bullrich, S. (1997). Systematic chaos: Self-organizing systems and the process of change. In F. Masterpasqua & P. Perna (eds.), *The psychological meaning of chaos: Translating theory into practice* (pp. 199–224). Washington, DC: APA.

Krause, K. L., Bochner, S. & Duchesne, S. (2006). *Educational psychology for learning and teaching* (2nd ed). Melbourne: Thompson.

Krumboltz, J. D. (1979). A social learning theory of career decision making. Revised and reprinted in A. M. Mitchell, G. B. Jones, and J. D. Krumboltz (eds.), *Social learning and career decision making* (pp. 19–49). Cranston, RI: Carroll Press.

Krumboltz, J. D. (1994). Improving career development theory from a social learning perspective. In M. L. Savickas & R. L. Lent (eds.), *Convergence in career development theories* (pp. 9–31). Palo Alto, CA: CPP Books.

Krumboltz, J. D. (1998). Serendipity is not serendipitous. *Journal of Counseling Psychology, 4,* 390–392.

Krumboltz, J. D. & Levin, A. S. (2004). *Luck is no accident: Making the most of happenstance in your life and career*. Atascadero, CA: Impact.

Kuhn, T. (1962). *The structure of scientific revolutions*. Chicago, IL: University of Chicago Press.

Kurzweil, R. (1999). *The age of spiritual machines: When computers exceed human intelligence*. New York, NY: Penguin.

Laszlo, E. (1991). *The age of bifurcation: Understanding the changing world.* Philadelphia, PA: Gordon & Breach Science Publishers.

Lefcourt, H. M. (1966). Internal versus external control of reinforcement: A review. *Psychological Bulletin, 65(4),* 206–220.

Lefcourt, H. M. (1976). Locus of control: Current trends in theory and research. In *Locus of control: Current trends in theory and research* (pp. 3–17). Hillsdale, NJ: Erlbaum; New York: Distributed by Halsted Press.

Lent, R. W., Brown, S. D. & Hackett, G. (1994). Towards a unifying social cognitive theory of career and academic interest, choice and performance. *Journal of Vocational Behavior, 45,* 79–122.

Lent, R. W., Brown, S. D., Talleyrand, R., McPartland, E. B., Davis, T., Chopra, S. B., Alexander, M. S., Suthakaran, V. & Chai, C.-M. (2002). Career choice barriers, supports and coping strategies: College students' experiences. *Journal of Vocational Behavior, 60,* 61–72.

Lenz, J. (2008). Translating theory to practice: A Cognitive Information Processing (CIP) approach to career development and services. Keynote Address to the Annual Conference of the Australian Association of Career Counsellors. March, Hobart, Australia.

Leong, F. (1996). Challenges to career counseling. In M. L. Savickas & W. B. Walsh (eds.), *Handbook of career counseling theory and practice* (pp. 333–346). Palo Alto, CA: Davies-Black.

Lewin, K. (1951). *Field theory in social science: Selected theoretical papers.* D. Cartwright (ed.). New York, NY: Harper & Row.

Lewis, J. & Coursol, D. (2007). Addressing career issues online: Perceptions of counselor education professionals. *Journal of Employment Counseling, 44(4),* 146–153.

Lewis, M. D. & Junyk, N. (1997). The self-organization of psychological defenses. In F. Masterpasqua & P. A. Perna (eds.), *The psychological meaning of chaos: Translating theory into practice* (pp. 41–73). Washington, DC: American Psychological Association.

Li, T. Y. & Yorke, J. A. (1975). Period three implies chaos. *American Mathematical Monthly, 82,* 985–992.

Lindley, D. (2008). *Uncertainty: Einstein, Heisenberg, Bohr, and the struggle for the soul of science.* New York, NY: Anchor.

Lips-Wiersma, M. (2002). The influence of spiritual "meaning-making" on career behavior. *Journal of Management Development, 21(7),* 497–520.

Livneh, H. & Parker, R. M. (2005). Psychological adaptation to disability: Perspectives from chaos and complexity theory. *Rehabilitation Counseling Bulletin, 49(1),* 17–28.

Loader, T. (2009). Careers Collage: Applying an Art therapy technique to career development in a secondary school setting. *Australian Careers Practitioner,* Summer, 16–17.

Lorenz, E. (1993). *The essence of chaos.* Seattle, WA: University of Washington Press.

Maccoby, M. (1976). *The gamesman: The new corporate leaders.* New York, NY: Simon and Schuster.

Mandelbrot, B. (1975). *Les objets fractals: Forme, hazard et dimension.* Paris: Flammarion.

Mandelbrot, B. (1977). *Fractals: Form, chance and dimension.* San Francisco, CA: WH Freeman and Company.

Mandelbrot, B. (1982). *The fractal nature of geometry.* San Francisco, CA: WH Freeman and Company.

Masterpasqua, F. (1997). Toward a dynamical developmental understanding of disorder. In F. Masterpasqua & P. A. Perna (eds.), *The psychological meaning of chaos: Translating theory into practice* (pp. 23–40). Washington, DC: American Psychological Association.

Marecek, J. & Frasch, C. (1977). Locus of control and college women's role expectations. *Journal of Counseling Psychology, 24(2),* 132–136.

Marks-Tarlow, T. (1995). The fractal geometry of human nature. In R. Robertson & A. Combs (eds.), *Chaos theory in psychology and the life sciences* (pp. 275–283). Mahwah, NJ: Erlbaum.

Masterpasqua, F. & Perna, P. A. (eds.) (1997). *The psychological meaning of chaos: Translating theory into practice.* Washington, DC: American Psychological Association.

Maxwell, J. C. (1873). *A treatise on electricity and magnetism.* Oxford, UK: Clarendon Press.

McCormick, R., Amundson, N. & Poehnell, G. (2006). *Guiding circles: An Aboriginal guide to finding career paths.* Richmond, BC: Ergon Communications.

McCrae, R. R. & Costa, P. T. (1987). Validation of the five factor model of personality across instruments and observers. *Journal of Personality and Social Psychology, 56,* 81–90.

McIlveen, P. & Patton, W. 2006. A critical reflection on career development. *International Journal for Educational and Vocational Guidance, 6,* 15–27.

McKay, H., Bright, J. E. H. & Pryor, R. G. L. (2005) Finding order and direction from chaos: A comparison of complexity career counseling and trait matching counselling. *Journal of Employment Counseling, 42(3),* Sep 2005, 98–112.

McMahon, M. & Patton, W. (1995). Development of a systems theory framework of career development. *Australian Journal of Career Development, 4,* 81–88.

McMahon, M. & Patton, W. (2002a). Assessment: A continuum of practice and a new location in career counselling. *International Careers Journal, 3(4)* (The Global Careers-Work Café). Available: www.careers-cafe.com.

McMahon, M. & Patton, W. (2002b). Using qualitative assessment in career counselling. *International Journal of Educational and Vocational Guidance, 2(1),* 51–66.

McMillan, E. (2008). *Complexity, management and dynamics of change: Challenges for practice.* Oxford, UK: Routledge.

Mealey, L. Bridgstock, R. & Townsend, G. C. (1999). Symmetry and perceived facial attractiveness: A monozygotic co-twin comparison. *Journal of Personality and Social Psychology, 76(1),* 151–158.

Medawar, P. B. (1967). *The art of the soluble.* Oxford, UK: Oxford University Press.

Mercer, R. T., Nichols, E. G. & Doyle, G. C. (1988). Transitions over the life cycle: A comparison of mothers and nonmothers. *Nursing Research, 37(3),* 144–151.

Mieromont, J. (ed.) (1995). *The dictionary of family therapy*. Oxford, UK: Blackwell Reference.

Miller, M. J. (1983). The role of happenstance in career choice. *Vocational Guidance Quarterly, 32(1)*, 16–20.

Miller-Tiedeman, A. (1997). The Lifecareer process theory: A healthier choice. In D. P. Bloch & L. J. Richmond (eds.), *Connections between spirit and work in career development* (pp. 87–114). Palo Alto, CA: Davies-Black.

Minbashian, A., Bright, J. & Bird, K. (2009). A comparison of artificial neural networks and multiple regression in the context of research on personality and work performance. *Organizational Research Methods, 13(3)*, 540–561.

Minear, P. (1954). Work and vocation in scripture. In J. O. Nelson (ed.), *Work and vocation*. New York, NY: HarperCollins.

Mitchell, K. E., Levin, A. S. & Krumboltz, J. D. (1999). Planned happenstance: Constructing unexpected career opportunities. *Journal of Counseling and Development, 77(2)*, 115–125.

Mitroff, I. I. & Denton, E. (1999). A study of spirituality in the workplace. *Sloan Management Review, 40(4)*, 83–93.

Mlodinow, L. (2009). *The drunkard's walk: How randomness rules our lives*. New York, NY: Vintage.

Moore, P. (2002). *E=mc²: The great ideas that shaped our world*. London, UK: Burlington.

Moore, T. (1997). *Meaningful work* (Audiobook): Audible.com.au.

Moran, M. G. (1998). Chaos theory and psychoanalysis. In L. L. Chamberlain & M. R. Butz (eds.), *Clinical chaos: A therapist's guide to non-linear dynamics and therapeutic change* (pp. 29–40). New York: Brunner/Mazel.

Morowitz, H. J. (2002). *The emergence of everything: How the world became complex*. New York, NY: Oxford University Press.

Neault, R. A. (2002). Thriving in the new millennium: Career management in the changing world of work. *Canadian Journal of Career Development, 1(1)*, 11–22.

Nevo, O. (1987). Irrational expectations in career counseling and their confronting arguments. *Career Development Quarterly, 35*, 239–250.

Nixon, Richard (1962). *Six Crises*, Garden City, NY: Doubleday.

Oliver, L. W. & Spokane, A. R. (1988). Career-intervention outcome: What contributes to client gain? *Journal of Counseling Psychology, 35*, 447–462.

Ormerod, P. (2005). *Why most things fail: Evolution, extinction and economics*. Hoboken, NJ: John Wiley.

Ortberg, J. (2007). *When the game is over, it all goes back in the box*. Grand Rapids, MI: Zondervan.

Osipow, S. H. (1973). *Theories of career development* (2nd ed.). New York, NY: Appleton-Century-Crofts.

Osipow, S. H., Carney, C. G., Winer, J., Yanico, B. & Koschier, M. (1987). *Career decision scale* (3rd ed.). Odessa, FL: Psychological Assessment Resources.

Parsons, F. (1909). *Choosing a vocation*. Boston MA: Houghton Mifflin.

Patton, W. & McIlveen, P. (2009). Practice and research in career counseling and development—2008. *Career Development Quarterly, 58(2)*, 118–161.

Patton, W. & McMahon, M. (1999). *Career development and systems theory: A new relationship*. Pacific Grove, CA: Brooks/Cole.

Patton, W. & McMahon, M. (1999). *Career development and systems theory: Connecting theory and practice* (2nd ed.). Rotterdam, The Netherlands: Sense Publishers.

Patton, W. & McMahon, M. (2006). *Career development and systems theory: Connecting theory and practice* (2nd ed.). Rotterdam: Sense Publishers.

Peat, F. D. (1987). *Synchronicity: The bridge between matter and mind*. New York, NY: Bantam.

Peat, F. D. (2002). *From certainty to uncertainty: The story of science and ideas in the twentieth century*. Washington, DC: Joseph Henry Press.

Peck, M. S. (1978). *The road less traveled: A new psychology of love traditional, values and spiritual growth*. London, UK: Arrow.

Peck, M. S. (1983). *People of the lie: The hope for healing human evil*. New York, NY: Simon & Schuster, Inc.

Peck, M. S. (1993). *Further along the road less traveled: The unending journey toward spiritual growth*. New York, NY: Touchstone.

Peck, M. S. (1997). *The road less traveled and beyond: Spiritual growth in an age of anxiety*. New York, NY: Touchstone.

Peters, E. E. (1994). *Fractal market analysis: Applying chaos theory to investment and economics*. New York, NY: Wiley.

Peters, T. (1987). *Thriving on chaos: Handbook for a management revolution*. New York, NY: Random House.

Pink, D. (2005). *A whole new mind*. Sydney, NSW: Allen & Unwin

Placher, W. C. (ed.) (2005). *Callings: Twenty centuries of Christian wisdom on vocation*. Cambridge, UK: Eerdmans.

Plowman, D., Solanksy, S., Beck, T., Baker, L., Kulkarni, M. & Travis, D. (2007). The role of leadership in emergent, self-organization. *Leadership Quarterly, 18*, 341–356.

Poole, M. E. & Langan-Fox, J. (1992). Conflict in women's decision-making about multiple roles. *Australian Journal of Marriage & Family, 13*, 2–18.

Poole, M. E., Langan-Fox, J., Ciavarella, M. & Omodei, M. (1991). A contextual model of professional attainment: Results of a longitudinal study of career paths of men and women. *Counseling Psychologist, 19*, 603–624.

Poole, M. E., Langan-Fox, J. & Omodei, M. (1993). Contrasting subjective and objective criteria as determinants of perceived career success: A longitudinal study. *Journal of Occupational & Organizational Psychology, 66*, 39–54.

Pors, F. (2007). The perils of prediction. Retrieved July 2, 2008, from www.econ-omist.com/blogs/theinbox/2007/07/ the_perils_of_prediction_june.cfm.

Porter, M. (1980). *Competitive Strategy: Techniques for analysing industries and competitors*. New York, NY: Free Press.

Priesmeyer, H. R. (1992). *Organizations and chaos: Defining the methods of non-linear management*. Westport, CT: Quorum Books.

Prigonine, I. (1997). *The end of certainty: Time, chaos, and the new laws of nature*. New York, NY: Free Press.

Prigonine, I. & Stengers, I. (1984). *Order out of chaos: Man's new dialogue with nature*. New York, NY: Bantam Books.

Pryor, R. G. L. (1979). In search of a concept: Work values. *Vocational Guidance Quarterly, 27,* 250–258.

Pryor, R. G. L. (1987). Differences among differences: In search of general work preference dimensions. *Journal of Applied Psychology, 72,* 426–433.

Pryor, R. G. L. (1991). Assessing people's interests, values and other preferences. In B. Hesketh & A. Adams (eds.), *Psychological perspectives on occupational health and rehabilitation* (pp. 17–52). Marrickville, NSW: Harcourt Brace Jovanovich.

Pryor, R. G. L. (1995a). Assessing personality: What is it and what influences it? *Australian Journal of Career Development, 4,* 30–32.

Pryor, R. G. L. (1995b). *Congruence Interest Sort (CIS).* Sydney, NSW: Congruence Pty Ltd.

Pryor, R. G. L. (2002). Review: Holland, J., Shears, M & Harvey-Beavis, Self Directed Search: Manual and related materials. *Australian Journal of Career Development, 11,* 74–77.

Pryor, R. G. L. (2003). Mind mapping for medico-legal vocational assessment. In M. McMahon & W. Patton (eds.), *Celebrating excellence in Australian career practice: Ideas for career practitioners* (pp. 152–156). Brisbane: Australian Academic Press.

Pryor, R. G. L. (2007). Assessing complexity: Integrating being and becoming. *Journal of Employment Counseling, 14,* 126–134.

Pryor R. G. L., Amundson, N. & Bright, J. E. H. (2008). Possibilities and probabilities: The role of chaos theory. *Career Development Quarterly, 56(4),* 309–318.

Pryor, R. G. L. & Bright, J. E. H. (2003a). The chaos theory of careers. *Australian Journal of Career Development, 12(2),* 12–20.

Pryor, R. G. L. & Bright, J. E. H. (2003b). Order and chaos: A twenty-first century formulation of careers. *Australian Journal of Psychology, 55(2),* 121–128.

Pryor, R. G. L. & Bright, J. E. H. (2004). "I had seen order and chaos but had thought they were different": Challenges of the Chaos Theory for career development. *Australian Journal of Career Development, 13(3),* 18–22.

Pryor, R. G. L. & Bright, J. E. H. (2005a). Occupational stereotypes. In J. E. Greenhaus & G. A. Callanan (eds.), *Encyclopedia of career development* (pp. 567–571). Thousand Oaks, CA: Sage.

Pryor, R. G. L. & Bright, J. E. H. (2005b). *The Luck Readiness Index.* Sydney, NSW: Congruence Pty Ltd/Bright and Associates.

Pryor, R. G. L. & Bright, J. E. H. (2005c). *The Luck Readiness Index: Manual.* Sydney, NSW: Congruence Pty Ltd/Bright and Associates.

Pryor, R. G. L. & Bright, J. E. H. (2006), Counseling chaos: Techniques for careers counselors. *Journal of Employment Counseling, 43(1),* 2–17.

Pryor, R. G. L. & Bright, J. E. H. (2007a). Applying chaos theory to careers: Attraction and attractors. *Journal of Vocational Behavior, 71(3),* 375–400.

Pryor, R. G. L. & Bright, J. E. H. (2007b). The Chaos Theory of Careers: Theory, practice and process. *Career Planning and Adult Development Journal, 23(2),* 46–56.

Pryor, R. G. L. & Bright, J. E. H. (2008). Archetypal narratives in career counselling: A chaos theory application. *International Journal for Educational and Vocational Guidance, 8(2),* 71–82.

Pryor, R. G. L. & Bright, J. E. H. (2009). Good hope in chaos: Beyond matching to complexity in career development. *South African Journal of Higher Education, 23(3)*, 521–537.

Pryor, R. G. L. & Hawkins, T. K. (2009). Medico-legal employability assessment: Myths, mistakes and misconceptions. *Australian Journal of Career Development, 18(1)*, 45–53.

Reardon, R. C., Lenz, J. G., Sampson, J. P. & Peterson, G. W. (2000). *Career development and planning: A comprehensive approach*. Belmont, CA: Wadsworth, Brooks-Cole.

Rescher, N. (1995). *Luck: The brilliant randomness of everyday life*. Pittsburgh, PA: University of Pittsburg Press.

Richmond, B. (2000). *The "thinking" in systems thinking: Seven essential skills*. Williston, VT: Pegasus.

Richmond, L. J. (1997). Spirituality and career assessment: Metaphors and measurement. In D. P. Bloch & L. J. Richmond (eds.), *Connections between spirit and work in career development* (pp. 209–236). Palo Alto, CA: Davies-Black.

Roberts, K. (1977). The social conditions, consequences and limitations of career guidance. *British Journal of Guidance and Counselling, 5*, 1–9.

Roe, A. (1956). *The psychology of occupations*. New York, NY: John Wiley.

Roe, A. (1972). *Perspectives on vocational development*. Washington, DC: American Personnel and Guidance, Association.

Roe, A. & Baruch, R. (1967). Occupational changes in the adult years. *Personnel Administration, 30(4)*, 26–32.

Rojewski, J. W. (1999). The role of chance in the career development of individuals with learning disabilities. *Learning Disability Quarterly, 22(4)*, 267–278.

Ross, L. & Nisbett, R. E. (1991). *The person and the situation. Perspectives of social psychology*. New York: McGraw Hill.

Rotter, J. B. (1966). Generalized expectancies for internal versus external control of reinforcement. *Psychological Monographs (General and Applied), 80(1)*, 1–28.

Rousseau, D. M. (1996). *Psychological contracts in organizations: Understanding written and unwritten agreements*. Newbury Park, CA: Sage.

Rubin, S. & Roessler, R. (2007). *Foundations of the vocational rehabilitation process*. Austin, TX: Pro-ed.

Sagar, S. S., Lavallee, D. & Spray, C. M. (2007). Why young elite athletes fear failure: Consequences of failure. *Journal of Sports Sciences, 25(11)*, 1171–1184.

Sagaria, M. D. (1989). Toward a women-centered perspective of careers: The quilt metaphor. *Journal of Employment Counseling, 26(1)*, 11–15.

Salomone, P. R. & Slaney, R. B. (1981). The influence of chance and contingency factors on the vocational choice process of nonprofessional workers. *Journal of Vocational Behavior, 19(1)*, 25–35.

Sanders, T. I. (1998). *Strategic thinking and then new science: Plain in the midst of chaos, complexity and change*. New York, NY: Free Press.

Sartre, J.-P. (1966). *Existentialism and humanism*. London, UK: Methuen.

Savickas, M. L. (1992). New directions in career assessment. In D. H. Montross & C. J. Shinkman (eds.), *Career development: Theory and practice* (pp. 336–355). Springfield, IL: Charles C. Thomas.

Savickas, M. L. (1993). Career counseling in the postmodern era. *Journal of Cognitive Psychotherapy: An International Quarterly, 7*, 205–215.

Savickas, M. L. (1995). Constructivist counseling for career indecision. *Career Development Quarterly, 43*, 363–373.

Savickas, M. L. (1997). The spirit in career counseling: Fostering self-completion through work. In D. Bloch and L. Richmond (eds.), *Connections between spirit and work in career development: New approaches and practical perspectives* (pp. 3–26). Palo Alto, CA: Davies-Black Publishing.

Savickas, M. L. (2001) A developmental perspective on vocational behaviour: career patterns, salience, and themes. *International Journal for Educational and Vocational Guidance 1, 49–57.*

Savickas, M. L. (2005). The theory and practice of career construction. In S. D. Brown & R. W. Lent (eds.), *Career development and counseling: Putting theory and research to work* (pp. 42–70). Hoboken, NJ: Wiley.

Savickas, M. L. (2006). Career construction theory. In J. E. Greenhaus & G. A. Callanan (eds.), *Encyclopedia of career development* (pp. 84–88). Thousand Oaks, CA: Sage.

Savickas, M. L. (2009). Interview. Afternoon tea with the Center on Education and Work: A conversation series on career and workforce development policies and practice. Retrieved, March 23, 2009 from www.cew.wisc.edu/news/afternoon-tea.aspx.

Savickas, M. L. & Baker, D. B. (2005). The history of vocational psychology: Antecedents, origin, and early development. In B. W. Walsh and M. L. Savickas (eds.). *A handbook of vocational psychology* (3rd ed.). London: Routledge.

Savickas, M. L. & Glavin, K. (2008). The Vocopher Project. Retrieved July 2, 2008, from www.vocopher.com/.

Savickas, M. L. & Lent, R. W. (1994). *Convergence in career development theories.* Palo Alto, CA: Consulting Psychologists Press.

Savickas, M. L. & Spokane, A. R. (1999). Introduction. In M. L. Savickas & A. R. Spokane (eds.), *Vocational interests* (pp. 1–13). Palo Alto, CA: Davies-Black Publishing.

Savickas, M. L., Nota, L., Rossier, J., Dauwalder, J. P., Duarte, M. E., Guichard, J., Soresi, S., Van Esbroeck, R. & van Vianen, A. E. M. (2009). Life designing: A paradigm for career construction in the 21st century. *Journal of Vocational Behavior, 75(3), 239–250.*

Schaffer, W. M. & Kott, M. (1985). Nearly one dimensional. Dynamics in an epidemic. *Journal of Theoretical Biology, 112,* 403–427.

Schein, E. H. (1968). Personal change through interpersonal relationships. In W. G. Bennis, E. H. Schein, F. I. Steele & D. E. Berlew (eds.), *Interpersonal dynamics* (rev. ed.) (pp. 406–426). Homewood, IL: Dorsey Press.

Schein, E. H. (1987) *Process consultation* (Vol. 2). Reading, MA: Addison-Wesley.

Schein, E. H. (1988) *Process consultation* (Vol. 1) (rev. ed.). Reading, MA: Addison-Wesley.

Schein, E. H. (1996). Kurt Lewin's change theory in the field and in the classroom: Notes toward a model of managed learning. *Systems Practice, 9(1),* 27–47.

Schuurman, D. J. (2004). *Vocation: Discerning our callings in life.* Grand Rapids, MI: Eerdmans.

Scott, J. & Hatalla, J. (1990). The influence of chance and contingency factors on career patterns of college-educated women. *Career Development Quarterly, 39(1),* 18–30.

Sears, S. (1982). A definition of career guidance terms: A national vocational guidance association perspective. *Vocational Guidance Quarterly, 31,* 137–143.

Seligman, M. (1992). *Learned optimism.* Sydney, NSW: Random House.

Seligman, M. E. P. (1998). *Learned optimism.* New York NY: Pocket Books (Simon and Schuster).

Seligman, M. E. P. (2002). *Authentic happiness: Using the new positive psychology to realize your potential for lasting fulfillment.* New York, NY: Free Press.

Senge, P. (1990). *The fifth discipline: The art and practice of the learning organization.* Sydney, NSW: Random House.

Sensoy-Briddick, H. (2009). The Boston Vocation Bureau's first counseling staff. *Career Development Quarterly, 57(3),* 215–224.

Sertl, J. & Huberman, K. (2010). *Strategy, leadership and the soul: Resilience, responsiveness and reflection for a global economy.* Devon, UK: Triachy Press.

Shahnasarian, M. (1994). *Decision time: A guide to career enhancement.* Location unspecified, USA: Psychological Assessment Resources.

Shahnasarian, M. (2006). Holland's theory of vocational choice. In J. E. Greenhaus & G. A. Callanan (eds.), *Encyclopedia of career development* (pp. 353–355). Thousand Oaks, CA: Sage.

Shamir, B. (1991). Meaning, self and motivation in organizations. *Organization Studies, 12(3),* 405–424.

Shapiro, S. M. (2006). *Goal free living: How to have the life you want now!* Hoboken, NJ: Wiley.

Sideridis, G. D. & Kafetsios, K. (2008). Perceived parental bonding, fear of failure and stress during class presentations. *International Journal of Behavioral Development, 32(2),* 119–130.

Smith, G. T. (1999). *Courage and calling: Embracing your God-given potential.* Downers Grove, IL: Intervarsity Press (IVP).

Spain, A. & Hamel, S. (1993). The tree metaphor: A new tool for career counselling for women. *Canadian Journal of Counselling, 27(3),* 165–176.

Spokane, A. R., Meir, E. I. & Catalano, M. (2000). Person–environment congruence and Holland's theory: A review and reconsideration. *Journal of Vocational Behavior, 57,* 137–187.

St Augustine (2005). *The confessions of St. Augustine.* (Modern English Version). Grand Rapids, MI: New Spire.

Stacey, R., Griffin, D & Shaw, P. (2000). *Complexity and management: Fad or radical challenge to systems thinking?* London, UK: Routledge.

Stacey, R. D. (1992). *Managing the unknowable: Strategic boundaries between order and chaos in organizations.* San Francisco, CA: Jossey Bass.

Starbuck, W. H. (1992). Strategizing in the real world. *International Journal of Technology Management, Special Publication on Technological Foundations of Strategic Management, 8,* 77–85.

Stewart, T. C. & West, R. L. (2007). Cognitive modeling: Deconstructing and reconstructing ACT-R: Exploring the architectural space. *Cognitive Systems Research, 8(3),* 227–236.

Stone, Harold T. (n.d.) quote as retrieved from http://thinkexist.com/quotation/i_try_to_keep_an_open_mind-but_not_so_open_that/209355.html

Strogatz, S. H. (2003). *Sync: The emerging science of spontaneous order.* New York, NY: Hyperion.

Stumpf S. A., Colarelli, S. M. & Hartrnan, K. (1983). Development of the Career Exploration Survey (CES). *Journal of Vocational Behavior, 22(2),* 191–226.

Super, D. E. (1953) A theory of vocational development. *American Psychologist, 8,* 185–190.

Super, D. E. (1957). *The psychology of careers.* New York, NY: Harper & Row.

Super, D. E. (1980). A life-span life-stage approach to career development. *Journal of Vocational Behavior, 16,* 282–298.

Super, D. E. (1993). The two faces of counseling: Or is it three? *Career Development Quarterly, 42,* 132–136.

Super, D. E., Osbourne, W. L., Walsh, D. J., Brown, S. D. & Niles, S. G. (1992). Developmental career assessment and counseling: the C-DAC. *Journal of Counseling and Development, 71,* 74–80.

Super, D. E., Savickas, M. L. & Super, C. M. (1996). A life-span life-stage approach to careers. In D. Brown & L. Brooks (eds.), *Career choice and career development* (3rd ed.) (pp. 121–178). San Francisco, CA: Jossey-Bass.

Szymanski, E. M. & Hershenson, D. B. (1998). Career development of people with disabilities: An ecological model. In R. M. Parker & E. M. Szymanski (eds.), *Rehabilitation counseling: Basics and beyond* (3rd ed.) (pp. 327–378). Austin, TX: Pro-ed.

Szymanski, E. M. & Parker, R. M. (2003) *Work and disability: Issues and strategies in career development and job placement.* Austin, TX: Pro-ed.

Taleb, N. N. (2007). *The black swan: The impact of the highly improbable.* New York, NY: Random House.

Taylor, K. M. (1982). An investigation of vocational indecision in college students: Correlates and moderators. *Journal of Vocational Behavior, 21(3),* 318–329.

Taylor, K. M. & Betz, N. E. (1983). Applications of self-efficacy theory to the understanding and treatment of career indecision. *Journal of Vocational Behavior, 22(1),* 63–81.

Tiedeman, D. V. (1997). Ready, set, grow: An allegoric induction into quantum careering. In D. P. Bloch & L. J. Richmond (eds.), *Connections between spirit and work in career development* (pp. 61–86). Palo Alto, CA: Davis-Black.

Tillich, P. (1952). *The courage to be.* London, UK: Collins.

Tinguely, J. (1959). Für Statik. Dussedorf. (Thrown from a plane).

Torre, C. A. (1995). Chaos, creativity, and innovation: Toward a dynamical model of problem solving. In R. Robertson & A. Combs (eds.), *Chaos theory in psychology and the life sciences* (pp. 179–198). Mahwah, NJ: Erlbaum. As cited in H. Livneh, & R. M. Parker (2005), Psychological adaptation to disability: Perspectives from chaos and complexity theory. *Rehabilitation Counseling Bulletin, 49(1),* 17–28

Tranberg, M., Slane, S. & Ekeberg, E. (1993). The relation between interest congruence and satisfaction: A meta-analysis. *Journal of Vocational Behavior, 42,* 253–264.

Tseng, M. S. & Carter, A. R. (1970). Achievement motivation and fear of failure as determinants of vocational choice, vocational aspiration, and perception of vocational prestige. *Journal of Counseling Psychology, 17(2)*, 150–156.

Tubbs, M. (1986). Goal setting: A meta-analytic examination of the empirical evidence. *Journal of Applied Psychology, 71(3)*, 474–483.

Tulving, E. & Thomson, D. M. (1973). Encoding specificity and retrieval processes in episodic memory. *Psychological Review, 80*, 352–373.

Uldrich, J. (2008). *Jump the curve: 50 essential strategies to help your company stay ahead of the emerging technologies*. Avon, MA: Platinum Press.

Vallence, K. & Deal, R. (2001a). *Sometimes magic (cards)*. Bendigo, Vic: Innovative Resources.

Vallence, K. & Deal, R. (2001b). *Sometimes magic: Celebrating the magic of everyday learning. (Manual)*. Bendigo, Vic: Innovative Resources.

Violand-Hobi, H. (1995). *Jean Tinguely: Life and work*. New York, NY: Prestel.

Vondracek, F., Lerner, R. & Schulenberg, J. (1986). *Career development: A lifespan developmental approach*. Hillsdale, NJ: Erlbaum.

Vygotsky, L. S. (1962). *Thought and language*. New York NY: Wiley.

Waldrop, M. M. (1992). *Complexity: The emerging science at the edge of order and chaos*. New York, NY: Simon & Schuster.

Warnath, C. F. (1975). Career development theories: Directions to nowhere. *Personnel and Guidance Journal, 53*, 422–428.

Warren, R. (2002). *The purpose-driven life*. Grand Rapids, MI: Zondervan.

Watson, M. (2006). Voices off: Reconstructing career theory and practice for cultural diversity. *Australian Journal of Career Development, 15(3)*, 47–53.

Watson, M. & McMahon, M. (2006). My system of career influences: Responding to challenges facing career education. *International Journal for Educational and Vocational Guidance, 6(3)*, 159–166.

Watts, A. G. (1996). The changing concept of career: Implications for career counseling. In R. Feller & G.Walz (eds.), *Career transitions in turbulent times: Exploring work, learning and careers* (pp. 229–236). Greensboro, NC: ERIC/ CASS.

Weiler, N. W. & Schoonover, S. C. (2001). *Your soul at work. Five steps to a more fulfilling career and life*. Mawah, NJ: Hidden Spring.

Wheatley, M. (1991). *Leadership and the new science* (2nd ed.). San Francisco, CA: Berret- Koehler.

Whiston, S. C. (2000). Individual career counseling. In D. A. Luzzo (ed.), *Career counseling of college students* (pp. 137–156). Washington, DC: American Psychological Association.

White, M. (2007). *Maps of narrative practice*. New York. W. H. Norton & Co.

Whyte, W. H. (1956). *The organization man*. New York NY: Simon & Schuster.

Wilder, B. (Producer & Director) (1960). *The Apartment* [Motion Picture]. United States. The Mirisch Company.

Williams, E. N., Soeprapto, E., Like, K., Touradji, P., Hess, S. & Hill, C. E. (1998). Perceptions of serendipity: Career paths of prominent academic woman in counseling psychology. *Journal of Counseling Psychology, 45(4)*, 379–389.

Williams, G. (1997). *Chaos theory tamed*. Washington, DC: Joseph Henry Press/ National Academy Press.

Williamson, E. G. (1950). *The clinical method of guidance*. In Arthur H. Brayfield (ed.). *Readings in modern methods of counseling* (pp. 22–26). East Norwalk, CT: Appleton-Century-Crofts.

Wiseman, R. (2004). *The luck factor*. London, UK: Arrow Books.

Wood, D. (1988). *How children think and learn*. Oxford UK: Blackwell.

Wood, J., Wallace, J., Zeffane, R., Chapman, J., Fromholz, M. & Morrison, V. (2004). *Organisational behaviour: A global perspective* (3rd ed.). Milton, Qld: John Wiley & Sons.

Wrzesniewski, A. (2003). Finding positive meaning in work. In K. S. Cameron, J. E. Dutton & R. E. Quinn (eds.), *Positive organizational scholarship* (pp. 296–308). San Francisco, CA: Berrett-Koehler.

Wrzesniewski, A. & Tosti, J. (2005). Career as a calling. In J. H. Greenhaus & G. A. Callanan (eds.), *Encyclopedia of career development*. Thousand Oaks: Sage Publications.

Young, G., Tokar, D. M. & Subich, L. M. (1998). Congruence revisited: Do 11 indices differentially predict job satisfaction and is the relation moderated by person and situation variables? *Journal of Vocational Behavior, 52*, 208–223.

Young, R., Valach, L. & Collin, A. (1996). A contextual explanation of career. In D. Brown & L. Brooks (eds.), *Career choice theory and development* (3rd. ed.) (pp. 477–512). San Francisco, CA: Jossey-Bass.

Young, R. A. & Collin, A. (2004). Introduction: Constructivism and social constructionism in the career field. *Journal of Vocational Behavior, 64*, 373–388.

Zajonc, R. B. (1980). Feeling and thinking: Preferences need no inferences. *American Psychologist, 35*, 151–175.

Zander, R. S. & Zander, B. (2000). *The art of possibility: Transforming professional and personal life*. New York, NY: Penguin.

Zunker, V. G. (2006). *Career counseling: Applied concepts of life planning* (7th ed.). Pacific Grove, CA: Brooks/Cole.

Zytowski, D. G. (1970) The concept of work values. *Vocational Guidance Quarterly, 18*, 176–186.

INDEX

In this index tables, figures and illustrations are indicated in **bold** type. Appendices are indicated by a.

Printed in Great Britain
by Amazon